"Ed Stetzer has written the new standard in church planting books. He has a story to tell, and he tells it with both precision and passion. Those who are already sold on the kingdom activity of church planting will be encouraged by this. But this book reads like a recruiting manual. It will charge up those who haven't yet gotten the bug."

Steve Sjogren
Launching Pastor, Vineyard Community Church Cincinnati, Ohio
Author, *Community of Kindness: A Refreshing New Approach to Planting and Growing a Church*

"Church planting has truly come of age. Ed Stetzer has masterfully engaged the priority of church multiplication with the Church's need to be culturally relevant. This work is comprehensive and, more importantly, it is integrative. Drawing from hundreds of sources, he has helped us all step into a new era that decompartmentalizes the sodalic work of the Church. He deals realistically with common obstacles for planting churches and gives leaders a compelling motivation for the highly focused mission of expanding the witness of Christ through church planting."

Kevin W. Mannoia
Dean, Haggard School of Theology
Azusa Pacific University
Author, *Church Planting: The Next Generation*

"Stetzer helps the new church developer think missionally, theologically, and practically about the process of starting new churches. I encourage you to read carefully, glean insights, and prayerfully apply the principles to your unique situation."

Bob Logan
Executive Director, CoachNet International Ministries
Co-developer, *The Church Planter's Toolkit*

"I give Ed Stetzer's *Planting New Churches in a Postmodern Age* a five-star rating. His treatment of the topic is theologically grounded, mission focused, well researched, richly referenced, and bears the mark of authenticity from someone who writes out of his own experience. If I could buy only one book on church planting this would be my first choice."

Eddie Gibbs
Donald A. McGavran Professor of Church Growth
Fuller Theological Seminary
Author, *ChurchNext*

"I like this book! In *Planting New Churches in a Postmodern Age*, Ed Stetzer provides us with a fresh mind-set as he tackles church planting from a postmodern perspective. He blends well Scripture and theology in what is an extremely practical hands-on approach to church planting."

Aubrey Malphurs
Pastoral Ministries Deptartment
Dallas Theological Seminary
Author, *Planting Growing Churches*

"Ed Stetzer is a wonderful theologian-practitioner, and he has provided a blueprint for church planting that is at once faithful to the message we proclaim and relevant to its proclamation in our fragile, changing world. This book is a timely gift to the church of Jesus Christ. No one should try to plant a church without it!"

Timothy George
Dean, Beeson Divinity School of Samford University
Executive editor, *Christianity Today*

"Ed Stetzer has done a great service for the churches of North America. In this book he has laid out a practical strategy for evangelizing North America by planting new churches. Stetzer's book successfully integrates biblical revelation, theology, postmodern philosophy, and sound, practical application. He explains why new churches are needed, and he teaches the reader how to start these churches. All those with a passion to see North America come to Christ would do well to read and heed this book."

John Mark Terry
Professor of Missions
Billy Graham School of Missions, Evangelism, and Church Growth
The Southern Baptist Theological Seminary

"In this one book, Ed Stetzer has taken the complex issue of postmodernity and given church leaders a handle to address the need and opportunity. This book gives the reader basic how-to's of planting a church which will effectively evangelize and congregationalize. It addresses why and how church leaders should be planting churches. Ed Stetzer leads the reader through all the steps and issues which must be addressed to plant a church that can thrive in the twenty-first century."

Richard H. Harris
Vice President, Church Planting
North American Mission Board

"For long years we have had few books on church planting. Then, beginning in the 1970s, various helpful titles began to appear. Now we have one of the very best of them. Ed Stetzer's book grows out of extensive experience, thoroughgoing research, and the kind of dynamic involvement that has been evidenced by many evangelical groups in recent years. For solid preparation and step-by-step know-how, read this book before undertaking a church plant. For in course correction and direction, keep it close at hand from start to finish."

David Hesselgrave
Emeritus Professor of Missions
Trinity International University
Author, *Cross-Cultural Church Planting*

"Ed Stetzer has written a church planting book that will be effective in reaching the postmodern, i.e., the new emerging generation in America. Look carefully; he does not instruct us how to build "the church of yesterday," nor does he instruct us how to plant "the church of yesterday," nor does he instruct us how to plant "the church of today;" but Stetzer's focus is on "the church of tomorrow." He does not give us the principles that worked in the 50s; but with careful research into statistics, case studies, and from the vast field of authority, the author has given us practical steps in planting a church that will reach Generation-Next."

Elmer L. Towns
Dean, School of Religion, Liberty University
Author, *Starting a New Church*

"*Planting New Churches in a Postmodern Age* is comprehensive and practical, deals with both strategy and tactics, and is relevant, addressing this age between modernity and postmodernity most helpfully. It sets church planting in biblical and historical perspective, seeing North America and Europe as genuine mission fields demanding that Christ's followers make disciples and gather new congregations. Church planters, denominational executives, mission administrators, and missiologists should read and reread this book."

Charles L. Chaney
Author, *Church Planting at the End of the Twentieth Century*

"*Planting New Churches in a Postmodern Age* by Ed Stetzer simultaneously blends the information of a theoretician with the insight of a practitioner while stressing both the content of Scripture and context of ministry. This book is the best to date on the subject of church planting in our emerging culture and is invaluable to all concerned with the mission of God and ministry of new churches."

Mark Driscoll
Pastor, Mars Hill Church, Seattle WA
Co-founder, Acts 29 Church Planting Network

"Ed Stetzer has done an important service to the church by 'breaking the code' in terms of how to evangelize people and people groups in today's world. The implications of this work move us one step closer to impacting effectively the North American mission field. *Planting New Churches in a Postmodern Age* moves beyond simply teaching church planters how to plant churches. It teaches them how to be missionaries, an absolute must in today's context. This work forces us to rethink how we approach our mission and gives us both practical and missional insights into achieving it."

David Putman
Team Leader, Strategic Readiness, Church Planting Group
Contributing author, *Church Planting at the End of the 20th Century*

"As both a seasoned church planter and a respected scholar, Ed Stetzer delivers an exceptionally practical and well-integrated approach to the vast challenge of planting healthy, reproducing churches. Drawing insights from theology, culture and his years of experience in the church planting trenches, Stetzer shares helpful and innovative ways to communicate the gospel in a postmodern age without falling prey to compromise. This book is now required reading in all my seminary courses on church planting. I highly recommend it!"

Steve Childers
Professor of Practical Theology
Reformed Theological Seminary-Orlando
Director of U.S. Center for Church Planting, Inc.
www.churchplantingcenter.com

PLANTING NEW CHURCHES IN A POSTMODERN AGE

PLANTING NEW CHURCHES

IN A

POSTMODERN AGE

ED STETZER

BROADMAN
&HOLMAN
PUBLISHERS

NASHVILLE, TENNESSEE

0–8054–2730–9

Published by Broadman & Holman Publishers,
Nashville, Tennessee

Dewey Decimal Classification: 254.1
Subject Heading: CHURCH PLANTING \
EVANGELISTIC WORK \ CHURCH GROWTH

Scripture is quoted from the Holy Bible,
New International Version,
copyright © 1973, 1978, 1984
by International Bible Society.

5 6 7 8 9 10 08 07 06 05 04

Dedication

To John Mark Terry:
I knew the "hows" of church planting,
but you taught me the "whys" of missions.

Contents

The Mastery of Space and Place

Two of the most famous words of history are these: *Know Thyself.* The Socratic injunction "know thyself" is another way of asking two separate but inseparable questions: "Do you know who you are?" and "Do you know where you are?"

To ignore your own history, not to start from home, is the path of treason. But failure to transcend your own history is the path of idolatry. Space and place, character and context overlap in complex and mystifying ways.

Poets have understood this double allegiance to space and place perhaps better than anyone else. Wallace Stevens defined a poem as "the cry of its occasion." One of my favorite lines from the poet Czeslaw Milosz is not found in a poem, but in an interview about his 1943 poems "The World" and "The Voices of the People": "It would certainly be very nice to view a poem apart from its date and circumstances, but that can't be done. Besides, what do we want—marble, unshakable canons, beauty? . . . Dates are important."[1] Church planters must practice dated crying with the best of poets.

Timeliness is the only route to timelessness. Space as spiritual and place as physical is the fulcrum of incarnation. Aleksandr Solzhenitzyn argues that from time to time in history we come across a "knot"—"a moment when trends and issues are neatly tied together; an hour when alternatives are clear; that brief period before decisions harden into fate."[2] When space and place, character and context are in harmony—when individual and the instant, the human and the here-and-now come together—the axis between heaven and earth comes into alignment.

To some degree, "Where are you?" even comes before "Who are you?" Kentucky farmer/poet/philosopher Wendell Berry has made a career of reminding us that "if you don't know where you are, you don't know who you are."[3] Just as poets know that "good poems come from roots,"[4] good persons come from roots as well. Each person needs to have a history, to recognize and remember the rock from whence they were hewn.

But for the disciple of Jesus, it's not our history that seals our fate. It's our heritage. The determining factor of a Christian's existence is no longer our history, but our heritage; it is not our past, but Christ's risen and regnant presence that shapes who we are. Too many Christians are living out of their personal histories and not out of our shared heritage as redeemed, reconciled people.

Ed Stetzer's book on *Planting New Churches in a Postmodern Age* is a marvelous resource that makes these two questions "Who are you?" and "Where are you?" hold hands. At the same time he teaches us to root ministries in our apostolic heritage which can transcend and triumph over our "dated" personal or cultural histories.

Everyone is looking for the next "killer app" (computerese), the next "category killer" (consumerese)—that one-stop, one-shop wonder that renders obsolete all the alternatives. Ed Stetzer has written the "killer app" and "category killer" for church planting in this emerging culture.

Leonard Sweet
Drew Theological School
George Fox University
www.preachingplus.com

Preface

I believe in church planting. More importantly for this book, I believe in church planters. For three years, I invested many hours recruiting, teaching, training, and encouraging potential church planters while I was teaching at a major theological seminary. Now, I recruit planters in a denominational capacity. My passion is to involve people in and equip people for church planting.

I am a church planter (currently on hiatus serving as a recruiter). As a church planter, I will share with you examples of my own church plants, particularly Calvary Christian Church (Buffalo, New York) and Millcreek Community Church (Erie, Pennsylvania). These two church planting experiences were formative to my knowledge and experience. Many of the resources in this book come from these churches. *Don't skip this—it is not the usual yada yada. It explains how to read the chapters.*

Church planting, the process of starting new churches or congregations, is not a new concept. Recently, many evangelical denominations have experienced a heightened awareness and practice of church planting. This return to New Testament missiological practice is good news. However, training in church planting principles is sporadic and often incomplete.

Today, there is great interest in and need for church plants that will reach a changing postmodern world. Being a missionary in a new culture, whether that culture is in another country or emerges in our own, takes discernment and wise planning. This book is written with the hope that its readers will become better equipped to engage in the task of church planting in today's world.

In order to write a reasonably sized book, I have limited the book to the basics. The companion Web site to this book is www.newchurches.com.

There you will find additional resources, other articles, and links related to the topic. The Web site is divided by topic following the outline of this book. Your contributions are welcome.

Also, church planting is still an emerging field in North America. People have been planting churches for two millennia, but in the last few decades, church planting has risen to prominence among evangelicals. The literature began with how-to tapes and practical books. Recently, more thoughtful books that examine culture and church planting in the light of missions have begun to emerge. I will try to include some of that here, but the Web site will have much more.

Finally, the greatest challenge in writing this book is including the principles of church planting (for example, how to gather a core group) from an analysis of emerging churches and trends (that is, what is working in new churches reaching postmoderns). I have already written a course on how to plant a church. I have done many conferences describing emerging postmodern generations. The challenge has been to combine the two emphases.

You will note that all the chapters except 2 and those in part 3 are fairly straightforward without many footnotes. These chapters are more practical and come from my own observations, teaching, and experiences. They are intended to be a complete explanation of how to plant a church. If you are a church planter, you will need this information.

Chapter 2 and the chapters in part 3 are more frequently footnoted and more in-depth. They spring from research, surveys, and evaluation of the work of others. These chapters address cultural issues that are specific to planting among postmodern North Americans. They are intended to look at emerging trends and patterns. Hopefully, the combination will be helpful to you.

This book is far from perfect, but it is my best attempt at providing the tools to plant and analyze those new plants. My hope is that it will generate good missionary thinking about how to reach people in this new age. I have intentionally tried to do both and include what did not make the "cut" on the Web site. The companion Web site will provide all of the examples that are not included in the book. (If they were included, the book would be about three thousand pages.)

I do not try to address every trend or idea. This means there will certainly be things that I have missed. Instead, I will also suggest additional reading at the end of each chapter. I hope this book will provide a resource to help planters start culturally relevant and biblically faithful churches across North America.

In writing this book, my approach is not driven by models, but by missions. Instead of just telling you about the wonderful things that Mars Hill, NextLevel Church and Ekklesia are doing (and they are good things), I will instead try to look at the culture through the lens of missions. I will try to help you think like a missionary to the people living in the culture of postmodernism.

Therefore, the approach of this book is missiological. In other words, we will look at postmodern North America as missionaries would when entering a new culture. In order to do this, I will draw on four sources:

1. A study of six hundred denominational church planters.

2. A study of one hundred church plants reaching postmoderns.

3. My own experience planting churches.

4. The current literature about the emerging postmodern church.

The question is not whether the church will reach postmodern people. Clearly, Jesus promised that the church and the gospel will prevail. The question is actually, "Will we (and the traditions we represent) be the groups that reach postmodern culture, or will God have to bypass us and use others?"

More complete information about these surveys can be found at www.newchurches.com/research.

Our basic question then becomes, "Who will God use to reach postmoderns?" and not "Will he reach postmoderns?" If you are a denominational or church leader, my hope is that you will protect church planters who think outside the methodological box but still hold to the truths of the faith. If you are thinking of planting a church, I hope to encourage you to be biblically faithful while radically engaging the postmodern culture around you.

Part 1

Basics of Church Planting

CHAPTER ONE

Introduction

*M*y own experience in church planting began in June 1988. I had just graduated from college with an undergraduate degree in natural sciences. I arrived in Buffalo, New York, to start my first church at twenty-one years of age. I had a vision to reach the entire city but little experience and no training. The church was not the great success I thought it would be. Although the church grew and we saw people changed by the power of the gospel, I could have avoided countless mistakes with proper training.

When I was planting this church, our district association was strategizing to plant seven new churches. All seven began within a three-year time frame. Of those seven churches, none would be considered a great success. The church I started, Calvary Christian Church, continues to this day with a faithful part-time pastor, but it is not a large church. Wheatfield Bible Church is the only other church of the seven planted that is still in existence. It is currently merging with an established congregation because of its weak average attendance in the twenties and thirties. The church planting effort that began with great enthusiasm ended with merely a whimper. Untrained and discouraged pastors left the field for better salaries and better possibilities in established churches elsewhere.

My attempt at church planting did not fail because of lack of effort. I personally knocked on thousands of doors. With the help of partnership churches, we knocked on tens of thousands of doors to start Calvary Christian Church in inner-city Buffalo. When Calvary decided to sponsor a new congregation, Lancaster Bible Church, we did so with what we assumed was an innovative strategy using billboards. My team generated many ideas and worked many hard hours, but little success followed.

At this time in western New York (and across North America), some strategies had succeeded. Successful church plants had shared their methods of success with others. Practices such as direct mail, telemarketing campaigns, and large grand openings had appeared infrequently but had become hot topics of discussion. At the first church I started, we began a direct-mail campaign and experienced some success. This piqued my interest in new techniques. However, many of these early methods no longer work as well as they once did. The rapidly changing cultural landscape required that we use different methods to be successful.

Today, there is much more material on church planting available. Church planting conferences meet regularly with hundreds in attendance. There are thousands of churches planting Web sites (a Google search produces 244,000 pages at the time of this writing). My own church planting Web site received over ten thousand hits last year. Many evangelical denominations have placed a renewed emphasis on the subject. The Southern Baptist Convention has committed to plant sixty thousand new churches by the year 2020. Other denominations have adopted similarly aggressive strategies.

In spite of this, some people in church circles are not enthusiastic about this new emphasis on church planting. Some people still object to church planting and church planters for several reasons. Some people misunderstand the purposes and intentions of church planters and new church starts.[1] To some people, church planting is a task for a great visionary pastor, one with the vision to go "where no one has gone before." To others, church planting is an alternative for problem pastors to start their own churches without meddlesome lay leaders. Still others see church planting as a waste of valuable time and money, resources that could be used to revitalize declining churches. Finally, some see church planting as merely a way of stealing the members of nearby churches.

While all of these problems may be true in some instances, biblical church planting is concerned with growing the kingdom of God and developing healthy churches with new converts. Nearby churches may be old, small, and traditional, but they have paved the way for new churches to move ahead. Biblical church planters focus on the Great Commission by reaching the unchurched, not by seeking to attract area Christians.

Furthermore, without church planting, Christianity will continue to decline in North America. "Studies show that if a denomination wishes to reach more people, the number of new churches it begins each year must equal at least 3% of the denomination's existing churches. Based on this formula, mainline denominations are failing to plant enough churches to offset their decline."[2] Without church planting, denominations will decline, but more importantly, the number of Christians will continue to decline.

There *should* be a struggle. We do want to see dying churches revitalized. God has allowed me the privilege of leading two churches through the process of revisioning, and it is a wonderful experience. But we must also start new churches. In order to do that, we need to address and overcome objections to church planting.

Common Objections to North American Church Planting

How did Christianity change from a faith spread primarily through church planting to a faith in which church planting has become an unusual practice? The obvious answer is that the church became *established*. As the church became established, it began to protect its *establishment*. Existing churches began to see a church plant as a competitor.

Many pastors understand the need for a charismatic, Presbyterian, and Baptist church in each community to serve the needs of members in these denominations. But many of those same pastors are hesitant to plant another church similar to their own in the same geographical area even though a different music style or congregational approach might reach an entirely different population segment.

Therefore, as a denomination establishes a number of churches in a certain area, it develops an antimissional mentality for its own community. The church may be very mission-oriented for Africa or Asia—anywhere but home. The fear of competition becomes more important than concern for the unchurched. Even the smallest denomination within a few years is likely to say, "We already have a church in that town; we don't need another congregation there." The community may contain five hundred thousand people, but one church will be considered enough for this denomination.

Critics of church planting usually do not voice their objections in such a straightforward manner. They typically raise a predictable series of objections. We will consider these objections on an individual basis.

Large Church Mentality

For many, the idea of one large church is more attractive than multiple churches. Large churches have the resources and programs to be full-service congregations. Thus, many leaders think the most efficient denominational strategy is to help medium churches become large churches.

Despite this bigger-is-better mentality, statistics do not support the assumption that size is necessarily the best way to reach people. Though large churches *are* often more cost effective than small churches, *new* churches are more effective than large churches, particularly in evangelism. On a per-capita basis, new churches win more people to Christ than established churches. Bruce McNichol explained the findings of his research in *Interest Magazine:*

- Churches under three years of age win an average of ten people to Christ per year for every one hundred church members.
- Churches three to fifteen years of age win an average of five people per year for every one hundred church members.
- Churches over fifteen years of age win an average of three people per year for every one hundred church members.[3]

Clearly, the newer a congregation is, the more effective that church is in reaching those who do not know Christ.

So if we know new churches reach more people per capita, and if we value reaching the unchurched, we *must* agree with C. Peter Wagner: "The single most effective evangelistic methodology under heaven is planting new churches."[4] Church planting is gaining new attention because it is a biblical method that works.

Parish Church Mind-set

Both the large church mentality and the parish church mind-set limit the number of churches possible in an area. The large church mentality focuses on developing *larger* congregations for a region. As described earlier, the parish church mind-set advocates the presence of only *one* denominational church for a region.

A parish is simply a geographical region (Louisiana still calls its counties "parishes"). A denominational parish has historically been defined as a region needing only one church to meet the spiritual or congregational needs of its people in that area. Roman Catholics, Lutherans, and Episcopalians formally follow the parish model when planning the placement of new churches, but most other denominations follow it informally.

These groups expect one church to meet the denominational and spiritual needs of a specific area. Proposals for new churches meet resistance because a church already exists in the area proposed for a new congregation. That resistance shows the parish church mind-set—if a denomination has one church in a "community," the denomination has sufficiently reached that community.

Parish mentality is a primary reason the church-to-population ratio is declining. Churches often die because people move out of rural areas to urban and suburban settings. Yet new churches are not often started in the new urban and suburban areas because they are too close to other established churches of the same denomination. This and other factors have caused a decline in the church-to-population ratio. According to Thomas Clegg and Warren Bird:

- In 1900, 27 churches existed for every 10,000 Americans.
- In 1950, 17 churches existed for every 10,000 Americans.
- In 1996, 11 churches existed for every 10,000 Americans.[5]

In 1900, the Census Bureau counted 212,000 churches. In 1995, the number of churches that existed in the United States was 345,406. Although the number of churches has increased by just over 50 percent during the past century, the U.S. population has increased by 300 percent! Today, an increasing population has fewer churches than in 1906.[6] This decline in church-to-population ratio may help explain the decline of the North American church during the past century.

Professional Church Syndrome

One of the greatest hindrances to church planting in North America is the notion that all churches must have seminary-trained pastors to be legitimate.[7] Roland Allen states that evangelistic growth in new churches is often inversely proportional to educational attainment.[8] Allen believes the more education a pastor has, the less effective he is likely to be in the evangelistic task.

With the increased professionalization (education) of the clergy, church planting has suffered. Seminary-trained pastors often expect full-time salaries provided by established churches. During their years of education, seminarians sometimes accumulate significant debt that makes bivocation-alism[9] or volunteer ministry following graduation impossible. On the other hand, denominational leaders often consider pastoral candidates without seminary training to be ineligible or unprepared to plant new churches. These biases hurt church planting.

However, both history and present-day practices of several faith groups tell another story. American history records that lay preachers effectively planted many Baptist and Methodist churches along the American frontier.[10] Today, charismatic and Pentecostal churches encourage "anointed" persons, regardless of their level of theological training, to start churches. It is not surprising that Calvary Chapel, Vineyard, and Open Bible Standard churches are some of the most effective church planting denominations in North America today. This is specifically because of their openness to using God-called, though not formally trained, leaders in founding new churches.[11]

See "Lay Church Planting on the Western Frontier, 1795-1810" and "Calvary Chapel and Vineyard Church Planting" at www.new-churches.com/history.

If we limit ourselves by assuming that pastors and church planters must be seminary graduates in order to plant new churches, we will never reach some unreached areas of North America. These areas include, but are not limited to, expansive apartment complexes, mobile home villages, marinas, townhouse communities,[12] and sparsely populated rural areas. Because of their poverty, transience, size, or support base, many of these areas cannot support a "professional" seminary-trained pastor expecting a full-time salary. The Professional Church Syndrome is a difficulty which denominations must overcome while simul-taneously providing theologically sound and practical training for church planters.

"Rescue the Perishing" Syndrome

Another significant impediment to church planting is the idealistic assumption that denominations should first rescue dying churches before planting new ones. Every church planter has heard the refrain, "Why should we start new churches when so many struggle and die?" However, saving dead and dying churches is much more difficult and ultimately more costly than starting new ones. Some authorities even argue that changing a rigid, tradition-bound congregation is almost *impossible.* As Lyle Schaller has indicated, even if it is possible, nobody knows how to do it on a large-scale basis.[13] Starting new churches is much easier and, perhaps, a better overall stewardship of kingdom resources.

Perhaps a better strategy is to do both—help revitalize dying churches and simultaneously plant new churches. Stuart Murray addresses the issue well: "It should be candidly acknowledged that current initiatives to plant thousands of new churches are ill-conceived unless these are accompanied by a significant reversal of the decades of decline. . . . There is no empirical evidence to support such an expectation at present."[14]

Murray proposes, and I would agree, that we need a strategy to revitalize established churches and, at the same time, to plant thousands of new churches. He explains: "Churches have been leaking hundreds of members *each week* for many years. Planting more of these churches is not a mission strategy worth pursuing. But planting new kinds of churches may be a key to effective mission and a catalyst for the renewal of existing churches."[15]

Both are needed. Unfortunately, many who call for the revitalization of dying churches are doing so as they seek for "convincing" objections to church planting. We need strategies to revitalize those churches that desire change. We also need to plant thousands of new churches throughout North America. If growing the kingdom is our ultimate objective, we must admit that one can't be accomplished without the other.

"Already Reached" Myth

Among the strongest myths that discourage church planting is the flawed understanding that the United States and Canada are already evangelized. Certainly, North American *Christians* have access to abundant resources of information. Evangelicals read Larry Burkett for financial information, listen to James Dobson for advice on raising children, sing along with Third Day, and purchase Tim LaHaye's fiction. But unchurched persons in North America remain generally untouched by this evangelical subculture and abide in darkness because the evangelical subculture is not providing a culturally relevant gospel witness.

While there are many Christian resources in North American, *unchurched* North Americans have a unique need in that they no longer have a biblical worldview or understanding. There is some question if they ever did. Instead, their religious ideas tend to be distorted reflections of biblical truth. In other words, secular people may be familiar with some religious terminology or ideas, but their familiarity is often different from its original meaning. For example, the most-quoted Bible verse by secular North Americans consists of two words, "Judge not." Though they know the *verse,* their understanding of its *meaning* is skewed. They believe it is wrong to judge another person's choices as wrong or immoral, as long as those choices hurt no one. (Generally speaking, in twenty-first-century North America, the *only* unforgivable sin is intolerance.)

Unchurched North Americans know Jesus said not to judge, but they seriously misunderstand biblical teachings on morals. For example, they have no understanding of the teaching on church purity in 1 Corinthians and the command that the church *should* judge in a redemptive spirit. When secular culture moves further and further from biblical norms, perceptions develop shadows—even corruptions—of biblical reality.

George Hunter believes:
- There are 120 million secular undiscipled people in the United States.
- The U.S. is the largest mission field in the Western hemisphere.
- The U.S. is the fifth largest mission field on earth.[16]

The spiritual deadness of North America appears not only in its culture but in its churches as well. Churches in the first decade of the twenty-first century are closing at a phenomenal rate. Eighty to eighty-five percent of American churches are on the downside of their life cycle.[17] Win Arn reports 3,500 to 4,000 churches close each year.[18] Our churches are dying, and our culture is changing. We know new churches can make a difference.

Conclusion

Obviously, powerful ideas work against church planting. The North American church has not caught a vision for church planting and New

Testament reproduction—yet. Most Americans and Canadians are not connected to any local church. The North American church is in trouble. It
needs to plant new churches, or it will continue to decline.

Even though some people are opposed to the idea of church planting, we
are to do it anyway—because it is biblical. In the following pages, you will
discover three compelling reasons to enact the biblical mandate for church
planting: the command of Jesus, the need for new churches to reach North
Americans, and the ineffectiveness of our present methodologies. Without
church planting, we will not fulfill the Great Commission. Detailed explanations of the practical how-tos of church planting will also be included.

Church planting is slowly regaining its biblical prominence in evangelical life. Between 1980 and 2000, over fifty thousand churches were planted
in North America. Christians are beginning to realize, once again, the need
to place an emphasis on church planting in North America. Even though
there is resistance to church planting, evangelicals have begun to realize the
value and priority of planting. This book is written to inform, to clarify, to
encourage, and to persuade evangelicals to embrace church planting. May
your passion for planting churches and growing the kingdom of God be
enhanced as you read.

Resources for Further Reading

Below are some of the more popular church planting books or tapes.
At www.newchurches.com, there is an annotated bibliography of all the
major church planting books with a focus or application on North
America.

Childers, Steve L. *Gospel-Centered Church Planting Manual.* Orlando,
    Fla.: U.S. Center for Church Planting, Inc., 2002.

Malphurs, Aubrey. *Planting Growing Churches for the 21st Century:
    A Comprehensive Guide for New Churches and Those Desiring
    Renewal,* 2d edition. Grand Rapids: Baker Book House, 1998.

Murray, Stuart. *Church Planting: Laying Foundations.* Scottsdale, Pa.:
    Herald Press, 2001.

Logan, Robert E. and Steven L. Ogne. *Church Planter's Toolkit* (tapes and
    workbook). St. Charles, Ill.: ChurchSmart Resources, 1991.

Hesselgrave, David J. *Planting Churches Cross-culturally.* Grand Rapids: Baker Book House, 2000.

http://www.churchplanting.com

http://www.coachnet.org/

http://www.churchplantingvillage.com/

http://www.dcpi.org/

CHAPTER TWO

Redeveloping a Missional Mind-set for North America

Any book on church planting must be a book about missions. Church planting is done properly when leaders make a decision to engage an unchurched world in radical fashion. Good missionaries always study the culture as they develop their strategy. This chapter will discuss the missionary methodologies every good church planter needs.

More and more Christian leaders are recognizing a distinct shift:

- "Today North America needs to be treated as a mission field in the same way that we in the West have approached much of the rest of the world for the past several centuries."[1]
- "Christians living in modern culture face a fundamental challenge. That challenge is to learn to think about their culture in Missional terms."[2]
- "Just as God is a missionary God, so the church is to be a missionary church."[3]

An Emerging Movement

The development of a North American missiology (the study of missions) caught the attention of the Christian community in the last two decades of the twentieth century. As new models of church arose, they forced the church to address issues not considered in the prior decades—issues about how the church can relate to contemporary culture and contextualize the gospel in that setting.

As the church has considered these theological/missiological issues (perhaps *because* the church has considered these issues), church planting is on the mind of evangelical Christians. Charismatic and Pentecostal groups plant the majority of new churches. Baptists also continue to plant a significant number of churches.[4] Even outside of the free-church tradition, mainline denominations are beginning to reemphasize church planting. Christians are beginning to realize, once again, the need to place an emphasis on church planting in North America.

Theologian Richard Mouw explains we are in a missionary "location"—that North America needs to be considered a mission field in the same way we once considered the underdeveloped world.[5] Though this situation is discouraging, it does present the church with a missiological challenge and opportunity.

"Christendom"[6] has come to an end. No longer is Christianity the "chaplain" to the broader culture. Christianity was universally assumed as the American religion even though it was not widely embraced. It was once perceived as part of our national ethos. No longer can that claim be made. This "humiliation" of Christendom has been underway for two centuries.[7] It is no longer appropriate, if it ever was, to speak of "Christian America."[8]

The end of Christendom allows the church to recognize that the gospel is distinct from Western culture. Thus, the gospel must be addressed in fresh ways to the ever-changing culture that has disassociated itself from any "pseudo-Christian" roots. The task of being *missional* is not just the task of bringing the gospel to the "primitives" outside our borders. The new challenge is to bring the gospel to Western culture, since it has become more resistant to the gospel.[9]

Therefore, I will speak of a "missional" church and North American church planting. The terminology can be confusing, so a word of explanation seems appropriate. A church and denomination can be "mission-minded" without being "missional." It is always easier to *support* missions than to *be* missional.[10]

A missional church is a church that is "on mission" in its setting. A church or church planter that is missional is focused on the mission of God (*missio Dei*) as its goal. A missional church is willing and eager to engage the culture with the truths of the gospel. Today, we desperately need persons, churches, and denominations to apply the lens of missiology to the

North American context, not just to international fields.[11] Christendom is dead and missionaries are needed.

The death of Christendom is not all bad news according to Hall: "Our Lord's metaphors for his community of witness were all of them modest ones: a little salt, a little yeast, a little light. Christendom tried to be great, large, magnificent. It thought itself the object of God's expansive grace; it forgot the meaning of its election to worldly responsibility."[12]

An increasing number of Christian leaders are beginning to understand that the church must not rework its programs; it must rediscover its mission—in short, it must become *missional.*

Obstacles to Missional Thinking

Two parallel problems keep many believers from engaging the unchurched culture. Christians tend to love or despise the culture too much.[13] Put another way, Christians tend to love either techniques or traditions to the detriment of the Christian mission.

The gospel never fits properly within a culture.[14] As such, persons within the church will always find reasons to criticize (or polemicize) those who try to contextualize the gospel. It is always easier to adopt church-culture norms rather than prevailing-culture norms.

Lesslie Newbigin explains:

Everyone with the experience of cross-cultural mission knows that there are always two opposite dangers, the Scylla and Charybdis, between which one must steer. On the one side there is the danger that one finds no point of contact for the message as the missionary preaches it, to the people of the local culture the message appears irrelevant and meaningless. On the other side is the danger that the point of contact determines entirely the way that the message is received, and the result is syncretism. Every missionary path has to find the way between these two dangers: irrelevance and syncretism. And if one is more afraid of one danger than the other, one will certainly fall into the opposite.[15]

There have always been those who have stood in opposition to the church being culturally relevant. This is not an unexpected response. When one sees the religious symbols and traditions recast in a manner that is seemingly disrespectful, it is normal for one to respond negatively. Many are unable to see that high content (being biblically sound) and high culture (being culturally relevant) are not mutually exclusive categories.

The gospel does not spread in a cultural vacuum, but it is always incarnated in a specific cultural context.[16] However, many Christians have been unable to distinguish churches that are culturally relevant and biblically based from those that are compromised by the culture. For many, any movement toward the culture must be inappropriate.

Consider the following illustration known as The Hughes Scale.[17] The goal of the missional church plant is to be securely in Quad B—committed to cultural relevance and to biblical authority. Instead, churches tend to polarize around two axes of the scale. (Quad A churches are Bible focused but are unable to relate to the lost world around them. Quad D churches can relate to the world but have abandoned the basic tenets of the faith.)

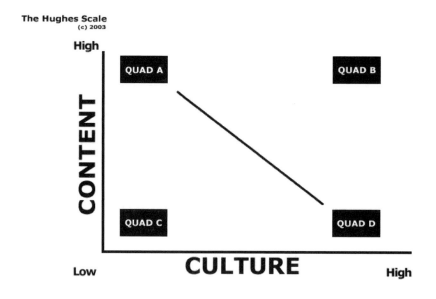

The New Testament church recognizes that we are never permitted to stop thinking missiologically.[18] But the church that considers itself committed to biblical authority and opposed to cultural compromise (represented in Quad A), often is unable to understand a biblically faithful, culturally relevant, missional church. Quad D churches are rightly labeled as "liberal"—compromised by the world and coopted by the culture. But the Christian church is often unable to distinguish the Quad B (missional church) and Quad D churches (the trendy or faddish church). Furthermore, the Quad A church is unable to see that contextualization is not necessarily the slippery slope to compromise. Lest we forget them, Quad C churches tend to focus on their traditions without any commitment to biblical fidelity.

Ironically, these reactions spring from modernity. The church has become deeply subverted by the values of the modern era.[19] As it engages the culture, it does so in a way that is reactionary. Two responses are common—an appeal to *tradition* or an appeal to *technique*. Neither is the response of the missional congregation.

The missional church rejects the false hopes of tradition and technique, repositioning itself as a body of people sent on mission. The Reformation provided the concept of the church where right things happen—correct preaching, administration of the sacraments and other practices. A "correct" church understood and administered these things correctly. Contemporary methodologies provide the concept of the church as a vendor of religious goods and services. The church with the correct management structure to deliver said goods is the most successful.[20] Both methodologies are unsatisfactory ways to plant New Testament churches in a postmodern age.

Tradition

For most people, a vision for the future tends to involve re-visioning an effective past experience. The difficulty seems obvious, but often it is not. To *what* preferred past do we return? Do we return to the Reformation and use it as the touchstone of revival? Some seem to think so. Why? Would not the early church be a better option? New churches have an opportunity that established churches often do not. They have the opportunity to contextualize the unchanging message of the gospel without any preexisting patterns to copy. They do not return to a romanticized past but they reincarnate it in a biblical present.

The unmet challenge is to separate ourselves from any unnecessary and traditional cultural wrappings.[21] Many among the conservative evangelical churches retreat to a preferred past in order to maintain a sense of spiritual nostalgia. Yet the church must never get too comfortable with any culture,[22] whether it existed five, fifty, or five hundred years ago.

Technique

Perhaps the greatest indicator of the inadequacy of our current missiology is its lack of theological depth.[23] Malphurs explains that one of the "accurate criticisms of (the church growth) movement" is its overemphasis on the practical.[24]

Van Gelder explains:

> The continued drift toward the development of large, independent community churches, with their focus on user-friendly, needs oriented, market-driven models described by George Barna in *User Friendly Churches,* is in need of careful critique. While celebrating their contextual relevance, we need to be careful that we are committed in using these approaches to maintaining the integrity of both the gospel and the Christian community. These churches may just be the last version of the Christian success story within the collapsing paradigm of modernity and Christian-shaped culture.[25]

If we do not have a missional strategy driven by solid theological and ecclesiological principles, we simply perpetuate culture-driven models of church and mission.[26]

The false hope of technique continues to undermine solid missiological thinking. There is a great lack of theological depth in many of the contemporary church planting and church growth movements because these are movements of technique, paradigms, and methodologies rather than genuine missiological movements.

Denominations are attracted to such methodologies. Denominations and churches want growth. These techniques have produced results, so they are often seen as the solution. Thus, denominations and churches flounder under the influence of myths, unable to think missiologically in their setting.[27]

A fascinating article provided a window into this church of technique. *Atlantic Monthly* provided an in-depth report on churches reaching people in the 1990s. The new church movement "constitutes, its champions believe, a distinctly American reformation of church life, one that transcends denominations and the bounds of traditional churchly behavior." Such churches are described as shopping-mall churches with new "product lines" asking, "Who is our customer?"[28]

The article explains that some of these churches "are dramatizing a truth that missionaries have known for decades." The article cites church growth author George Hunter: "To reach non-Christian populations, it is necessary for a church to become culturally indigenous to its mission field"—whether in Asia, Africa, or Exurbia.[29] Indigenous means to be "native" to an area. An indigenous plant grows naturally in a given area. An indigenous church grows naturally in its setting. Hunter calls for the church to be indigenous and Hunter is correct, but his solutions fail to satisfy.

Hunter refers to these churches as "apostolic congregations," an important term we will address shortly. By his definition these are large, growing congregations that reach the unchurched. Of course, apostolic churches should and would reach the lost and grow, but that is not their defining characteristic. Hunter basically defines an apostolic church as one that reaches the unchurched and is contextualized in a North American setting. He then devotes most of the article to describing the techniques of those churches.

Technique may be the more dangerous of the extremes. The church bound by tradition often recognizes its problem. The tradition-bound church may even bemoan its condition. But the traditional church is often unable to break out of its negative patterns. On the other hand, the church absorbed in technique is convinced that it *is* missional—that its techniques are actually expressions of mission, while they are actually methods that replace missional thinking.

Overcoming the obstacles of tradition and technique requires an openness that is often absent among believers mired in cultural expressions of Christianity. Developing missional thinking requires us to have our own cultural presuppositions challenged, regardless of the era from which they are derived.

There is always a need for balance. We can't abandon tradition simply because it is traditional. Many traditional church expressions are finding new life in church plants reaching postmodern generations. But tradition or denominational distinctives must never take the place of being missional.

Cal Guy wrote some profound words that describe the nature of keeping a healthy balance between theology and contextualization: "We apply the pragmatic test to the work of the theologian. Does his theology motivate men to go into all the world and make disciples? Does it so undergird them that they, thus motivated, succeed in this primary purpose? Theology must stand the test of being known by its fruit."[30] Guy was simply saying that if theology does not lead to mission, it is an incomplete theology.

As a counterbalance, Murray cautions: "In some recent church planting literature, the scope and level of theological discussion and engagement with biblical teaching has been disappointing. Responding to the objection we are considering here requires advocates of church planting to move beyond selected proof texts and develop a hermeneutically responsible and theologically coherent framework for the practice they are advocating."[31]

There is a New Testament balance. We need new churches, not because they are trendy or provide places to try all the "cutting edge" techniques. Instead, we need new churches that are fresh expressions of the unchanging gospel—new missional contextualized churches in every setting across the globe. This is balance.

Embracing a Missional Theology

A church becomes missional when it remains faithful to the gospel and simultaneously seeks to contextualize the gospel (to the degree it can) so the gospel engages the worldview of its hearers. The most obvious example is Paul and his encounter with the Greeks at Mars Hill. Paul attempted to connect with the worldview of his hearers.[32]

> Paul then stood up in the meeting of the Areopagus and said: "Men of Athens! I see that in every way *you are (already)* very religious. For as I walked around and looked carefully at your objects of worship, I even found an altar with this inscription: TO AN UNKNOWN GOD. Now what you worship as something unknown I am going to proclaim to you" (Acts 17:22–23, emphasis added).

Paul is an excellent example of what it means to be a missionary. He sought to understand the people he was reaching and relate to them in their cultural context. His approach was controversial then, and it still is.

Paul did four things in his effort to be culturally relevant:

- He understood the Athenian position on reality.
- He understood an underlying spiritual interest.
- He looked for positive points within their worldview.
- He encouraged them to find true fulfillment in Christ.[33]

Acts indicates that Paul approached Jews and Gentiles differently. He engaged them based upon their culture and preunderstanding of gospel truths. With the Jews, Paul reasoned about the saving role of the Messiah and his resurrection (17:1–4). With the Gentiles, Paul's reasoning was more foundational—addressing issues of resurrection, morality, and judgment.[34] In all cases, the culture of the hearer impacted Paul's evangelistic methods.

Culturally appropriate evangelism answers the actual questions being asked by a given culture, rather than those questions the church believes the culture should ask. The *sine qua non* is found in 1 Peter: "But in your hearts set apart Christ as Lord. Always be prepared to give an answer to everyone who asks you to give the reason for the hope that you have. But do this with gentleness and respect" (1 Pet. 3:15). The world's questions, in fact, should help determine the evangelistic methodologies and expressions of the indigenous church.

Understanding Missiological Thinking

Missiological thinking is not the same as missionary support. Many churches will support cross-cultural missions, yet oppose missiological thinking within their own context. Missiological thinking requires an understanding of the church's biblical identity, its loss of that identity, and its need to rediscover an indigenous expression of that identity in each culture.

The Church's Missional Identity

Ninety years ago, Martin Kähler stated "mission is the mother of theology."[35] In order to live out a missional mandate, the church must rediscover that part of its nature. The church will not play its proper role in the new missional movement until it understands the biblical and theological basis for such.[36] God is a missionary God in this culture and in every culture. His nature does not change with location. Therefore, a missionary posture should be the normal expression of the church in all times and places.[37]

The church needs to realize that mission is its fundamental identity.[38] Paul's letters contain instructions for the churches he helped start. These churches struggled with the issues that all new churches face, yet they were challenged to be on mission. The text defines the mission, and the church must live that mission at all costs. A nonmissional church misrepresents the true nature of the church.[39] As Schenk points out, "The Great Commission institutionalizes mission as the raison d'être, the controlling norm, of the church. To be a disciple of Jesus Christ and a member of his body is to live a missionary experience in the world. There is no doubt that this was how the earliest Christians understood their calling."[40]

The source of missionary identity is located in the nature of the triune and "sending" God; this identity is connected ontologically with the very existence of the church. Furthermore, the fact that Jesus was the "sent one" is the most fundamental identification of Jesus.[41] Jesus said, "As the Father has sent me, I am sending you" (John 20:21). Because of our identity in Christ, we are to continue the mission of Jesus.[42] "There is no participation in Christ without participation in His mission to the world. That by which the Church receives its existence is that by which it is also given its world mission."[43]

The concept of *missio Dei,* the mission of God, is recognition that God is a sending God, and the church is sent. It is the most important mission in the Scriptures.[44] Jesus Christ is the embodiment of that mission; the Holy Spirit is the power of that mission; the church is the instrument of that mission; and the culture is the context in which that mission occurs.[45] Larkin expresses it well: "The Triune God is the sending One par excellence, enabling and guiding faithful witness through adversity, the crossing of cultural thresholds, and any other impediment to the progress of the gospel to the ends of the earth."[46]

Scripture identifies the elect as being chosen for the purpose of "declaring the praises," a missional task carried over from the unfulfilled (and unappreciated) task of missionary Israel. The apostle Peter explains, "But you are a chosen people, a royal priesthood, a holy nation, a people belonging to God, that you may declare the praises of him who called you out of darkness into his wonderful light" (1 Pet. 2:9).

What Went Wrong?

How did the church lose its missional focus? The church of western European Christendom was a church without mission.[47] As the Reformation took hold, the mission of the church was often neglected. Roman Catholics were energized by "new lands" to reach. But Protestants lost this missionary zeal. This loss did not go unnoticed. Counter-Reformation Catholics pointed to the lack of missionary participation among Protestants as evidence of a defective Protestant church.

This loss of missionary focus was evident both confessionally and practically. Although the Reformation restored much of primitive Christianity, it also lost much. The consequences of this loss of missional focus continue today.

There has been substantial debate regarding the nature of the Reformation church—was it a missionary church, did it value missions? These are valid questions with regard to whether the Reformation church engaged in the task of missions. They are, unfortunately, the wrong questions. The Reformers were trapped within geographic Christendom, while their Catholic counterparts were engaged in colonial expansion. Protestant "mission" became missions to Catholics.[48] While Protestants focused on Catholics, Catholic missions flourished.

Pre-Reformation confessions referred to the church as "one holy, apostolic church." Such is not found in the confessions of the Reformation. Instead, the Reformation confessions reacted to the errors of apostolic succession. By de-emphasizing the "apostolic" nature of church, the Reformers also diminished the apostolic–sending nature of the church. The church that "reformed" lost touch with the God who sends, and the mission of the church suffered.

Van Gelder makes this observation: "Lost in this deletion was an emphasis on the church's 'being authoritatively sent' by God into the world to participate fully in God's mission. The Reformers downplaying of the apostolic attribute and their shifting of authority from the Pope to the Bible were reinforced by . . . the establishment of state churches within their various nations."[49]

The Protestant church lost some of its missional focus due to geography and polemics. Geography caused it to look inward. Polemics against Catholicism forced it away from the apostolic nature of the church. The Protestant churches had to regain a missionary focus and then understand the missionary purpose—to present the unchanging gospel in a changing culture. Protestants, and eventually evangelicals, are left with the unfinished task of sending the gospel to every people and culture. This is a task for which we are often unprepared.

This loss of missional focus also led to a loss of missional thinking. Evangelicals continue to struggle with presenting the unchanging gospel in an ever-changing cultural setting. Churches must parallel, in some ways, their host cultures. This process is called "indigenization."

The Process of Indigenization

According to Beyerhaus, "To be indigenous means that a church, in obedience to the apostolic message that has been entrusted to it and to the living guidance of the Holy Spirit, is able in its own particular historical situation, to make the gospel intelligible and relevant in word and deed to the eyes and ears of men."[50]

Being indigenous was not the standard practice of the church from the fourth century until the seventeenth. The imperial church was accustomed to conquest by the sword, not by mission and evangelism. But a truly indigenous church seeks to become incarnate within the culture in which it finds itself.

Every culture is imperfect, and thus, at times hostile to the gospel. But cultures remain the contexts in which Jesus Christ meets persons by grace.[51] We must pay attention to the culture if we are to be truly missional.[52] Just as we exegete or interpret the biblical text, we must exegete (analyze) the culture where we seek to proclaim that text.

Roland Allen (1868–1947) was an Anglican priest and a missionary to China. His monograph *Missionary Methods: St. Paul's or Ours?* played a significant role in challenging paternalistic approaches to indigenization. Allen promoted the idea (radical at the time) that we must learn to trust the Spirit's work in and through new believers. This idea requires a mutual trust between missionaries and new converts as well as confidence in the Holy Spirit to guide both.[53]

The church always struggles with the need to enculturate while guarding against syncretism.[54] The North American church is no different. Modern voices echo similar concepts: "We need to exegete that culture in the same way that missionaries have been so good at doing with the diverse tribal cultures of previously unreached people."[55] But evangelicals have generally forbidden North American churches from doing the very thing we require international churches to do. While engaging in this struggle, there will always be antimissional forces that cannot separate their own culture (or the culture they pine for) from the actual *kerygma* (gospel) and *didache* (teaching) of the scriptural text.

> An indigenous church, young or old, in the East or in
> the West, is a church which, rooted in obedience to Christ,
> spontaneously uses forms of thought and modes of action
> natural and familiar in its own environment. Such a church
> arises in response to Christ's own call. The younger
> churches will not be unmindful of the experiences and
> teachings which the older churches have recorded in their
> confessions and liturgy. But every younger church will seek
> further to bear witness to the same Gospel with new
> tongues.[56]

Indigenous churches look different from culture to culture. Thus, one would expect that a biblically faithful indigenous church would look different in Senegal from an indigenous church in Singapore. One must also expect an indigenous church in Seattle to look different from one in Sellersburg, Indiana. Indigenous churches look different from location to location. Further, they look different from generation to generation. Faithful indigenous churches take their teaching from the unchanging biblical text and apply it to the ever-changing cultural milieu.

Ecclesia Semper Reformanda

The Reformation was rooted in the concept that the church would continuously reform. It would never arrive. Such remains true today. As the culture changes, the church is compelled to change. But individual churches often face sociological and institutional pressures that hinder such reform. Local churches often struggle just to change the color of the carpet in the worship center! They are not dealing with cultural and epistemological shifts that are going on in North America today.

Even cross-cultural missionaries struggle with the task of contextualization. Even at their best, most cross-cultural evangelists are not noted for their contextual successes.[57] Thus, it is no wonder that North Americans, with a genuine love for missions and the lost, find it difficult to contextualize in a changing culture at home.

Most established churches are unwilling, or at least unable, to change. They are unable to become and remain indigenous. How can we then create churches that are faithful to biblical teaching and also indigenous? In other words, where can we find solid *missiological* churches? Church planting is, and should be, the locus for missiological thinking in North America. New churches can indigenize in ways that established churches cannot.

The reason for this inability to reach a changing culture should be clear. Many churches die because they make choices and adopt patterns of tradition that cause them to decline. Traditions and patterns which were meaningful years ago become contextually outdated. Yet churches continue to practice those same traditions for sentimental reasons. These traditions and patterns can create barriers to surrounding neighbors who do not understand the traditions and who feel alienated by them.

Jerusalem and Antioch

The church's separation from the practices of Judaism began at the resurrection of Jesus, but Christians remained a part of Jewish faith communities for decades to follow. The transition[58] from Jewish Christian to Gentile church was complete by 135 C.E. By 180 C.E. the church added even Jewish Christians (the Ebionites) to its list of heretics.[59] Such a transition cannot go unnoticed. The early church used the Jewish religious system, in some places superceded it, and eventually outgrew it. The Jerusalem church was unable to break from Judaism. The Jerusalem church was unable to become indigenous in its changing context.

Three decades later, Justin, responding to Trypho, begrudgingly affirmed the faith of (early Ebionite) Christians, who followed the teachings of Mosaic law as long as they did not try to persuade others to their view.

> And Trypho again inquired, "But if some one, knowing
> that this is so, after he recognises that this man is Christ, and
> has believed in and obeys Him, wishes, however, to observe
> these [institutions], will he be saved?"
>
> I said, "In my opinion, Trypho, such a one will be saved, if
> he does not strive in every way to persuade other men,—I
> mean those Gentiles who have been circumcised from error by
> Christ, to observe the same things as himself, telling them that
> they will not be saved unless they do so. This you did yourself
> at the commencement of the discourse, when you declared that
> I would not be saved unless I observe these institutions."[60]

Justin, however, already considered non-Christian Jews to be powerful
enemies.

> For other nations have not inflicted on us and on Christ
> this wrong to such an extent as you have . . . you not only
> did not repent of the wickedness which you had committed,
> but at that time you selected and sent out from Jerusalem
> chosen men through all the land to tell that the godless heresy
> of the Christians had sprung up, and to publish those things
> which all they who knew us not speak against us. [61]

Some Jewish Christians did not want to make the change. They desired
to remain *both* Jewish and Christian. The Ebionites were such a group, but
they were condemned by Irenaeus:

> Those who are called Ebionites agree that the world was
> made by God; but their opinions with respect to the Lord are
> similar to those of Cerinthus and Carpocrates. They use the
> Gospel according to Matthew only, and repudiate the Apostle
> Paul, maintaining that he was an apostate from the law. As to
> the prophetical writings, they endeavour to expound them in
> a somewhat singular manner: they practise circumcision, per-
> severe in the observance of those customs which are enjoined
> by the law, and are so Judaic in their style of life, that they
> even adore Jerusalem as if it were the house of God.[62]

What happened? The culture changed, Jerusalem was sacked, and the
rest of the Christian world went forward. Antioch became the great

mission-sending church. But Jerusalem decided it would not change; it would not compromise its traditions by accommodating culture; and it would not be the church that God would use to evangelize the world.

Conclusions

The Christendom model of church inhibited the church from interacting in a missional manner.[63] The church was handicapped because it did not have to be missional. It was, after all, Christendom, and it was commonly acknowledged as the preferred spiritual path within its geographical boundaries. But that is no longer the case. We are no longer on "home turf." Instead, we are in a missionary setting and need to focus on reaching the unchurched around us. We have seen that church planting is the most effective way to reach those outside the faith.

Thus, a North American missiological movement is, and should be, engaged in planting new churches. New churches can engage text and culture in their setting because they are required to think missiologically; they are missional entities.

As mentioned earlier, C. Peter Wagner asserts, "The single most effective evangelistic methodology under heaven is planting new churches."[64] That is because church plants can often engage persons within the lost culture in a way that established churches cannot or will not.

There is no basis, biblically or theologically, for the territorial distinction of missions and evangelism.[65] Though this has been assumed since Gustav Warneck, there is no evidence in the biblical text to warrant a separation between missions and evangelism. On the contrary, their separation has caused harm to the church. While missions became the task of reaching those outside of Christendom, evangelism became the task of reaching those within its boundaries.[66] Like a bear fed by the tourists, the church was unable to fend for itself when the food was removed and Christendom was lost. Thus, in an attempt to promote the importance of missions, missiologists have often undermined the church by removing missional thinking from its rightful place.

Instead, the church must learn to exegete its culture and reflect on the culture from a biblical perspective.[67] If we take seriously theology of mission, the Word must become flesh in every new context.[68]

Solid, disciplined, and prolonged intellectual work in
the context of missionary encounter between the gospel and
contemporary cultures is an essential part of the mission of
theology.[69]

True theology is the attempt on the part of the church to
explain and interpret the meaning of the gospel for its own
life and to answer questions raised by the Christian faith,
using the thought, values, and categories of truth which are
authentic to that place and time.[70]

Church planting is always on the cutting edge of North American missiology because it has no emotional investment in the patterns of tradition.
But it is also in danger of unspiritual pragmatism. In its attempt to become
culturally relevant, it can often become culturally bound. Van Gelder
observes:

We need to exegete . . . culture in the same way that missionaries have been so good at doing with diverse tribal cultures of previously unreached people. We need to exegete . . .
the themes of the Rolling Stones . . . , Dennis Rodman,
Madonna, (and) David Letterman. . . . We need to compre-
hend that the Spirit of the Living God is at work in these cultural expressions, preparing the hearts of men and women to
receive the gospel of Jesus Christ. We have to find, in good
missionary fashion, those motifs and themes that connect
with the truths of the gospel. We need to learn how to proclaim, "That which you worship as unknown, I now proclaim to you." This is the missionary vision at its best.[71]

We do this by taking risks. We risk condemnation of those who are
comfortable within the crumbling walls of Christendom. They may never
understand the necessity of taking these risks because they choose to equate
contextualization with compromise. They cannot understand because they
love their churched culture too much.

For too long, theology has had philosophy as its only partner in discourse.[72] Instead, theology needs to reengage missional thinking by asking
questions such as, "How can the gospel best become incarnate in this setting?" and, "What cultural values and symbols can be used to illustrate

gospel truth?" Steffen provides a detailed list of questions to be used when entering every culture:

- What is the worldview of the target audience?
- What is the culture's decision-making pattern?
- What does it cost a person in this culture to become a Christian?
- What redemptive analogy is best for this culture?
- How does this culture view Christianity?
- What does this culture understand about the basic components of the gospel story?
- Is this culture a shame-culture or guilt-culture?
- How will this culture understand Christian rituals?
- What is the best delivery system for exposing the people of this culture to the gospel?[73]

Questions such as these force the church to analyze biblical truth in the light of culture and vice versa. The alternative is to lose the correct focus of the church. As Bosch declares, "Just as the church ceases to be the church if it is not missionary, theology ceases to be theology if it loses its missionary character."[74]

Church planting can reach those untouched by the established church.[75] New churches approach evangelization in a way that tends to be more culturally indigenous than established churches. If new churches can avoid the trap of technique, they can engage the changing culture effectively with the unchanging gospel of Jesus.

North America desperately needs a true spiritual awakening. This can come, in part, from the planting of new churches. Misinformed and fearful people will always resist what they do not understand. But without church planting, we will not fulfill the words of the Great Commission. The sending nature of God has not changed. He sends us to new and emerging cultures even here in North America. We are most like Christ when we join him in the mission of reaching the unchurched by planting new churches.

There is always risk, and many churches are unwilling to take those risks. Gilliland observes:

Contextualization [is] a delicate enterprise if ever there was one . . . the evangelist and mission strategist stand on a razor's edge, aware that to fall off on either side has terrible

consequences . . . Fall to the right and you end in obscuran-
tism, so attached to your conventional ways of practicing and
teaching the faith that you veil its truth and power from
those who are trying to see it through very different eyes. Slip
to the left and you tumble into syncretism, so vulnerable to
the impact of paganism in its multiplicity of forms that you
compromise the uniqueness of Christ and concoct "another
gospel which is not a gospel."[76]

The end result, at least for our purposes, is to establish new churches
that are culturally relevant. If the church is willing to be missional and its
theologians and thinkers are willing to assist in this process, the potential is
unlimited. As the church rediscovers its missional nature, it will acquire a
renewed passion to be a people on mission. Effective, missional, and biblically sound churches can be planted. These churches will engage the culture
while remaining faithful to the "faith once delivered to the saints." The
result may look different to us but not to God. From his perspective, the
word has become flesh in a new setting. We will truly become missionaries
to a postmodern age.

Resources for Further Reading

Below are some resources focusing on emerging North American missiology. You can find a longer bibliography at www.newchurches.com/
reading.

Bosch, David J. *Transforming Mission*. Maryknoll: Orbis Books, 1998.

Hunsberger, George R. and Craig Van Gelder, eds. *The Church Between
Gospel & Culture*. Grand Rapids: Wm. B. Eerdmans Publishing Co.,
1996.

Newbigin, Lesslie. *The Gospel in a Pluralist Society*. Grand Rapids:
Eerdmans, 1990.

Van Gelder, Craig, ed. *Confident Witness—Changing World*. Grand
Rapids: Eerdmans, 1999.

_____. *The Essence of the Church*. Grand Rapids: Baker Books, 2000.
An excellent resource is the "Gospel and Culture Network,"
http://www.gocn.org/.

CHAPTER THREE

The Biblical Basis of Church Planting

*W*e would be wrong to send out planters with marketing tools but not the fundamental truths of God's Word and the principles of Scripture from which to work. There are some clear New Testament patterns of church planting. The Book of Acts is the most important book ever written on the subject. Moreover, the rest of the New Testament was written to new churches in their respective life situations. The New Testament is an anthology of church planting books!

How did the New Testament church plant churches, and how can we rediscover their passion? Amberson observes:

> We, today, need to recapture the note of spontaneity which existed in the New Testament and, therefore, produced churches as the believers witnessed to the Lord Jesus Christ. Church planting does involve specific and deliberate intent to start new churches, but the New Testament points to the fact that new churches and church planting are the direct and inevitable consequences of believer's involvement in witnessing and proclamation.[1]

One way to regain our passion may be to view the commands of Jesus the way the early church did.

The Commissionings of Jesus

> Then Jesus came to them and said, "All authority in heaven and on earth has been given to me. Therefore go and make disciples of all nations, baptizing them in the name of the Father and of the Son and of the Holy Spirit, and

teaching them to obey everything I have commanded you. And surely I am with you always, to the very end of the age" (Matt. 28:18–20).

The Great Commission in Matthew 28 lists several tasks related to congregations—baptizing, teaching, and making disciples. Often in our North American settings, we do not relate these responsibilities to planting new congregations. Instead, we view these activities as concerns only for existing churches. But the earliest church believed they were fulfilling the Great Commission by planting new congregations. The Great Commission calls us to evangelize and to congregationalize.

But evangelizing and congregationalizing is only one of Jesus' four sending commands. Elmer Towns provides a helpful grid to understand the multiple commissions of Jesus.[2]

SCRIPTURE	WHERE	WHEN	TO WHOM	WHAT	KEY
John 20:21	Upper room Jerusalem	Resurrection	10 disciples	I am sending you	Commission
Matt. 28:18–20	Mountain in Galilee	At least two weeks after the resurrection	11 disciples	Disciple all "peoples" then baptize and teach	Strategy
Luke 24:46–48	Jerusalem	40th day	11 disciples	Preach repentance and forgiveness of sins based on the resurrection of Christ	Content
Acts 1:8	Mt. Of Olive	40th day	11 disciples	Jerusalem to uttermost part of earth	Geography[3]

I Am Sending You

Each subsequent expression provides more details for the central task. In its simplest form, Jesus explained, "As the Father has sent me, I am sending you" (John 20:21). Since the Father had sent Jesus to "seek and to save what was lost" (Luke 19:10), we are sent *in the same manner* as Jesus—by the Father, to seek and save the lost.

Up until the late eighteenth century, most Protestant Christians believed Jesus' commissions applied only to those disciples who actually *heard* his words. Church leaders proclaimed, "That was for the apostles. It doesn't refer to us." They failed to understand the implications of such a hermeneutic. Eliminating one part of the Scripture diminishes the impact of all Scripture. Scripture was always written to specific people in specific places. On the other hand, if we understand the Bible applies to the immediate hearer *and to us,* then *all* believers are called and sent by God to go wherever and for whatever purpose God chooses.

Disciple All People Groups

Two weeks following his commission in John 20, Jesus spoke the Great Commission, which was the second of the sending commands. (Matt. 28:18–20). The Great Commission in Matthew is Jesus' best-known word of sending and clearly explains that the task of world evangelization is given to His disciples—then and now.

The Great Commission explains that the gospel is intended to reach every nation. The word *nation* is better translated every "people" or "ethnic group." Jesus commanded believers to "seek and save the lost" among every people and ethnic group.

In applying Jesus' commission to the arena of church planting, we need to ask whether different people groups live on the North American continent. Think of a person born in the Great Depression era in conversation with a person born only twenty years ago. The contrast between these two persons easily demonstrates that different people groups, even among the same racial and ethnic groups, populate North America.

One would think that because there are different kinds of Anglos, it would be acceptable to plant churches to reach each people group within the broad category of Anglos. However, existing churches often say, "No, they all can come to our church, grow up and mature, and learn to appreciate the music and style we have chosen."

Jesus' command emphasized going to all people groups. People groups have different values. The gospel is designed by God so the unchanging message can be put into changing "cultural containers" to reach people where they are and to take them where they need to go. All methods and worship styles should be centered on God and focused on the Bible. "All peoples" means we must work within the culture of those people groups we wish to reach. This process is called *contextualization*. Contextualization is a skill that North American missionaries, like international missionaries, must use.

Disciple, Baptize, Teach

The Great Commission *is* church planting because Jesus called us to several activities. The Great Commission *is* church planting first because it calls us to *disciple*. Discipleship is the task of the New Testament church. Discipleship is not working when Christians must find their opportunities for spiritual growth outside the church. When a Christian says, "I can't get discipleship at church; I must get it at home (or elsewhere)," it is likely that the believer belongs to an unhealthy church.

God expects the church to provide discipleship. Discipleship is not just a course or a series of studies. Discipleship centers on the salvation event. Discipleship begins with conversion and continues as an ongoing process. "Make disciples" means that the church is to win people to Christ and grow these new converts in the faith. That process is meant to take place in the local church.

Second, the church is to *baptize*. Baptism is an ordinance of the local church. Baptism takes place in or among the local church. I say *among* because it does not have to take place *within* a church building. Many planters have baptized in bathtubs, lakes, or swimming pools. Baptism takes place wherever we can gather the church and wherever there is enough water to perform the ordinance. The Greek word *baptizo* means ongoing baptizing—immersing each new believer. Baptism is a local church ordinance with local church purposes. The Great Commission is given to the local church.

The third part of Jesus' commission instructs the church to *teach*. We observe the fulfillment of this command to teach in Acts 2:42: "They devoted themselves to the apostles' teaching" which was the basis for their growth and fellowship. The Great Commission is fulfilled in churches through the planting of new churches, and by the teaching of biblical precepts.

Some people note that the Great Commission does not use the term *church planting*. Thus, they argue that the Great Commission is fulfilled only through existing congregations (particularly in highly churched areas). But the early church was filled with the Holy Spirit, according to the Book of Acts (2:4; 4:8; 4:31; 9:17; 13:9). These Spirit-filled disciples planted churches. Thus, it is evident that the first hearers of the Great Commission assumed its fulfillment required multiplying disciples and forming new congregations.

The early church fulfilled the Great Commission by planting churches. The first believers heard the commission, left their homes, and went out to plant. When we hear the Great Commission, we should also be motivated to go out and plant new congregations. The best indication of what Jesus meant can be found in how the hearers responded.

Preach Repentance and Forgiveness

Just before his ascension, Jesus again reminded the disciples of their task. The third command describes the *content* and *location* of their proclamation: "repentance and forgiveness of sins . . . to all nations" (Luke 24:47). The only way lost persons can be found is through the preaching of repentance and forgiveness. This is the message of every genuine messenger of the gospel. But this command contained Jesus' instruction to wait until they had received the power of the Holy Spirit in Jerusalem. Jesus' command to preach repentance and forgiveness of sins rested upon his resurrection. This is the content of the commission.

Church planting and church growth are sometimes criticized because the content of the message is not Christ and Christ crucified. This criticism is, at times, true because the content of the message is at times more opinion than proclamation of God's Word. On the other hand, many persons criticize any new innovation. I have planted contemporary, seeker-sensitive churches that reach unchurched people with the Good News. We achieved success by using creative methods. Criticism followed. We determined that one particular criticism would never be true of us—that we preached anything other than Christ.

The message church planters present should never be anything other than the Word of God. Jesus expressed this axiom when he said to "preach repentance and forgiveness based upon the resurrection." Regardless of how seeker-sensitive we wish to be, we can never justifiably remove the stumbling block of the cross. The most biblical church is the one in which the cross is the *only* stumbling block for the unchurched.

Lost people should face no church-culture stumbling blocks that keep them from Christ. Lost people need no additional reasons to stay away from church. The unchurched need to hear the Good News of Jesus Christ—and that includes the stumbling block of the cross. Planters must not present any message other than Christ, and they should present it in a style that is culturally appropriate to the hearers.

The Acts Account

The final sending passage from Jesus provides the geography. "You will receive power when the Holy Spirit comes on you; and you will be my witnesses in Jerusalem, and in all Judea and Samaria, and to the ends of the earth" (Acts 1:8). In addition, the power that Jesus promised in the sending account in Luke appears here. When that power is present, the disciples—then and now—find themselves able to spread the gospel with confidence locally, regionally, and globally.

Early believers were sent (as we are) for the same purpose for which Jesus was sent: to disciple all people groups and to seek and save the lost—both locally and around the world. New Testament Christians acted out these commands as any spiritually healthy, obedient believers would: they planted more New Testament churches. The Great Commission instructs us to evangelize and congregationalize people. Furthermore, Jesus even supplied the content of the message as Paul described it—only Christ and Christ crucified (1 Cor. 1:23).

The sending God sent the Son. We join him in his mission of seeking and saving the lost. Then we become God's sent people to proclaim the message of repentance and forgiveness in the power of the Holy Spirit both locally and worldwide to all people groups.

New Testament Patterns

While differences do exist in the way churches were planted in the New Testament, this section will demonstrate patterns of church planting used throughout the New Testament. Church planting convictions and endeavors should begin with the heart of God. Luke 19:10 states that Jesus "came to seek and to save what was lost." In focusing on unchurched persons, we align our lives with Jesus, who modeled and claimed, "It is not the healthy who need a doctor, but the sick. I have not come to call the righteous, but sinners" (Mark 2:17).

Many churches in North America have "called the righteous" with better teaching and more programs. Advertising claims of "programs for the whole family," "quality Bible teaching," and "full-featured choirs" seem designed to attract members from other churches. But *Jesus* claimed that he had come to call outcasts rather than the righteous. Like Jesus, the planter must seek the unchurched. In fact, through Luke's trilogy of parables (chapter 15) about the lost sheep, the lost coin, and the lost son, Jesus underscored the importance of seeking those who are lost in order to share God's Good News with them.

> Now the tax collectors and "sinners" were all gathering around to hear him. But the Pharisees and the teachers of the law muttered, "This man welcomes sinners and eats with them." Then Jesus told them this parable: "Suppose one of you has a hundred sheep and loses one of them. Does he not leave the ninety-nine in the open country and go after the lost sheep until he finds it? And when he finds it, he joyfully puts it on his shoulders and goes home. Then he calls his friends and neighbors together and says, 'Rejoice with me; I have found my lost sheep.' I tell you that in the same way there will be more rejoicing in heaven over one sinner who repents than over ninety-nine righteous persons who do not need to repent. Or suppose a woman has ten silver coins and loses one. Does she not light a lamp, sweep the house and search carefully until she finds it? And when she finds it, she calls her friends and neighbors together and says, 'Rejoice with me; I have found my

lost coin.' In the same way, I tell you, there is rejoicing in the presence of the angels of God over one sinner who repents" (Luke 15:1–10).

The angel's response indicates the importance of conversion. Jesus promises in Luke 15:7, "I tell you that in the same way, there will be more joy in heaven over one sinner who repents, than over ninety-nine righteous persons who need no repentance" (NASB). Following the parable of the coin, he continues, "In the same way, I tell you, there is joy in the presence of the angels of God over one sinner who repents" (Luke 15:10, NASB). Although Jesus' words ending the parable of the prodigal son are attributed to the father in the story, he clearly is a symbol for God. In the story, the father pleads with his "righteous son" to "be merry and rejoice, for this brother of yours was dead and has begun to live, and was lost and has been found" (15:32, NASB).

Luke's Gospel certainly emphasizes heaven's joy at the conversion of lost ones. Luke continues this theme in Acts 15:3 with his reference to the early church's joy over the conversion of lost sinners when Paul reported his success among the Gentiles.

The New Testament Planter

Through the ministry of the apostle Paul, the New Testament provides a great example of the way we can minister to unchurched persons. Paul invited the recipients of his letters to "be imitators of me, just as I also am of Christ" (1 Cor. 11:1, NASB). What did Paul do that was worthy of imitation? What did he want his readers—including us—to imitate? Identifying the values and actions of Paul can enrich the ministry of every modern-day church planter.

Paul the Planter

1. Paul was personally prepared for his church planting ministry.

- His world-class formal training gave him a broad understanding of divine history.
- He was vitally connected with God (2 Cor. 12:7–9).
- He became prepared by stepping out in ministry from the start (Acts 9:20–22).

- He was teachable. He apprenticed under Barnabas. He was willing to be under authority before God put him over others (Acts 11:25–26).
- He lived an exemplary life (1 Thess. 2).

2. Paul was an evangelist.
- He began preaching the gospel right after conversion (Acts 9:19–22).
- He was a net fisherman in two ways: he led whole families to Christ (Acts 16:25–33), and he conducted large-group evangelistic meetings (Acts 13:44; 14:1; 19:9–10).
- He looked for those who were most receptive (Acts 18:6).

3. Paul was an entrepreneurial leader.
- He had a vision and call from God (Acts 9:15; Rom. 15:20–23).
- His vision was to be the apostle to the Gentiles through leading missionary teams into new territories to plant churches. He combined quick-strike evangelism with church planting. The wedding of these two powerful methodologies sparked movements that made an impact for generations.
- He selected the workers and apprentices he wanted on his team. He was not afraid to ask others to make sacrifices for the cause of Christ (Acts 16:2–3). Sometimes he would not let people on his team (Acts 15:38). Paul also appointed long-term leaders for the churches he started (Acts 14:23). He even gave direction to his teammates as to where they should minister (Acts 18:19; 19:22).
- He received direction from God as to where his team should plant, and his teammates had confidence in his decisions (Acts 16:6–10).
- He was a proactive strategist (Acts 13:14, 44–49). He established a reproducible pattern for his church planting (Acts 14:1, 17:2).
- He deliberately did advanced planning (Acts 19:21).

4. Paul was a team player.
- He was willing to be on a team (Acts 13:1–5).

- He always planted with a team (Acts 15:40; 16:6; 20:4).
- He had a sending base church to which he reported back (Acts 14:26–28).

5. Paul was a flexible, risk-taking pioneer (1 Cor. 9:19–21).
- He constantly penetrated new territory (Rom. 15:20).
- He targeted a new group (Rom. 11:1).
- He pioneered new methods of ministry (Acts 13).

6. Paul cared for people (shepherd role).
- He invested personally in the lives of people (Acts 20:31).
- He was like a nursing mother and an encouraging father (1 Thess. 2:7–11).
- He was vitally concerned with the growth and development of converts (Acts 14:22).
- He drew close to coworkers (2 Tim. 1:2).

7. Paul empowered others (equipper role) (Acts 16:1–3).
- In order to lead this rapidly growing movement, he risked delegation to young Christians.
- His team planted churches on their first missionary journey, and then a few months later came back to these new churches and appointed elders (Acts 13:13, 21; 14:21–23).
- He recognized his own strengths and weaknesses and delegated to others according to their strengths (Titus 1:5).

8. Paul stayed committed to fulfilling God's calling and vision even at the cost of extreme personal sacrifice (Acts 14:19–20; 2 Cor. 11:23–28).
- He never backed down, and he never gave up.
- He maintained a thankful attitude in the face of cruel and unfair treatment (Acts 16:25).

9. **Paul was willing to let go of his plants and move on to plant more (Acts 16:40).**

- It seems that Paul needed special encouragement to stay in a city for very long (Acts 18:9–11).
- The longest he ever stayed in any one place was three years (Acts 20:31).
- Ephesus was possibly his strongest plant and our best model (Acts 19:10).
- He had faith in God's ability to keep the churches he started strong (Acts 20:32).
- He was willing to let his best teammates leave his team in order to benefit best the kingdom of God (Acts 17:14).
- He followed the example of Barnabas, who was willing to let go of the top position on the church planting team (Acts 13:6–12).
- He modeled the church at Antioch that was willing to let go of its top leaders (Acts 13:1–4).[4]

A couple of things bear repeating. One component of Paul's example worthy of our imitation was his *entrepreneurial personality.* An entrepreneur starts new ventures from scratch. The fact that Paul was entrepreneurial is central to understanding his church planting ministry. Effective church planters always demonstrate entrepreneurial leadership skills. As an entrepreneur, Paul was always thinking of new ways to evangelize and new areas to enter. We will look further at entrepreneurial leadership later in this book.

A second trait worthy of imitation was Paul's *desire to remain a team player.* Maintaining the balance between being an entrepreneur and being a team player challenges many contemporary planters. These two traits fit together poorly unless the Holy Spirit is allowed to guide an entrepreneurial planter to be a team player. Church planting, though profoundly entrepreneurial, is *not* a solitary effort; church planting must be a *partnership.*

Finally, Paul instructed others to follow the model he presented. For us to follow, we need to understand his strategy and his passion. Paul always asked, "How can I best reach unbelievers?" To reach them, he was willing to pay any price and change any methodology short of compromising the gospel. This willingness included the risk-taking of entrepreneurship and the accountability of partnership. Such traits are worthy of our imitation.

New Testament Church Planting

Church planting appears not only in the life of Paul but also throughout the New Testament, particularly in the Book of Acts. Indeed, Acts becomes a remarkable document when read with an eye toward church planting. Take a look at the outline below through the lens of a church planter.[5]

Church Planting in the Book of Acts

I. Church Planting in Jerusalem (Acts 1–7)

    A. Its Origin

        1. Born in prayer (1:12–14)

        2. Bathed in the Spirit (2:1–4)

        3. Begun with proclamation (2:14–39)

        4. Baptized in the name of Jesus (2:41)

    B. Its Functions

        1. Doctrinal Teaching (2:42)

        2. Fellowship (2:42)

        3. Worship (2:42, 46)

        4. Prayer (2:42; 4:29–31)

        5. Benevolence (2:44–45; 4:34–35)

        6. Identification with the community (2:47)

        7. Witness (4:33; 5:42)

    C. Its Growth

        1. Three thousand baptized at Pentecost (2:41)

        2. People saved daily (2:47)

        3. Two thousand saved on Solomon's Portico (4:4)

        4. Multitudes added (5:14)

        5. Priests believe (6:7)

D. Its Organization
    1. Apostles (6:2)
    2. Deacons (6:3)
    3. Congregation (6:5)
    4. Elders (15:6, 22)

II. Church Planting in Judea and Samaria (Acts 8–12)

A. Church planting done by laity (8:1, 4)
B. Mass evangelism (8:5–6, 12)
C. Village evangelism (8:25)
D. Churches multiplied (9:31)
E. Growth enhanced by miracles (9:35–42)
F. Salvation extended to Gentiles (10:44–48)

III. Church Planting in the World (Acts 13–28)

A. Scattered laity started Jewish churches (11:19)
B. Christians from Jerusalem plant Gentile-Jewish church in Antioch (11:20–21)
C. Antioch became the great missionary church
    1. Sensitive to the Holy Spirit (13:2)
    2. Submissive to the Spirit (13:3)
    3. Sending church (13:3)

D. Paul's First Missionary Journey (13–14)
    1. Preached first in synagogues (13:5; 14:1)
    2. Shifted to the Gentiles (13:46)
    3. Moved from city to city (13:13–14)
    4. Appointed elders to lead the churches (14:23)
    5. Returned to check on the new churches (14:21)

E. Paul's Second Missionary Journey (15:40–18:22)
    1. Employed a team ministry (15:40)
    2. Returned to visit new churches (15:41)
    3. Guided by the Holy Spirit (16:9–10)

4. Evangelized households (16:15, 33)
5. Taught in the marketplace (17:17)
6. Contextualized the message (17:22–23)
7. Emphasized responsive peoples (18:6)

F. Paul's Third Missionary Journey (18:23–21:17)
    1. Returned to visit the churches (18:23)
    2. Established mother churches in urban areas (19:10; 1 Thess. 1:8)
    3. Started house churches (20:20)
    4. Encouraged stewardship in new churches (1 Cor. 16:1–3)

Church planting began in Jerusalem. Acts 1–7 describes the founding, growth, and early challenges of the Jerusalem church. The church was born in prayer (1:12–14), immersed in the Spirit (2:1–4), and bathed in the miraculous (2:5–13). God brought about a powerful ministry in Jerusalem, the center of the earliest church. It did not take long for the "found" of the church to preach the Word to the lost.

A study of Acts reveals that laypersons affected early church planting (8:1, 4). They performed mass evangelism (8:5–6, 12) as well as village evangelism (8:25). Through this lay movement churches multiplied (9:31). Miracles enhanced the growth of the church (9:35–42), and salvation reached increasing numbers of Gentiles (10:44–48). Later, lay Christians from Jerusalem witnessed about Christ and planted a Gentile-Jewish church in Antioch (Acts 11:20–21).

The founding of the Antioch church may be the most important moment in church planting history. Antioch would send missionaries throughout the world. Under the leadership of the Holy Spirit, the Antioch church became the first great missionary-sending church (Acts 13:3). On the other hand, the Jerusalem church turned increasingly inward and lost much of its vision, finally disappearing like the Judaizers of the early Christian movement. In contrast, the Antioch congregation reached the world by becoming the first church planting church!

Few church planters have been blessed by the sponsorship of an Antioch congregation, a church that willingly sponsors new churches. Very few churches volunteer, as Antioch, to send the *best* of their leaders and to contribute *significant* amounts of money for the establishment of new congregations. The Antioch church did just these things.

Redeemer Presbyterian Church in New York City is an Antioch church today. Redeemer knows that "no single church, no matter how large and active, can all by itself change an entire city. (Therefore) saturating greater New York with gospel-centered new churches is the only way to truly insure the transformation of our city that we so much desire."[6] As a result of their commitment, the Redeemer Church helps plant churches in New York and around the world. For the enduring success of church starting, planters need more Antioch churches to provide support.

Acts records that the church at Antioch sent Paul on his first missionary journey (chs. 13–14). He began by preaching the Good News of Jesus Christ in Jewish synagogues (13:5; 14:1) to receptive and responsive people. Synagogues existed in almost every major community in the Roman Empire. Smaller communities hosted places of prayer where no synagogue had yet been established. Paul approached these people whom he hoped to be receptive and responsive, telling them the Good News of Jesus Christ.

Eventually, as Jews became more resistant to this approach, Paul began to emphasize reaching Gentiles (Acts 13:44–47). He began with God-fearers. These were Gentiles who demonstrated a hunger for true spirituality and authentic religion, and they worshiped with the Jews in their community synagogues. Although these "seeker" Gentiles could not become full members of a synagogue without undergoing the initiation rite of circumcision, they desired to worship the one true God of the Jews. Paul's move toward the more receptive Gentiles began with the God-fearers. To the Gentiles, the gospel (without circumcision) was Good News indeed.[7]

During Paul's second missionary journey (15:40–18:22), he began to focus on contextualization. Much like North Americans today, the Athenians were people in search of spiritual truth. At Mars Hill in Athens, Paul took the revolutionary step of starting where the people were: "I see that in every way you are very religious" (Acts 17:22). Beginning at the point of their search, Paul provided them with a reasoned witness about the truth of Christ.

In the last few decades, a new movement—postmodernism—has been born in the West. One of its attributes is "spirituality," although it is expressed in ways foreign to most evangelical Christians. Postmodern generations are turning away from institutional Christianity in a way not seen in several generations.[8] Church planters who immerse themselves in the new culture without a commitment to traditional patterns will be the best change agents.[9] New churches are contextualizing as Paul did. This enables them to reach this new cultural expression—understanding that postmodern "spirituality" lacks the truth of the Holy Spirit.

On his third missionary journey (18:23–21:17), the apostle returned to the churches he had founded earlier (18:23). He also established strategic mother churches in major cities (Acts 19:10; 1 Thess. 1:8). These congregations would later become sending churches in their own right.[10] Paul even encouraged stewardship in these new churches (1 Cor. 16:1–3; 2 Cor. 8:1–6; 9:1–5) so they could become self-supporting and reproducing, learning to serve others. Paul was concerned that these churches avoid developing external dependency.

Conclusion

The accounts and details which we have considered in Acts demonstrate that Paul and other early Christians believed in and practiced church planting as a normal part of their lives. Planting new churches was not a novel or unique concept for particularly zealous believers. Rather, church starting was the normal expression of New Testament missiology. Intentional church planting, under the guidance of the Holy Spirit, was the method of the early churches. Church planting explains how the early church exploded across the Roman Empire during the decades following the resurrection of Jesus.

The life of Paul and the action of the early church demonstrate that church planting was a primary activity. Any church wishing to rediscover the dynamic nature of the early church should consider planting new churches. Furthermore, the means that Paul and the early church used provide principles for us to apply in our current methodology. Though many of their strategies were specific to their context, we should find their principles universally applicable.

Resources for Further Reading:

Allen, Roland. *Missionary Methods: St. Paul's or Ours?* Grand Rapids: Eerdmans, 1962.

Brock, Charles. *Indigenous Church Planting* (Neosho, Mo.: Church Growth International, 1981.

Shenk, David W. and Ervin R. Stutzman. *Creating Communities of the Kingdom: New Testament Models of Church Planting.* Scotdale, Pa.: Herald Press, 1988.

CHAPTER FOUR

Models of Church Plants and Church Planters

*T*here are many ways to plant a church, but there is not one "right" way that God blesses uniquely. The patterns or models that do seem to recur are explained below. These are based on observation and conversations with others. As each model is explained, a biblical example is provided (if available) followed by a modern example along with a discussion of strengths and weaknesses.

Model 1: The Apostolic Harvest Church Planter

Paradigm:	Starts churches, raises up leaders from the harvest, moves to new church
Biblical Model:	Paul
Historic/Modern Example:	Methodist circuit riders House church movement Networks of house churches

Principles:
- Planter starts and moves on.
- Pastor comes out of the church and then goes back into it.
- Pastor may or may not be classically educated.
- Churches may provide core for each new congregation.

The Apostolic Harvest church planter is the model that we are most familiar with in the New Testament. For example, Paul would go to an established urban center, teach and preach at the marketplace and/or synagogue, engage the intellectuals and elite, start worship, appoint elders-pastors, and then supervise the new elder/pastor via letter and occasional visits. In the graphic below, the Apostolic Harvest church planter goes to an area, plants a church, calls out and trains a new planter (the arrows come from and back to the new church), and then leaves to plant another church (possibly with some core members from the previous church plant).

(c) Edward J. Stetzer, 2002

The apostolic model is probably what most laypeople picture when imagining church planters. This planter is seen as an itinerant journeyman starting churches from town to town. The model has been widely used throughout history—from Gregory the Great's strategy in the sixth century to Methodist circuit riders of the U.S. Midwest in the eighteenth century.

You can download these graphics from www.newchurches.com/ resources.

Paul started an undetermined number of churches, primarily in Galatia, Asia, Achaia, and Macedonia. Many people think of this as the only model of church planting. It is not the only model, but it is certainly an important one.

Biblical Examples

A biblical example of this paradigm can be seen in Acts 13–14.[1] In this passage, Paul and his companions arrived at Pisidian Antioch (13:14).

Upon arrival, they preached and "as many as had been appointed to eternal life believed" (13:48, NASB). In Iconium, the pattern is repeated: they arrive, preach, and "a great multitude believed" (14:1, NASB). After preaching the gospel in Lystra (14:7) and Derbe (14:21), "they returned to Lystra and to Iconium and to Antioch, strengthening the souls of the disciples, encouraging them to continue in the faith. . . . And when they had appointed elders for them in every church, having prayed with fasting, they commended them to the Lord in whom they had believed" (14:21–23, NASB).

Concerning their return trip, John B. Polhill notes:

The two apostles [Paul and Barnabas] returned the way they had come, revisiting the newly established churches along the route—first Lystra, then Iconium, and finally Pisidian Antioch. In each congregation they performed three essential ministries. First, they strengthened the disciples (v. 22a). This probably refers to their further instructing the Christians in their new faith. Second, they encouraged them "to remain true to the faith" and pointed out the "many hardships" they might encounter for bearing the name of Jesus (v. 22b). . . . The final ministry of the apostles was to establish leadership in the new congregations. For these early churches there was no professional clergy to assume their leadership. Consequently, the pattern of the Jewish synagogues seems to have been followed by appointing a group of lay elders to shepherd the flock.[2]

Historic Example

A historic example of this paradigm can be seen in the rapid growth of the Methodist (and Baptist) denominations in nineteenth-century America. According to Justo L. Gonzalez, the use of itinerant ministers without formal education was a major factor in the growth of these churches:

While other denominations lacked personnel because they had no educational facilities on the frontier, Methodists and Baptists were willing to use whoever felt called by the Lord. The Methodist vanguard were lay preachers, many of them serving an entire "circuit," always under the supervision of the "Connection" and its bishops. The Baptists made use of farmers or others who made a living from their trade, and who also served as pastors of the local church. When a new area was opened for settlement, there usually was among the settlers a devout Baptist willing to take up the ministry of preaching. Thus, both Methodists and Baptists become strong in the new territories, and by the middle of the century they were the largest Protestant denominations of the country.[3]

According to John Mark Terry: "Circuit riders encouraged and appointed lay preachers to carry on the local ministry while they were busy along the circuit. These lay preachers played a great part spreading Methodism on the frontier. Normally, a young man who gave evidence of faith and speaking ability was encouraged to preach some trial sermons. If these efforts pleased the people, then the circuit rider gave the young man an 'exhorter's license.' Some of the exhorters became circuit riders, but many remained exhorters their whole lives."[4]

By the late 1800s, the Methodist churches were multiplying so many churches that they were averaging one new church per day with plans for two churches per day. When a speaker at a Free Thinker's Society meeting in Chicago stated that the churches were dying across the land, it resulted in the composition of a song to serve as a rallying-cry for churches to plant churches:

The infidels a motley band in council met and said,
The churches are dying across the land and soon will all be
    dead.
When suddenly the message came and struck them in dismay,
All hail the power of Jesus name, we're building two a day.
We're building two a day, dear Bob, we're building two a
    day,
All hail the power of Jesus name, we're building two a day.[5]

Also during the nineteenth century, one home missionary of the African Methodist Episcopal Church reported to the general conference in 1844 "that during four years he had covered three hundred miles in his itinerant preaching, establishing forty-seven churches with a total membership of two thousand. He had seven other itinerant preachers working with him, and twenty-seven local preachers had organized fifty Sunday schools with two hundred teachers and two thousand students."[6] As these itinerant preachers worked together, they appointed local preachers who pastored the churches they had started.

Contemporary Example

The house church movement is one of many examples of the Apostolic Harvest model today.[7] John Dee has spent some time in China and offers a description of a typical underground house church.

I thought you might be interested to learn a little about the house church system in China. This one church I will share about is typical. Its membership is approaching 100,000. Its radius is 300 miles.

The leader is 30 years old and he has a wife and a young son. I have been to this church and witnessed the brilliant young people in it. When a young person receives the Lord Jesus as Savior their immediate goal is to become a co-worker to be sent out for the Lord. They are not given an office with a computer, phone and fax machine. No retirement plans offered here or head Bishop post to shoot for. Without a doubt, they all know that sooner or latter, they will be arrested, tortured and put into prison for the Lord.

So the leadership is committed to teaching and raising up these young people to become full time gifted anointed evangelists for Christ. As the revival continues to multiply in the area, this church sends out 30 full time workers into the countryside. Their meetings start at 5:00 am and often last until dark. They gather in the dark and leave in the dark singing and praising the Lord in the Spirit as they go.[8]

Charles Brock, who founded Church Growth International, has served as a church planter both in North American and abroad. According to Brock, a normal process in the apostolic church planting experience (when working among receptive people) would take about eighty-two weeks. During this time, the group is led to Christ, congregationalized, taken through leadership training, and subjected to a study of the books of Galatians, John, and Romans.[9]

After proper leadership is in place, the Apostolic Harvest church planter moves on to begin another church. For Brock, his objectives have been threefold: (1) The salvation of individuals; (2) the birth of New Testament-principled churches; and (3) the birth of an indigenous association of New Testament-principled churches.[10]

Can It Work Today?

The model is still found in North America today, though to a much lesser degree than in the past. There are several reasons that there are fewer Apostolic Harvest church planters today. They include:

Paul was single. This type of church planting is difficult for a person with a family. Paul was able to move rapidly without the need to consider family issues. One must wonder how it worked for the people who traveled with him!

Synagogues are less open to itinerant evangelists. Paul had an instant crowd—both at the synagogue and in the marketplace. The Hellenistic culture encouraged and participated in open public discourse and debate. This is no longer the case. Politics and religion, once staples of debate, are now on the forbidden list for most people. Thus, the apostolic starter must generate a crowd because he will not have a ready-made crowd as Paul did.

Paul had apostolic authority. Paul could come to a town, plant a church, appoint pastors, and expect the laity to follow (read the epistles to see how well they followed . . . and Paul was an apostle.) Most "apostles," in non-authoritarian denominations, do not have the same level of authority. Thus, the process is not as effective.

Paul established the church with miraculous signs. Almost every reader will agree with one of two statements: signs and wonders have *ceased,* or signs and wonders have *decreased.* If the reader is a cessationist, he or she believes that the gifts have passed away. If the reader is from a perspective open to or practicing sign gifts, it is still unlikely that they have seen gifts at the apostolic level: people rising form the dead, regular healing, etc. With few exceptions, a new church is generally difficult to start based on miraculous signs.

Although the apostolic planter cannot operate in the same manner as Paul, there are both similarities to today's world and advantages to Paul's model in a postmodern age.

Cities are larger. An apostolic planter does not need to move from Philippi to Ephesus to Rome to start multiple churches. Today, Steve Childers at Reformed Seminary outside Orlando, Florida, can help to start churches throughout Central Florida, the United States, and even in Japan, without moving his family from Altamonte Springs.[11]

People can be reached en masse. Although there are no receptive synagogues waiting for us to engage them, there are people who are receptive and responsive. Today we can reach thousands of people at the same time through direct mail, phone campaigns, E-mail, and other means. Gathering a crowd has almost become commonplace: this many mailings produce this result, this many calls produce this result, etc. An effective apostle can gather a crowd, evangelize and equip laypeople, raise up a pastor, and move on effectively in the postmodern age.

Pastors are readily available (for most areas). Ask the typical pastor, "How would you like to pastor a one-year-old church filled with new believers ready to have a long-term pastor?" Most will jump at the prospect. So if a leader does not emerge immediately from the group, other leaders are often available nearby.

The apostolic planter can be most effective when *not* serving a local church (although the planter might be on staff at a local church). Instead, the Apostolic Harvest planter's main focus is on reproducing congregations. This is seen today when church planters work as denominational church-starter strategists or catalytic church planters, bivocational or lay church starters, or itinerant apostolic church planters.

Laypeople can also be involved in apostolic church planting. God has gifted many laypersons with full-time work in a secular field and given them a passion to reach people. Such planters can gather a core group through a home Bible study, help mentor a pastor, and then allow that pastor to lead the new church.

Model #2: The Founding Pastor

Paradigm:	Starts a church, acts as a "church planter" for a short time, and remains long term to pastor the new church
Biblical Model:	Peter and the Jerusalem church
Historic/Modern Example:	Charles Spurgeon, Rick Warren

Principles:
- Planter starts and pastors the church long term.
- Pastor often moves from another location.
- Pastor often classically educated.
- New church hopefully sponsors new congregations.

Although the Founding Pastor is listed as the second model, it is the most common model in North American church planting. In this model, the pastor can come from outside the community to plant and stay. Or the planter might be a local layperson who plants a church, grows it, and becomes its pastor. (The lower right of the graphic emphasizes that even a founding planter needs to help plant other churches—keeping focused on kingdom growth.)

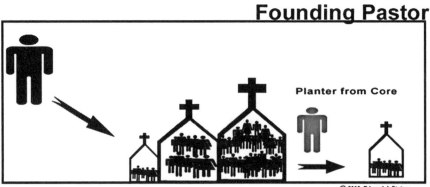

Founding Pastor

Planter from Core

© 2002 Edward J. Stetzer

The founding pastor has a great desire to plant, grow, and stay at a church long term. The pastor may be a "planted" pastor or an entrepreneurial planter (see below), but either way the founding pastor has a desire to stay at one church beyond the time that an apostolic harvest planter would. The founding pastor has a "pastor's heart," and therefore, he does not get as restless to move on to another location as the apostolic harvest planter. The pastor will hopefully lead the new church to start others, but the founding pastor is a "pastor with a missionary's heart" rather than a "missionary with a pastor's heart." The founding pastor often learns church planting because it is necessary to start the church. Then the planter moves on to the issues of pastoring, eventually raising up others to plant another church.

Biblical Example

Peter may be a biblical example. Over time, he emerged as the leader of the Jerusalem church after preaching its "founding" sermon in Acts 1. Peter was obviously the spokesperson for the apostles and the church in Jerusalem and is singled out many times from the apostles:

- His speech is recorded in Acts 1:15–22.
- Peter is said to have taken a stand with the eleven (Acts 2:14).
- Peter spoke in the portico of Solomon (3:11–12).
- Peter spoke to the rulers, elders, and scribes (4:8).
- Peter spoke to Ananias and Sapphira (5:1–11).
- People desired Peter's shadow to fall on sick (5:15).
- Peter and the other apostles answer (5:29).
- Apostles heard that the Samaritans had believed and sent Peter and John to check it out (8:14).
- Peter took the gospel to the Gentiles (10:48).

Under Peter's leadership, the Jerusalem church helped start churches in Antioch and throughout Asia Minor. Peter was involved in church planting and ministry (which got him in trouble later). We know that he visited Antioch, Corinth, and perhaps other places to establish or encourage new churches. Yet his focal point of ministry was Jerusalem. From that church, he impacted the others.

Historic Example

Among the thousands of historic examples of the founding pastor model is John Taylor. In 1783 Taylor and his family made a three-month journey by flatboat and horseback to Kentucky. After settling in Woodward County and establishing a farm, Taylor and several other Baptists formed Clear Creek Baptist Church. Taylor served as the pastor for nine years. He also had a part in founding seven other churches in Kentucky, Western Virginia, North Carolina, and Tennessee.[12]

Contemporary Example

C. Peter Wagner cites Rick Warren as an example of the founding pastor model. "As Rick was finishing his work in Southwestern Baptist Theological Seminary, he prayed, 'I'll go anywhere you send me, Lord, but please allow me to spend my whole life wherever that may be.' I have since heard him say in public that although he is not yet 40, Saddleback Valley Community Church is his last parish."[13] Rick may be an even better example because he did not just start one church—Saddleback is involved in planting daughter churches. At the time of this writing, they have sponsored thirty new churches in the United States alone—and many more internationally.

Other Types of Founding Pastors

There are at least two other types of founding pastors. The first I will call the "planted pastor" and the second the "entrepreneurial pastor."

The Founding Pastor: The Planted Pastor

Principles:
- Organization and vision for new church usually external—from an apostolic church planter, mother church, or denominational leadership.
- Planted pastor usually has a shepherding heart with administrative ability but not a church planter's gift mix.
- Planted pastor by definition does not quickly leave but stays long term.
- Planted pastor is usually classically educated and comes from outside the congregation.

- Frequently, the pastor reaches and disciples the core. The crowd is attracted or created by someone other than the pastor.
- Planted pastor hopefully helps sponsor new works.

"Me, a church planter?" is the frequent question of the planted church planter. The answer is yes and no. Yes, the planted pastor is the first/founding/starting pastor. No, the planted pastor is not necessarily a great church planting entrepreneur or strategic church planter. The planted pastor is generally a pastor with strengths typically thought of as ministerial: preaching, teaching, counseling, and related abilities. These strengths are often not found in other church planters who are more often task driven and outreach oriented.

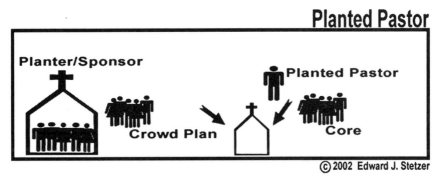

The planted pastor will lead the church as it is planted. The planted pastor may find and pastor the core while someone else (a larger mother church, an apostolic planter, or a denominational leader) provides the crowd. The diagram above illustrates the point. The planter comes from the outside and, preferably, has developed some leadership in the core. Then the crowd is generated—leading to a successful new church plant.

The planted pastor has many gifts but not planter gifts. These gifts must include people skills, preaching skills, and pastoring skills. However, the planted pastor does not need to have the ability to launch a crowd of hundreds. The planted pastor must be able to create a core and then pastor the crowd. Someone else can gather the crowd.

The planted pastor can come at different times in the church development process. If there is a strong sponsor church, laypeople may already be planning the new church and can participate in the selection of the pastor. In other cases, the planted pastor is a staff member at an established church.

Biblical Example

The closest biblical parallel to the planted pastor model would be that of Timothy's ministry in Ephesus.[14] Although Acts does not record the origins of the church at Ephesus, because of the ministry of Priscilla and Aquila (Acts 18:18–19), Apollos (Acts 18:24–26), and Paul, the disciples grew in the faith (Acts 19:1–21). Some time later, Paul sent a letter of instruction to Timothy, who was providing leadership to the Ephesian body of believers: "To Timothy, my true child in the faith. . . . As I urged you upon my departure for Macedonia, remain on at Ephesus, in order that you may instruct certain men not to teach strange doctrines nor to pay attention to myths and endless genealogies" (1 Tim. 1:2–3, NASB). We can conclude that others planted the Ephesian church, and then God (and Paul) planted Timothy there as the pastor.

Historic Example

Although Charles H. Spurgeon is known mostly for his pulpit skills, he had a passion for new churches. When Spurgeon arrived at Park Street Chapel, he found a dwindling congregation. Over time the congregation grew to megachurch size and Spurgeon established a ministerial school. Michael Nicholls has noted the impact of Spurgeon's involvement in church planting:

Twenty-seven churches were founded by students from the Pastor's College between 1853 and 1867. In the second half of the nineteenth century, the number of Baptist churches in London doubled and nearly all of these were founded, in one way or another, under Spurgeon's influence. Students were sent out to new areas or existing churches, normally at the command of "the guv'nor," as students called Spurgeon.[15]

Spurgeon joined with two other London ministers, Landels of Regent's Park and Brock of Bloomsbury, to found the London Baptist Association, with the clear intention that one new chapel should be erected each year. Both Brock and Landels had planted their churches and commenced local missions, but Spurgeon's vision was London-wide.[16]

Spurgeon impacted London the most, through church planting, during the 1860s and 1870s. New Baptist churches averaged more than eight per year between 1856 and 1860. Forty-eight churches had been planted under Spurgeon's guidance by 1878.[17] Spurgeon would send people out and set up places to plant new churches. Then he would plant one of his students there as the pastor of the new church. Spurgeon's students were planted pastors.

Contemporary Examples

The growth of church planting technology has enabled many people who do not have typical church planting gifts to plant growing churches. For example, Stonecreek Community Church[18] outside Atlanta was a church plant sponsored by Johnson Ferry Church. Johnson Ferry sent out two hundred people to be a part of the new church. They used direct mail to gather an additional three hundred persons at their first service. A total of five hundred people attended the first service. The pastor, Tommy Politz, is very gifted, but it was not necessary for him to have the gifts and skills found in most church planters who begin with few if any people. He needed skills for pastoring—he was a planted pastor.

In some cases, a new church can be so large that little or no church planting skills are required. Paul Yonggi Cho is pastor of the Yoido Full Gospel Church[19] of Seoul, Korea. In a letter, Cho wrote: "I have sent three of my associate ministers to other areas to start their own churches. Yet these faithful ministers were not sent out empty-handed. We gave each of them a starting congregation of 5,000 members plus the necessary funds to have a successful ministry in their area."[20]

As we look for church planters, not all of them have to be the types we would associate with the job. Instead, by planting pastors as well as churches, we open up the ministry for many who would have never considered the task.

The Founding Pastor: The Entrepreneurial Planter

Principles:

- Entrepreneurial planters love the challenge of starting churches but are often bored by pastoring the same church long term. However, Entrepreneurial planters are generally not attracted to the apostolic method because they love pastoring.

- The entrepreneurial planter often leaves before the congregationalizing is formalized (three years).
- The entrepreneurial planter is often classically educated and comes from outside the congregation but may have avoided education due to boredom.
- The entrepreneurial planter may sponsor new churches.

The entrepreneurial planter is another type of founding pastor. The entrepreneurial planter is usually an innovative and enthusiastic pastor who continually seeks a new challenge. That sometimes involves moving to a new church plant every few years, but that is often not the plan at the beginning!

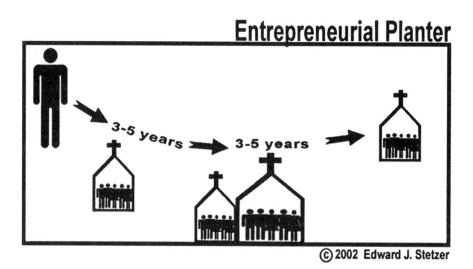

Entrepreneurial Planter

© 2002 Edward J. Stetzer

The entrepreneurial planter is more than a restless pastor. Entrepreneurial planters love to start, grow, and move forward. Sometimes the entrepreneur is not interested, willing, and/or able to lead the church through its post-plant phases. The entrepreneurial planter wants to build a core (year 1), launch and assimilate (year 2), outreach to unchurched (year 3), and growth (years 4 and 5). Sometimes the entrepreneurial planter does stay but is always starting new ministries, outreaches, and programs to keep the challenge alive.

Some entrepreneurial planters do not want to lead the church through the solidification phase (3–7 years) and thus leave before this phase begins. When this happens, the entrepreneurial planter has a real problem: job security. Since all ideas do not work, and all fields are not ready for harvest, there are times when the entrepreneurial planter will struggle financially. The same pastor can have different results in different communities even using the same methods. This person can often be viewed as unable to stay long term. Rather than recognizing the potential for church planting, many of these individuals will move from one established church to another.

Ron Hale, a church planter who at one time served as the denominational missions director in Pittsburgh, Pennsylvania, provided a model to empower the entrepreneurial planter. Most denominations simply do not have an appropriate mechanism for funding entrepreneurial planters. Ron proposed a Church Planting Evangelistic Association modeled after the organizations of itinerant evangelists. In such a system, a church planter would work with a group of supporters to provide ongoing funding for each additional church plant.

To download a copy of the Church Planting Evangelistic Association go to www.new-churches.com/resources.

John Shepherd is an example of an entrepreneurial planter who moved frequently. John planted Palm Coast Church in Florida, which grew from zero to 250 in three years.[21] John was the pastor there, the people loved him, and he could have stayed there for his entire ministry. Instead, he felt God leading him to found another church outside Nashville, Tennessee. River Oaks Church[22] had over three hundred at its first service and grew to five hundred in three years. John could have stayed there forever, but he felt God calling him to plant again.

Although many entrepreneurial planters tend to move every three to five years, some do not. They are *still* entrepreneurs and must constantly be involved in starting new projects. Those new things can be new ministries or new churches that the pastor does not lead. I would put myself in this category.

After planting Millcreek Community Church,[23] I felt the need for a new challenge. I was finding the weekly routine of pastoral ministry to be a little tedious. Instead of moving to another church, I began to start new ministries and to try new ideas—eventually starting two new churches, both with their own pastor.

Founding pastors, whether planted or entrepreneurial, are essential for kingdom growth. Statistics do show that longer tenured pastors tend to grow stronger churches. When founding pastors plant strong churches that plant other churches, church growth becomes exponential, and the kingdom benefits.

Model 3: Team Planting

Paradigm: A group of planters relocates into an area to start a church. Often the team has a senior pastor.

Biblical Model: Paul (at times)

Historic/Modern Example: Missionaries at Iona, team church plants

Principles:
- A team forms in, or relocates to, a specific area to plant a new church.
- Church planting vision often comes from one key member of the team.
- Good teams have a gift mix.
- Team may amicably split up the mother church into multiple daughter churches or become traditional staff members of the founded church.

The team concept of church planting is in vogue today. The method provides camaraderie, a division of gifts, and a strong leadership base. But this method is the most infrequently used of all the models. The reason is simple: money. The cost of funding three or more full-time staff members is prohibitive in most church-start situations. Unfortunately, most church plant team members are not willing to be bivocational. If more church planting teams were willing to work bivocationally, more new churches would be planted successfully. A powerful church planting team would involve a full-time senior pastor and a team of bivocational staff.

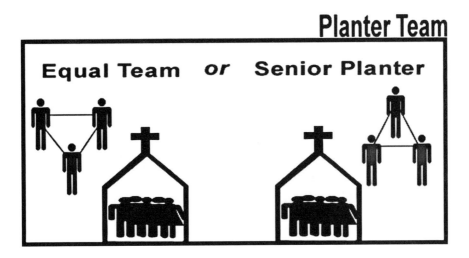

Biblical Support

The team method has strong biblical support. A large portion of Paul's ministry could also be described with this paradigm. The first example of this model found in Paul's ministry is seen in Acts 13:2–3; the church at Antioch sent out Paul and Barnabas to preach the gospel. In Acts 13:5, John Mark is seen as a helper. Eventually, Barnabas and John Mark traveled to Cyprus, and Paul departed with Silas to Syria and Cilicia (Acts 15:36–41). In Acts 16:1–5, Timothy joined Paul's team. In Acts 18:18–19, Paul traveled with Priscilla and Aquila to Ephesus. According to the scriptural account, Paul also had other traveling companions (Acts 19:29). We know that all of these people were involved in some form of ministry with Paul.

Historic Example

Columba's (521–597) ministry at Iona is a historic example of team planting. According to John Mark Terry:

[Columba] founded several monasteries. . . . In 563
Columba took twelve fellow monks and founded a new

monastery on the island of Iona near the coast of Scotland.
The monastery at Iona was a base from which to evangelize
the Picts, a tribe in northern Scotland. Even after Columba's
death, the monastery at Iona continued to send out evangelists. One monk won a prince named Oswald to faith in
Christ. When Oswald returned home to Northumbria, he
asked the monastery to send a missionary to evangelize this
people. The abbot sent Aidan, who not only evangelized the
people of Northumbria but also founded a new monastery
modeled after the one at Iona.[24]

In the Middle Ages, monasteries became centers of team planting.
Teams would go out and plant a monastery (for example, Augustine of
Canterbury) and then work together to plant churches in the surrounding
villages. After churches sprang up around monasteries, the monks would
move to a different location.

Contemporary Example

There are numerous contemporary examples of the team planting
model. Much of the current literature on the team approach is directed
toward urban church planting.[25] James E. Westgate has divided the urban
team approach into two categories: eastern model and western model. The
eastern model,

demonstrates the awareness of the need to develop a mini
community in the midst of an urban pressurized society.
Instead of sending one lone couple to face the difficulties and
adjustments of complex urban culture, this model provides a
network of supportive and complementary relationships to
deal with the diversity and complexity of an urban setting.
The focus of this team is not only to plant a church but to
reproduce themselves by training others to plant reproductive
churches.[26]

The eastern model "calls for a team of trainers equipping teams of
church planters. The primary role of the team is to train others."[27]

Regarding the western model, Westgate writes:

> The team is committed to a bivocational approach to
> church planting. The primary goal of the team is to plant a
> church in a strategic place in the city. The primary focus of
> the team is evangelism, with each team member committed to
> disciple five to ten people during the first year, a potential of
> fifty people for the beginning of the church. The second year,
> the church is organized and the couples concentrate on train-
> ing the new converts to share their faith while achieving their
> goal of leading ten more people to Christ. . . . During the sec-
> ond year the couples also choose someone to be trained in
> their own particular areas of skill, such as Bible study, or
> Christian education.
>
> The third year is a transitional stage for the church. Team
> members turn their responsibilities over to those whom they
> have trained. . . . Each team member then becomes the
> church planter for a new sister church and calls for four to
> six new couples to join them from a seminary or denomina-
> tional sister church.[28]

More and more church plants are using a team planting model—and
not just in urban settings. The nondenominational Kensington Community
Church in Troy, Michigan, began in such a manner.[29] In 1990, senior pastor Steve Andrews led a staff of four bivocational pastors, each assigned to
a different area: evangelism, exaltation, equipping, and exhortation. Over
five hundred attended the first service, and it became one of the strongest
churches in Michigan.

Rusty Corum planted New Hope Church[30] in suburban Washington,
D.C. Although he was the only paid staff member, he brought four others
with him to help plant New Hope—mainly friends from seminary who took
secular jobs as the church was planted. Today, several hundred people worship each week in the Hayfield Secondary School in Alexandria, Virginia.

My Ph.D. dissertation[31] focused on what causes a new church to have
a larger attendance. I compared the attendance of churches that did a
certain thing and those that did not. I also asked church planters to give
their thoughts on church planting issues. Over six hundred responded.

One of the recurring themes from the church planter surveys was the desire for church planting teams. The survey revealed that attendance was demonstrably higher in plants with more than one church planting pastor on staff. The attendance is almost double. This does not, of course, take into account the other factors that would also be elevated by the presence of multiple staff—in other words, if the church could afford multiple staff, perhaps they already have a large course, sponsor church, and ample funding. However, the mean attendance difference is clear.

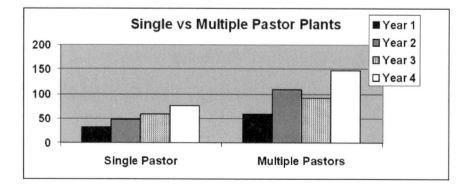

It is not just the presence of multiple pastors that makes a difference. Instead, this increased mean attendance is most present when there are two staff members—not three or more. The "missing" variable below would include churches without additional staff.

It seems that those who have two staff members are the most effective church planting teams. The survey did not address whether the teams were full-time or not. In most cases, I would guess that they were not. Thus, I think the most effective church planting team would be a full-time lead pastor with a part-time second pastor with worship and evangelism skills.

When three or more pastors are present, I have found that the new church struggles with making connections with the lost community. They build close team relationships, but perhaps because they have close friends on the team, they do not make as many evangelistic contacts and relationships.

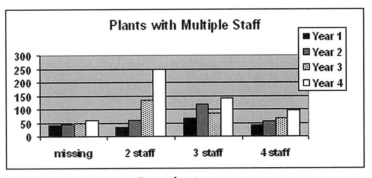

Conclusions

God uses many types of people and many different methods to plant churches. The list above is not intended to be complete, but it might help you think through your role in church planting. Perhaps you have not yet fully explored what being a church planter involves. Maybe you fit in one of the above categories, or maybe you see yourself as a combination of these models. The call of God and his provision of spiritual gifts will determine how each church planter accomplishes the work of starting new churches.

Resources for Further Reading

Cannistraci, David. *The Gift of Apostle.* Ventura: Regal Books, 1996.

Nevius, John L. *Planting and Development of Missionary Churches.* Nutley, N.J.: Presbyterian and Reformed Publishing Company, 1958.

Sanchez, Daniel R., Ebbie C. Smith, and Curtis E. Watke. *Reproducing Congregations: A Guidebook for Contextual New Church Development.* Cumming, Ga.: Church Starting Network, 2001.

Steffen, Tom. *Passing the Baton: Church Planting That Empowers.* La Habra, Calif.: Center for Organizational & Ministry Development, 1997.

Wagner, C. Peter. *Church Planting for a Greater Harvest.* Ventura: Regal Books, 1990.

Part 2

Basics of
New Church Life

What Makes a Church Planter?

*I*n order to engage in church planting effectively, it is important to consider who can plant a church. Do only churches plant churches? What about denominations? What about an individual? For that matter, must an individual be ordained, formally trained, and sent out by an agency of the denomination? In the New Testament, we see several patterns regarding the *who* of church planting.

Teams Plant Churches

Schenk and Stutzman declare, "In the book of Acts and in the Gospels, we find that the pattern of team ministry was followed consistently."[1] In many cases in the New Testament, God raised up apostolic teams to plant new churches. As we have seen, this was the apostle Paul's practice.

Paul consistently utilized team ministry in his church planting. In his intimate circle were Barnabas, Silvanus, and Timothy. Working with him as independent coworkers were Priscilla, Aquila, and Titus. Finally, Paul worked with a series of local church representatives that included Epaphroditus, Epaphras, Aristarchus, Gaius, and Jason.

> The churches, Ollrog argues, put these persons at Paul's disposal for limited periods. Through them the churches themselves are represented in the Pauline mission and become co-responsible for the work. As a matter of fact, not being represented in this venture constitutes a shortcoming in a local church; such a church has excluded itself from participating in the Pauline missionary enterprise.[2]

Individuals Plant Churches

When Philip went to Samaria (Acts 8:1–40), there is no indication that he was sent by anyone other than the Holy Spirit. As he won converts, the apostles sent Peter and John there, but Philip had already been baptizing converts and planting the new church.

Although an individual planting a church is the most common method today, it is the least common in the New Testament. This does not imply that it did not happen. Early church history reflects that several of the apostles set out in different directions to plant churches. This should remind us of the importance of bringing a team to plant—or developing one soon upon arrival.

Laypeople Plant Churches

Aquila and Priscilla are two names that appear frequently in the New Testament. They were laypeople, probably a married couple in business, and they probably started the church in Ephesus. They show up in several different cities (Rome, Corinth, and Ephesus; see Acts 18:2–3, 18–19, 26; 2 Tim. 4:19).

They hosted a church in their home at both Ephesus and Rome (1 Cor. 16:19; Rom. 16:3–5). Since there is no record of the church in Rome being "founded," it is logical to assume that Aquila and Priscilla helped start the church that met in their house.

They had a heart for church planting and the ministry of Paul, and they "may well have financed his trip"[3] to Ephesus. Richard Longenecker explains that they were probably traveling business owners:

[They] were either transferring their business from Corinth to Ephesus or leaving their Corinthian operation in charge of a manager (as possibly they did earlier at Rome) in order to open a new branch at Ephesus. Perhaps Aquila and Priscilla, who seem to have been fairly well-to-do, paid Paul's passage as they joined him on board the ship for Ephesus—and perhaps also paid his passage on to Jerusalem. Being themselves Jewish Christians, they would have appreciated Paul's desire to fulfill his vow at Jerusalem.[4]

The fact that laypeople can plant churches raises an interesting point. It reminds us that those not called to pastoral ministry can still be involved in the ministry of church planting. It is a ministry for laypeople as well as pastors.

Agencies and Denominations Plant Churches

Many people feel strongly that agencies and denominations should not plant churches. In one sense, they want to be careful about agency or denominational support for a new church. In my faith tradition, we believe in the autonomy of the local church, and we are very skeptical of outside ecclesiastical control. In most cases, however, agency/denominational church starting is not about control; it is about start-up.

> [The Bible does not speak against] the idea of people collectively gathering and sending out people to do the work of the gospel. Paul was not supported solely by the Jerusalem church, from which he went out of on his missionary journeys. Paul traveled and was supported by many different people and churches (ex., Philippians 4:16) that he might do the work that God had for him, and even had to support himself at times (Acts 18:3). Christians gathering resources and sending out workers into the harvest is what God has called His people to do, and while local church government seems to be restrictive, the work of the Gospel is not. God has worked in many different ways throughout history, and to place restrictions on God concerning this matter could cause many to miss out on the blessing of planting a new church.[5]

Churches Plant Churches

Although there is no requirement for "churches planting churches" in the New Testament, this method remains the preferred one today. In the New Testament, churches *did* commission people to plant churches, and some of their people *did* move from community to community in the process. But we cannot say that this is the only method of church planting described in the New Testament. "The real agent in the planting of the [church in] Antioch was the Holy Spirit. We see no evidence that the Jerusalem church as the 'mother church' or 'sponsoring church' took official action to send church planters to start a 'mission' or 'daughter congregation' at Antioch."[6]

But churches can and do plant churches. The best church planting occurs when a sponsor/mother church is actively involved in the planting of new churches. This has historically been called church extension—where a mother church "extends" itself into another location. Today, we prefer to call that church multiplication.

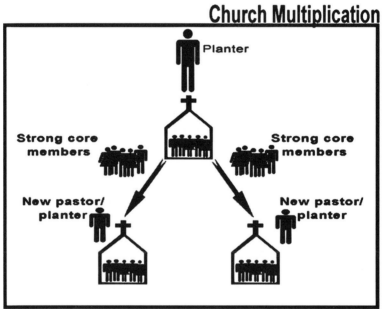

Church Multiplication

Planter

Strong core members

Strong core members

New pastor/ planter

New pastor/ planter

© 2002 Edward J. Stetzer

Mother churches tend to be involved at different levels. When new churches have a mother church sending out core members to help start the new church, it is obviously very involved. When it sends new members, the difference can be seen in the chart below. Each year the attendance of a new church with an involved mother church is higher than those without the participation of a sponsoring/mother church.[7]

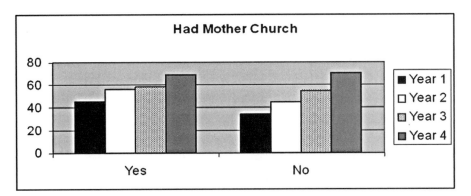

Beyond the attendance numbers, church planters can be encouraged and nurtured in the environment of a new church. On countless occasions, I have sat with church planters who were discouraged because they did not have the support and encouragement of a sponsor or mother church. On the other hand, I have visited with many church planters who had the support of a mother church—and they have shared a sense of enthusiasm and excitement. Having a supportive sponsor or mother church makes a big difference, and it is the best way to plant a daughter church.

So Who Can Plant?

A former student of mine explained the issue of "who can plant" like this: "What was the criteria that Barnabas used in making his judgments on the church at Antioch. The Bible says he 'saw the evidence of the grace of God' (Acts 11:23). That is the only criteria that the Bible mentions. Thus, what Barnabas did was he recognized God at work in that church plant."[8]

Ultimately, God calls church planters and blesses new churches. God can use teams, individuals, agencies, and other churches. But without the Holy Spirit's work we are not planting churches; we are starting religious clubs.

God can use different or multiple persons to plant churches. Over the last twenty years, persons have begun to notice and categorize certain characteristics of church planters. In the early 1990s, Joe Ratliff wrote about some of the characteristics of church planters. He explained: "Selling a vision is generally couched in the personality of the church planter. However, this does not necessarily mean the church planter has to have a vibrant, slap on the back gregarious personality. Rather, the church planter must have a communicating personality, a listening personality, a people personality. The church planter must be serious and sincere about the vision."[9]

Those ideas have been more fully developed in the last few years. Individuals and groups began to develop assessments to evaluate church planting potential.

What Does a Church Planter Look Like?

In the late 1980s church planting leaders began to speak of "assessments." Assessments come in many varieties. In some cases, an assessment lasts one week and involves intensive psychological testing, one-on-one interviews, group interactions, and follow-up meetings. On the other hand, some assessments are short and simple—intended to help the potential church planter clarify a sense of calling and giftedness.

For information about assessments, see www.new-churches.com/assessment. Also, see www.church-plantingvillage.net for an on-line self assessment called "The Discovery Tools."

The task of church planting requires people who are uniquely gifted. Since you are reading these words, you may be asking, "Am I a church planter?"

A planter's S.H.A.P.E. includes:

- **Spiritual gifts:** Gifts of ministry bestowed by the Holy Spirit
- **Heart or passion:** A burden to establish an outreach toward a specific people group, in a particular location, or through a specific type of ministry
- **Abilities:** Entrepreneurial talents useful in planting (or perhaps in generating income in a bivocational church plant)
- **Personality type:** Analysis of personality types often appearing in church planters
- **Experiences:** Tools for describing experiences to help the planter understand when, where, and how to plant a church

From his study of church planters from several Protestant denominations, Charles Ridley[10] developed a helpful process for determining the probability that a person will succeed in church planting. Denominations across North America use his work to assess their planter candidates.

Ridley determined that most successful church planters share thirteen behavioral characteristics. It is the Ridley assessment to which most people refer when they speak of a church-planter assessment.

Church planters who have gone through a Ridley assessment interview lead churches that are larger in attendance than those who do not. Attendance is a good indicator of church health (though not the only one). Although this graph only refers to attendance, most church planting leaders would acknowledge that a new church is more likely to fail when it is started by a planter who has not been assessed. All other factors being equal, an assessment assures the selection of better church planters with a higher likelihood of success.

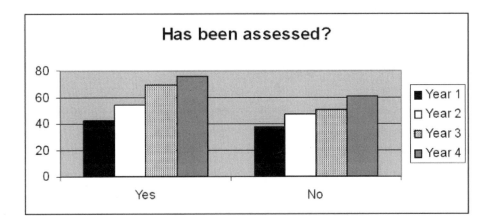

The Ridley Categories

1. *Visionizing Capacity* is the ability to imagine the future, to persuade other persons to become involved in that dream, and to bring the vision into reality.

2. *Intrinsically Motivated* means that one approaches ministry as a self-starter, and commits to excellence through hard work and determination.

3. *Creates Ownership of Ministry* suggests that one instills in others a sense of personal responsibility for the growth and success of the ministry and trains leaders to reproduce other leaders.

4. One Who *Relates to the Unchurched* develops rapport and breaks through barriers with unchurched people, encouraging them to examine

and to commit themselves to a personal walk with God. As an additional outcome, new believers become able to lead others to salvation in Jesus Christ.

5. *Spousal Cooperation* describes a marital partnership by which church planting couples agree on ministry priorities, each partner's role and involvement, and the integration and balance of ministry with family life.

6. *Effectively Builds Relationships* is the skill to take initiative in meeting people and deepening relationships as a basis for more effective ministry.

7. Starters *Committed to Church Growth* value congregational development as a means for increasing the number and quality of disciples. Through this commitment they increase numerical growth in the context of spiritual and relational growth.

8. *Responsiveness to the Community* describes abilities to adapt one's ministry to the culture and needs of the target area residents.

9. One who *Utilizes Giftedness of Others* equips and releases other people to minister on the basis of their spiritual giftedness.

10. A starter who is *Flexible and Adaptable* can adjust to change and ambiguity, shift priorities when necessary, and handle multiple tasks at the same time. This leader can adapt to surprises and emergencies.

11. *Builds Group Cohesiveness* describes one who enables the group to work collaboratively toward common goals, and who skillfully manages divisiveness and disunifying elements.

12. A starter who *Demonstrates Resilience* shows the ability to sustain himself or herself emotionally, spiritually, and physically through setbacks, losses, disappointments, and failures.

13. One who *Exercises Faith* translates personal convictions into personal and ministry decisions and resulting actions.

Other Qualifications

Besides the qualities addressed by the S.H.A.P.E. inventory and described by the Ridley categories above, we find other qualifications in the New Testament. For example, although the requirements in 1 Timothy 3 target pastor-elders, they also apply to church planters. But because church planters encounter issues typically not faced by pastors of established congregations, we need to consider several qualifications uniquely essential to church planters.

The first additional qualification is a *certainty of call to church planting*. In Ephesians 3:8, Paul wrote, "To me, the very least of all saints, this grace was given, to preach to the Gentiles the unfathomable riches of Christ" (NASB). In times of doubt, pain, and struggle, Paul could look back to a specific time of his calling. This certainty of being called to preach to the Gentiles reassured him in difficult times. In 1 Timothy 2:7 he wrote, "For this I was appointed a preacher and an apostle (I am telling the truth, I am not lying) as a teacher of the Gentiles in faith and truth" (NASB).

Just as a call to the Gentiles compelled the apostle Paul, part of the planter's call is to a certain people. That call may be to the people of a specific community or a specific culture or demographic group.

Ridley mentions *faith* as a qualification equal with a dozen others, but it deserves much greater emphasis. The author of Hebrews wrote, "Faith is the assurance of things hoped for, the conviction of things not seen" (Heb. 11:1, NASB). Though every pastor needs faith, the church planter needs *extraordinary* faith. Although the church does not exist and cannot be seen before it is started, the planter must possess the conviction that the new church is a reality—it will come into existence. The planter who does not have faith that God is planting a church through his efforts should not be a planter.

Conclusions

Many people plant churches for wrong reasons. One list of inappropriate reasons includes:

- A strong desire to preach—but no one will give you an opportunity.
- Frustrated where you are because you can't do what you want to do.
- Can't get an invitation to pastor an established church.
- Out to prove something.
- Need to get some experience—and church planting seems like a good opportunity to practice ministerial skills.[11]

None of these are adequate reasons—even if your personality sounds similar to the list above. But if a person has the right *reasons* and the right *wiring*, the combination can lead to great church planting potential.

After reading these categories, you might be encouraged or discouraged—depending on how you feel you "line up" with the categories. If you are encouraged, you might consider connecting with some church planting leaders in your church, fellowship, or agency. Share your interest in church planting with them. The remainder of this book will contain practical steps that can be used to plant the church God has called you to plant.

If you read the categories and were discouraged, do not give up yet. First, ask those who know you if you have some of these characteristics. If they, and you, agree that these categories do not describe you, you should reconsider being a lead church planter. However, you could still consider serving on a church planting team, and you can certainly encourage and support others in church planting.

Resources for Further Reading

Mannoia, Kevin. *Church Planting: The Next Generation.* Indianapolis, Ind.: Light and Life Communication, 1994.

Ridley, Charles R. *How to Select Church Planters.* Pasadena: Fuller Evangelistic Association, 1988.

CHAPTER SIX

Church Structure

*T*he typical church planter thinks a great deal about the new church's first service—envisioning the crowd and great attendance, rehearsing preaching, and "pre-living" the church's first service of worship. Most planters, on the other hand, have not considered the nature of the congregation's underlying governance or structure.

The noted church growth authority, Elmer Towns, considers changing, incorrect ecclesiology to be a frequent cause of new church failures. My own church planting experience is probably a good example. I started my first church, Calvary Christian Church, with a public launch service of twenty-one people, followed by a weekly attendance of nine people. Our plan was that the congregation would be cell-based and governed by a plurality of elders.

Following a challenging first year and pressure from *all* nine church members, I attended a conference on the effective Sunday school. Soon our church reorganized itself around Sunday school structures and had no cell groups. We did continue following a strong pastoral leadership model but deemphasized elder plurality.

Within a year we reorganized again and emphasized deacon leadership. I was unsure of what approach to governance was best. I did not know the Bible's counsel concerning church structure. I responded to whatever I learned at the latest conference or read in an influential book. (About this time in my life, I decided to attend seminary!) The church was quickly discouraged after each change.

Just as changing worship styles can divide churches, changing church structure and leadership styles can divide a congregation and sap morale. Changing plans for assimilation also frustrates people. The church planter must decide on church structure before the congregation begins. This section of our study centers on both ecclesiology and assimilation because each one heavily influences the other.

Many planters are young, idealistic, and recent college or seminary graduates. During their academic training, they learn about ecclesiological paradigms. They decide which model to adopt as their own. Many schools advocate one model over others. Many young church planters view their new church start as a way to demonstrate their chosen structure as the best. But planting a church to demonstrate an ecclesiological principle is a sure path to failure.

No Structure, or Too Much Structure?

Some planters downplay the importance of biblical church structures. They believe that structures are theological afterthoughts or traps to be avoided for the sake of encouraging a streamlined organization. But when these things are ignored at the beginning, they frequently become problems at a later date.

On the other hand, some churches discuss their ecclesiology so frequently that they tie up meetings with endless internal business. Visitors wonder whether these churches can decide any matter without the approval of some board or body. I must admit that is how I started. After the first service at my first church, we had a thirty-two-page constitution for nine regular attendees. We had three pages for each attendee! Our committees outnumbered our people. We held monthly business meetings because I thought that was God's design. When a church focuses on structure, the planter spends time servicing the structure.

The Bible does provide us with a solid middle ground for church structure. Churches do need *biblical* ecclesiology that enables them to function with efficiency and integrity.

Scholars and practitioners have identified several options for church governance in the Scriptures and in tradition.

- **Elders.** The pure-elder paradigm provides a true plurality for governance with no chief leader. It is practiced among Brethren denominations and in some Bible churches. Some biblical evidence supports this view.

- **Pastors and Elders.** This approach commends a plurality of leaders among which the pastor serves as an elder and is the "first among equals." Other elders may be laypersons or paid vocational (full-time) staff.[1]
- **Pastor and Board.** In this form of government, the pastor is seen as the leader, but looks to the church board to share in the tasks of leadership and major decision making. The board may be comprised of either deacons or elders. This pattern describes the most commonly practiced form of church governance, although little biblical support for this approach may be found.
- **Board and Pastor.** This form of church government acknowledges the pastor as an employee of the board. The pastor performs ministry at their direction. Although this model appears in many church settings, one finds no biblical evidence to commend its use.
- **Pastor.** Churches that follow this ecclesiological system clearly follow only the pastor. This style frequently appears among independent Baptists and in charismatic and Pentecostal congregations. The pastor is the decision maker for the church, sharing authority with no one—except, perhaps, with the entire church under a congregational form of government. Some proof texts may be interpreted to support this approach.

Scripture References to Consider

In order to determine what the best structure should be, we need to look to Scripture. A number of passages help us understand biblical teachings about ecclesiology. These passages include John 17:23; Acts 14:23; 20:17, 28–32; 21:18; 1 Corinthians 11:17–18; Galatians 6:10; Ephesians 4:3; 1 Timothy 3; 4:14; 5:1–2, 17–19; Titus 1:5–9; James 5:14–15; 1 Peter 5:1–5.

My best understanding of the biblical teaching is that the church should be led by a group of pastor-elders who serve in covenant relationships with one another. Generally, there will be a lead pastor-elder, but they will be drawn from the preaching team and the congregation as a whole. They might include pastors, bivocational pastor-elders, and lay pastor-elders.

Let Congregational Purpose Shape Ecclesiology

Churches should structure themselves for growth because the New Testament teaches that the church exists to evangelize the world, grow the body of Christ, and extend His kingdom.[2] Church structure functions like a human skeleton; it is a necessity for function and well-being, but structure should remain invisible to the naked eye. Church structure should be biblical yet remain out of sight in its functional routine. Ecclesiological structure helps the church to be orderly. Scripture emphasizes that churches must be orderly because of the very nature of God: "God is not a God of disorder but of peace" (1 Cor. 14:33).

Jesus most frequently pictured his followers as a "flock." Jesus called Christians his "sheep" and the church his "flock." This emphasis is also revealed in the term for a church leader known as "pastor." The Greek word *poimen* may be translated as either "shepherd" or "pastor." Pastors are to serve as shepherds—to feed, to protect, and to lead God's flock. The task of the pastor is to serve as assistant shepherd or under shepherd to the Good Shepherd (John 10:11, 14), whom Peter (1 Pet. 5:4) termed the Chief Shepherd. Thus, pastors embrace the call to "shepherd" the flock that God has placed under their care (Acts 20:28; 1 Pet. 5:2).

All of these biblical principles of leadership point to the biblical concept of eldership (also interchangeably called "pastors" in Scripture). Pastor-elders were said to choose deacons (Acts 15:22), to "rule" (1 Tim. 5:17), and to intercede on behalf of the sick (James 5:14). These leaders were said to have received appointment, in at least one instance, from a church planter (Titus 1:5).

Pastor-Elder

Several Scriptures explain the role. One of the clearest verses is 1 Timothy 5:17: "The elders who direct the affairs of the church well are worthy of double honor, especially those whose work is preaching and teaching." Another helpful text is 1 Peter 5:1–4:

> To the elders among you, I appeal as a fellow elder, a witness of Christ's sufferings and one who also will share in the glory to be revealed: Be shepherds of God's flock that is under your care, serving as overseers—not because you must,

but because you are willing, as God wants you to be; not
greedy for money, but eager to serve; not lording it over those
entrusted to you, but being examples to the flock. And when
the Chief Shepherd appears, you will receive the crown of
glory that will never fade away.

These two passages suggest that some pastor-elders teach and some do not (or else why the double honor?). The traditional "pastor" is not the only "elder" in the church. Some elders preach and teach; some do not. Furthermore, the "elder" is also called an "overseer" (Greek: *episkopos*, often mistranslated as "bishop") and the shepherd-pastor (Greek: *poimen*, translated as either "pastor" or "shepherd").

Therefore, a church is *led* by pastor-elders—some of whom function as teaching pastors. Pastors lead and feed the flock, help people find their place in ministry, and lead with an attitude of love found in loving families. A proper understanding of the nature of the church and relevant biblical passages helps us understand the leadership qualities called for in church planters.

Deacons

According to the New Testament, deacons are servants who assist the church in accomplishing its ministry. Their role is a *ministry* role. In Acts 6, deacons took responsibility to oversee the church's social ministry to widows who needed the daily distribution of food. Deacons are to conform to certain lifestyle and behavioral requirements (1 Tim. 3:8–13). Paul greeted them as church leaders (Phil. 1:1). Deacons are ministry leaders who serve under the leadership of the church's pastor-elders.

Neutral Names

At several of my church plants, we used neutral terms for the positions of elder and deacon. We called our pastor-elders the "administrative team" and our deacons "ministry leaders."

There are positive and negative aspects to this approach. First, if these functions are biblical offices, is it not better to use the biblical terminology? Neutral terms may overemphasize a businesslike appearance of the church; biblical terminology tends to emphasize the scriptural nature of the church.

On the other hand, neutral names can be understood by everyone. Because new evangelistic churches attract persons from other churches and denominations, this approach provides a great advantage for helping everyone make a fresh start in the new church. Thus, when a former Church of God member sees elders as leaders and deacons as servants of the church, he or she may conflict with the former American Baptist who sees deacons as the leadership "board" of the church. Neutral terminology may more clearly delineate the roles of each person in leadership.

The value of this approach is clear. Everyone can learn what title performs what function without having to unlearn old meanings. Furthermore, the case may be made that churches of the New Testament era understood elders as *leader*-servants and deacons as *ministry*-servants. Clarity in terminology today is just as important. Some authorities in church planting recommend using terminology that is understood by everyone in the culture of the church. Context determines terminology.

In spite of the practicality of neutral names, however, I have become convinced that using biblical terminology is best. This practice allows the church to look to biblical texts for explanation and descriptions of leadership roles. The practice takes more work, but it enables the church family to personalize the Scripture text. When they read about elders, there are specific people in mind. When they read about deacons, they have a face to go along with the name.

Applications

How does this understanding influence the structure of a new church?

1. *New churches should call out a few pastor-elders.* Pastor-elders serve in such an important role that they should be high in spiritual caliber and few in number. A smaller group promotes greater intimacy and higher mutual accountability within the leadership.

These leaders should be called out slowly. New churches don't need many committees to function appropriately. Perhaps one administrative committee to oversee the plans of the new church will be a helpful accountability structure.[3] Many new churches appoint a "steering committee" early. This steering committee is not yet a leadership body—they are an advisory team that helps provide direction. Some, if not all, of those on the early steering committee can become pastor-elders when the new church constitutes.

2. *The church should understand that pastors are elders.* Thus, if the congregation follows a team of three pastor-elders, one could serve as the vocational pastor while the other two may be lay pastors. On the basis of congregational growth, the church may want at a point in the future to call all of these pastor-elders as church staff or add other pastor-elders.

3. *The congregation should allow its pastor-elders to "direct the affairs of the church."* When congregations entrust most decisions to pastor-elders, those churches generally eliminate the need for constant church business meetings.

From the outset of the new church, the planter-pastor should tell the people that the pastor will lead the church and that a group of other pastor-elders will lead the church alongside the pastor. That biblical structure will allow the pastor to lead under predictable accountability, thereby maximizing the effectiveness of the church. With proper accountability and leadership, the church will become fully empowered for its purposes of growth and ministry.

Conclusion

Nothing can take the place of effective leadership. In the established church, this is important, but in the new church it is basically all that exists. Everything rises and falls based on leadership. God-led leaders will serve their church plants through equipping and empowering others.

Resources for Further Reading

Baxter, Richard. *The Reformed Pastor.* http://www.ccel.org/b/baxter/pastor.

Sanders, Oswald. *Spiritual Leadership.* Chicago: Moody Press, 1994.

Strauch, Alexander. *Biblical Eldership.* Littleton, Colo.: Lewis and Roth Publications, 1995.

Towns, Elmer L. *Getting a Church Started: A Student Manual for the Theological Foundation and Practical Techniques of Planting a Church.* Lynchburg, Va.: Church Growth Institute, 1985.

Warren, Richard. *The Purpose-Driven Church.* Grand Rapids: Zondervan Publishing House, 1995.

CHAPTER SEVEN

Planter-Pastor Leadership

Leadership is a big topic. There are hundreds of books on the subject from both secular and Christian viewpoints. I won't attempt to duplicate their work here. But if you are untrained in leadership, it would be well worth your time to learn more about the subject. Instead of repeating what is already well covered, I will address two subjects unique to church planting leadership: the daily routine and the challenge of cultural adjustment.

Daily Responsibilities and Schedule

The planter's schedule is an expression of priorities in ministry. Many planters complain about the pastor's forty-hour workweek. Church planters need to know that pastors do not ask church people to work just forty hours. We ask them to work an average of forty to fifty hours at their employment, and then to volunteer another five to ten hours of work per week for the church. If pastors are to model leadership, a fifty-hour pastoral workweek is not unreasonable. Many bivocational ministers work many more than fifty hours per week.

Mapping out a productive work schedule is always a challenge. Larry Lewis outlines a good system of time allocation by dividing the schedule into four sections: visitation, sermon preparation, administration, and meetings.[1] The following schedule is broken down for both full-time and bivocational starters.

Evangelistic Outreach: *fifteen hours per weeks (full time); three hours per week (bivocational).* You cannot plant a church without spending time with lost people. If the planter does not set evangelistic outreach as a priority, the church cannot grow. If there are no core group members in the beginning, the planter has *nothing else* to do but knock on doors, make phone calls, or meet people. A prospect file helps the planter focus upon a group of people who are receptive to follow-up visits.

Sermon and Study Preparation: *ten hours per week (full-time); two hours per week (bivocational).* Many seminary students have heard they need to spend thirty or more hours each week in sermon preparation. Realistically, you won't have that much time to devote to message preparation as a church planter, nor do most pastors! Nevertheless, one must take the requirement for study seriously. God mandates through Paul that we "preach *the Word*" (2 Tim. 4:2, emphasis added), not a series of opinions, or even opinions proof-texted with Scripture. Church planters should make strong biblical preaching a priority.

One good resource for many planters (particularly time-short bivocational planters) is the sermon resources of others. Church planters often use sermons prepared by others. This practice dates back to the first century. The Internet serves as a great resource for faster sermon preparation.[2]

Your seminary preaching professor probably advised against this—but in reality, this practice is acceptable as long as you do it with integrity. If you do use someone else's sermon outline, make sure it is authentic to the biblical text. It should also contain your personal style, theological understanding, and conviction. If you do not personalize the materials of others, even novice listeners will find the differences distracting and confusing. When using a prepared outline, let the Holy Spirit transform it into his and your message.

Administration: *ten hours per week (full-time); two hours per week (bivocational).* Administration, as all pastoral functions, is essential but must be balanced with other tasks. For those with the gift of administration, meetings and planning can quickly fill up a schedule. For church planters, this time may include development of outreach materials, strategy development and related planning tastes.

Ministry: *fifteen hours per week (full-time); three hours per week (bivocational).* Many church planters become bogged down in this task area. New churches attract all kinds of troubled people who want the care of an idealistic, energetic, people-loving, people-seeking church planter. As a result, the planter can get overwhelmed ministering to these troubled people.

As hard as it is, the church planter should focus on people who seem likely to become reproducing leaders and on those who are able to minister to others. Many planters focus on a small group of available people who are willing to spend much of their time with the planter. But in many cases these people will not become reproducing leaders. It makes more sense for the pastor to spend time with potential reproducers. Reproducers are people who can help develop a church in which more and more people are equipped and trained for ministry. Then the church is able to care for those who are needy. The pastor will also have more time to minister to people with greater needs as necessary. This is not a matter of ministry but a matter of priorities and timing.

Personal Adjustment Challenges

There are certain changes and challenges that every planter needs to prepare to face in starting a new church.

The planter must be prepared for *culture shock,* a cross-cultural disorientation that makes the planter feel like the proverbial fish out of water. No matter the location of the new start, when the starter leaves the confines of a home church and established Christian relationships, culture shock will inevitably follow.

Culture fatigue may be described as a low level of nagging culture shock. Repeated weariness from working as a "stranger in a strange land" wears down the optimism of the planter. The church planter finally feels worn out, weary of being unaccustomed to how the people of the new church think, talk, and react to life. The planter may feel overcome with emotional exhaustion and think, *I keep on telling them the right message, and they just don't get it.*

Because all church planters inevitably become vulnerable to culture shock and fatigue, they must prepare themselves emotionally to face this challenge. Even if you are planting in your hometown, it will be stressful to focus on the unchurched people in that town since they are in the unchurched culture; you are from a churched culture.

First, the planter must take the following warning seriously: *every planter will experience some form of this cross-cultural struggle.*

Second, the planter needs to identify an *Ebenezer* (1 Sam. 7:12). This marker is a memorial of God's help. It reminds the starter of God's call and

God's promise that planting a new church, and planting in *this* place is the divine call. The planter must be able, in the midst of doubt and weariness, to look back to that "Ebenezer" moment when God's direction had been clear and unmistakable.

Jim Dumont, a church planter in Erie, Pennsylvania, first moved to the town in 1981 to start Erie Christian Fellowship. He had nowhere to live and did not know anyone; he came solely in obedience to the call of God. He and his family lived in a campground for six weeks. Now, many years later, he says that every time he goes by the campground, "it reminds me of God's faithfulness." For Pastor Jim, this campground is his Ebenezer.

Third, the planter must *develop a network* of other planters and intercessors, a mentor, and a supervisor who can provide support during the high tides of weariness and hopelessness. An analysis of over six hundred church planters has shown that there is a significant value to having a mentor and a supervisor.[3]

Meeting with a supervisor has a surprising impact on the attendance of a new church. Frequent meetings may indicate a heavy involvement by the sponsoring entity—the planter would probably have a close relationship with the supervisor. Most church planters I know would chafe at the idea of a weekly meeting with a supervisor, but it clearly makes a positive difference. Accountability leads to productivity.

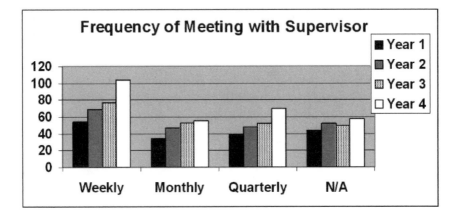

Meeting with a mentor has a similar positive impact on attendance. In my setting, we believe that a supervisor should focus on work issues and a mentor should focus on personhood issues. Meeting with a mentor means that the church planter has someone who is concerned about personal issues—providing encouragement and nurture to the church planter.

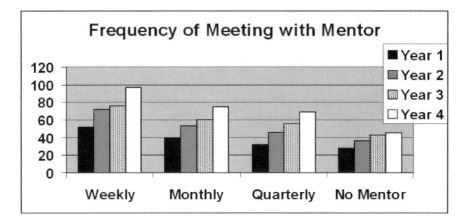

Relationships make leaders; wise leaders will also create learning relationships. This is not easy for most church planters, who tend to be free spirits and perhaps mavericks. But the best church planters combine innovation with learning and become leaders under accountability.

Finally, the planter must learn and remember, in spite of everything, that the God of eternity is faithful and that He is the God of the fiery furnace. He *always* accompanies his obedient servants into the midst of life's hottest fires (Dan. 3:19–30).

Conclusion

Leadership is essential. You may have plenty of funding, a full-time team, and a great location, but if your leadership skills are not developed, you will not be successful. On the other hand, you may have no funding, no team, and no place to live, and still be successful if God is at work through you as a leader. The full title of Elmer Towns's church planting book was *Getting a Church Started in the Face of Insurmountable Odds with Limited Resources in Unlikely Circumstances.* The only way to overcome such obstacles is with Spirit-filled and Spirit-led leadership.

Resources for Further Reading

Jones, Marge and E. Grant Jones. *Psychology of Missionary Adjustment.* Springfield, Mo.: Gospel Publishing House, 1995.

Hiebert, Paul G. *Anthropological Insights for Missionaries.* Grand Rapids: Baker Book House, 1985.

MacDonald, Gordon. *Ordering Your Private World.* Nashville: Thomas Nelson, 1985. See pages 64–88.

O'Donnell, Kelly, ed. *Missionary Care: Counting the Cost for World Evangelization.* Pasadena, Calif.: William Carey Library, 1992.

Sjogren, Steve and Rob Lewin, *Community of Kindness.* Ventura, Calif: Regal from Gospel Light, 2003.

http://www.asbury.edu/dept_sites/academic/psych/mis_care/index.cfm

http://www.aim-us.org/ministry_opportunities/missionary_care.htm

CHAPTER EIGHT

Involving Lay Leaders

Since most church planting teams have, at most, one full-time staff member, volunteer laypersons comprise most teams. As a result, the church planter needs to equip thoroughly and train those lay leaders before the new church opens for public worship.[1]

Trained, committed laypeople must become engaged in ministry before the church launch. This pre-launch stage resembles the period of human prenatal maturation during which a fetus develops systems to enable it to function after birth. A baby born without all of these systems developed and functional will not thrive. Similarly, certain operational systems *must* be fully functional by the time the church has its first public worship service. Otherwise, the church will be born prematurely and will not have the necessary parts to achieve success for the kingdom of God.

The church planting team can come into the community with the church planter; however, most planters will raise up a local team. The local team can give helpful input regarding the community in which the church is being planted. At least five lay leaders are needed to make the new church work.

Different church planting leaders suggest different team members. Lyle Schaller believes that all church planting teams should include at least three people: a pastor, an evangelist, and a music specialist. He also suggests a five-person team that would, in addition to the three just mentioned, include someone to minister to families with children and a person responsible for developing church life.[2]

Five Indispensable Leaders

You need at least five people heading up five systems.[3] Bob Logan identifies five key systems or processes (with volunteer leaders) that must be in place before the first public worship service: new member assimilation, network evangelism, spiritual gifts mobilization, a children's ministry team, and a worship team. Logan's systems could be "personalized" with the following team members: pastor (may also need an administrator), worship leader, preschool/children's minister, assimilation coordinator, evangelism networker, spiritual gifts mobilizer. At the end, I will add two more that I think are essential.

The *pastor* is a charismatic leader and vision-caster for the new congregation. This person does not need to be ordained. In the same way, although giftedness to be the chief administrator is helpful, if the pastor does not possess such skills, the team should complement the pastor and help supply those abilities.

The *worship leader* is a talented music director with the ability to lead the congregation toward a culturally appropriate encounter with God. If this person does not direct the church's music, he or she should have the ability to assess and empower other leaders for music ministry. His or her job is to put together a worship team.

The worship leader makes sure that attendees find the worship time appropriately structured, interesting, and meaningful—always pointing people toward God. Depending upon the type of church being started, the worship system may be so sophisticated that it includes a twelve-piece praise band and a worship leader, PowerPoint technology, and worship programs. On the other hand, the music may be so simple that it requires only one guitar and transparencies to show on an overhead projector. Whatever the level of sophistication, the church must have its worship system ready before launch day arrives. In today's sophisticated culture, people have grown to expect quality of presentation, even from volunteer organizations such as churches. Poor quality may mean that first-time guests will not return.

The *preschool children's minister* is a child care worker (probably a volunteer) who sacrifices personal fellowship with the adult group in order to serve the children who attend. This person should mature in the ability to delegate tasks as the church grows.

In most cultures, a preschool ministry system is crucial for effective church ministry. During a new church's early days, the planter should resist pressures to develop a full children's program immediately. Even with much effort, this ministry will not quickly become a quality program. Instead, the new church can start by providing something for the youngest children during the service.

Most parents will immediately want a full children's ministry. The best way to resist this pressure is to encourage parents to adopt the high quality of worship as *their* priority. If they can be convinced to follow that path, they should be able to wait for the children's ministry to become a higher church priority in the future. When resources are more plentiful and the needs for that ministry increase, the new church can invest more time, energy, and resources in developing a full-blown children's ministry.

Parents need to feel comfortable when they drop off their children at the nursery. The parent who signs a child in should be the same person who claims the child after the service. The new church should provide pagers for parents who leave their infants and toddlers in the church's care. Clean, easily identifiable uniforms for the workers, along with basic care focused on the needs of infants and toddlers, can assure parents of good child care long before the congregation can start a full, high-cost program of children's ministry.

The *assimilation coordinator* develops and oversees ways for involving church members and guests more deeply in the life of the congregation. Although we will consider the area of assimilation in greater depth later, I will define this layperson now as the organizer of small groups or Sunday school.

The assimilation system will involve guests and members in real relationships, ministries, and services within and beyond the congregation. Not having an assimilation system in place was one of the first mistakes I made while planting Millcreek Community Church. A total of 234 people attended our launch service. On the following Sunday, 167 people returned. Of the original 234 persons, we preserved 135. Although Millcreek outperformed the typical church plant (which averages 50 percent of the launch attendance one month later), it struggled without a well-developed, intentional assimilation system. A fully functional assimilation system of small groups can help new churches outperform the usual 50 percent rate of loss following launch day.

The *evangelism networker* promotes activities to reach the unchurched and also assists other leaders in evangelizing the unchurched through their existing networks. Riverside Church[4] in Cincinnati identifies this position as the "pastor of purpose." His job is to keep the church focused on the evangelistic purpose of the church.

Although evangelism should be the center of a new church's mission, it seems that evangelism is easily forgotten in the new church. There is so much focus on getting the music ready, recruiting nursery workers, and raising the finances that evangelism can become a low priority. The evangelism networker helps the church stay focused by providing evangelistic projects and reminding the core of their own evangelistic responsibility. Christians who are not evangelistic before the church launch day will not suddenly become experienced witnesses after the launch.

The church's *spiritual gifts mobilizer* is a coach who assists persons in identifying their spiritual gifts and their place in ministry within and beyond the congregation. Developing volunteers takes time—particularly if volunteers are recruited from among new believers. Taking the time to develop church systems during the prenatal stage will make postlaunch discipleship much stronger. To do this, new churches need a systematic process for spiritual gifts discovery and ministry placement. The new church should develop a strategy to match spiritual gifts with ministries that are needed in the community.

There are resources available to the church planting team for little or no cost to help people discover and utilize their spiritual gifts. A helpful program for the small church to develop a ministry placement system is *Team Ministry* (Church Growth Institute: 1-800-553-GROW). Saddleback Church also provides excellent small church resources through its *Discovering My Ministry* class (www.purposedriven.com). Finally, *Network* is an effective resource for larger churches (www.networkministries.com).

All of these processes for assimilation resemble one another to some extent. They:
- teach about spiritual gifts, passions, and personality types;
- provide a measurement instrument of spiritual gifts (a gifts "inventory");
- display a list of ministries that might match each gift; and
- recommend a way for one-on-one meetings by which leaders help new people find their place for ministry.

Once these volunteers are recruited, trained, and placed, they can take up the mantle of new church leadership. Some key positions need to be filled first so the church can have a successful start.

Two Other Important Leaders

In addition to the five leaders needed in Logan's systems, I would add two more:

A *welcome coordinator* organizes greeters, ushers, and other volunteers who make gathering with the church a warm and friendly experience for guests. Greeters help attendees feel welcomed and wanted. Volunteers must be able to tell arriving guests where to go and what to do.

These volunteers should be friendly, helpful people who smile. They should be trained to meet virtually every conceivable need. They should know the location of a first-aid kit, the site of the nearest water fountain, and the location of all departments, meeting rooms, and rest rooms in the church. Other tasks to consider for greeters are:

- Greeting guests in the parking lot
- Clearly marking entrances
- Providing name tags for all attendees
- Assigning "seat shepherds" to sit in a specific area each week to connect guests with nearby members to make them feel welcome
- Promoting the "Three-Minute Rule"—members must talk to someone they don't know for the three minutes following the end of worship

A church must *intentionally develop* its volunteer-staffed greeter and usher system. A welcome coordinator will help fulfill this vital ministry.

Finally, the *financial organizer* oversees the new church's finances. This is especially important if a sponsoring church does not coordinate these matters for the new group. If a sponsoring church takes care of finances, the prelaunch church still needs this organizer to plan for specific on-site management of offerings, counting, transferring of funds, and reporting to the sponsoring church.

Good financial organization protects the congregation and planter more than it achieves any other purpose. Congregational offerings must be safeguarded and handled appropriately in order to protect the integrity of leaders and the reputation of the congregation. In order to reassure givers, and even noncontributing guests, the congregation should inform attendees about the purposes for which their gifts are earmarked. The planter and core group should agree well ahead of launch day on a strategy for safeguarding and accounting for finances.

An Important Caution

One word of caution is in order. It is important to take the needed time to develop leaders. It is not enough to assign tasks; new churches must develop leaders. Pick leaders wisely—or suffer the consequences later.

Steve Sjogren warns churches to go slow in this process.

It is common to trust leaders in the early phase of a plant, only to discover in short order these were "LWAs"— leaders with an agenda. As church planters are in a conundrum for several years in a new plant—we need leaders desperately, but most of those available to lead aren't qualified. Why is it common for these faux leaders to find their way to new church plants? Those who have been rejected in the past from other churches find it attractive to start over at a new church where no one knows them. The challenge with leaders is this—to allow those who have failed in the past to get a fresh start, but at the same time make leadership decisions that will allow the church to grow in the years to come. This is my conclusion on this issue: I must more seriously take into consideration the larger work of God over individual leadership choices. It's a goose and golden egg question. The golden eggs (individual leaders) are wonderful, but I must protect the health of the goose (the local church) above all other considerations.[5]

Conclusion

The team outlined above does not have to move to the area with the church planter. As of this writing, I have never planted a church with a preexisting team. Instead, we formed the team on the field from the people we reached. They became the launch team, ready when we went public with our grand opening.

These team members and systems need to be prepared and implemented within the new congregation before its launch service. In rare instances, the team may have more than one paid staff member. Mostly, the team is made up of laypeople who often develop from a pool of new believers.

The church planter should limit prelaunch ministry positions to those essential for the new start based on its dreams, vision, giftedness, and systems for evangelism and ministry in the surrounding community. Save the plans for the men's and women's ministries until after the launch. All the new team members need to be focused on the launch until that is accomplished.

When these systems are well-grounded, the congregation is probably ready to begin public worship. With a good launch, the church should find itself able to progress quickly and grow rapidly. The indispensable role of laypersons in the development of these systems cannot be overstated.

Where do you find these laypersons? The next two sections, the culture and the contacts, will help explain where to find these people.

Resources for Further Reading

Cladis, George. *Leading the Team-Based Church: How Pastors and Church Staffs Can Grow Together into a Powerful Fellowship of Leaders.* San Francisco, Calif.: Jossey-Bass, 1999.

Cordeiro, Wayne. *Doing Church as a Team.* Ventura, Calif.: Regal Publishing, 2001.

Gangel, Kenneth O. *Team Leadership in Christian Ministry.* Rev. ed. Chicago: Moody Press, 1997.

Malphurs, Aubrey. *The Dynamics of Church Leadership.* Grand Rapids: Baker Books, 1999.

Part 3

Understanding Cultures and Models

CHAPTER NINE

The Builders and the Boomers

Church planting is missionary work. All potential missionary church planters must begin by determining their mission—exploring questions of personal call and conviction—and by learning missions principles. Following this, effective missionaries must seek to understand the culture they have been called to reach.[1] Cross-cultural understanding begins with an exegesis of the target culture.[2] By "exegeting" the culture, a planter learns assumptions and patterns already at work in the culture.

I am not a big fan of demographic segmentation, but there may be some value in looking at the Builder and Boomer generations. However, among emerging postmodern generations, these models tend to lose their usefulness.

Although the following outline is a broad generalization, most demographers divide North America into groups. The first group is composed of the two distinct generations:

1. *Builders* are those people who were born before 1946. At the turn of the millennium, there were more than 50 million of these people in the U.S. and 8 million in Canada.

2. *Boomers* were born during the two decades following World War II. As of 2000, this was the largest single segment of the population, with more than 70 million in the U.S. and 8 million in Canada.

The second group includes the emerging postmodern generations:

3. The generation known as *Busters*, totaling about 30 million (U.S.) and 7 million (Canada) as of 2000, were born from 1965 to 1976.

4. *Millennials* were born from 1977 to 1994. At the turn of the millennium, there were more than 70 million of this generation in the U.S. and 6 million in Canada.

5. Rounding out this generational tally are the *Babies,* born since 1994. At the time this book was written, this generation totaled about 10 million in the U.S. and 3 million in Canada.[3]

The Builders and Boomers are distinct generations. The Busters, Millennials, and Babies are the emerging postmodern generations. There were clear commonalities among the Builders and the Boomers, but these common patterns are less evident in emerging generations.

Since *individuals* comprise every demographic segment, many persons may not fit the general patterns found in that segment. Furthermore, each region (and even communities of a region) may demonstrate unique cultural characteristics that do not conform to national or continental patterns.

Not only do national cultures present exceptions within *age* segments, but they also present exceptions through racial, ethnic, and language differences. Effective church planters need to examine carefully and strategize for all of the cultural nuances and distinctives that they identify in their "cultural exegesis."[4]

Two Generations

In order to understand the sweeping patterns of demographic segmentation, let us consider the segments individually. These descriptions are very brief and are intended as snapshots. If you are planting a church, you are encouraged to look much deeper by studying the local area in much more detail.[5]

Builders

Although they are not the largest group in the general population, Builders (born prior to 1946) predominate in most churches. This group holds power in the majority of established congregations. Conflicts sometimes arise, even though they attempt to integrate younger groups with different cultural values into church life and leadership.

Builders are individualistic, since they were shaped by heroes such as John Wayne and Roy Rogers, champions of the cinema who single-handedly defeated their enemies. Builders value personal responsibility and individualism. The theme song for this generation could be Frank Sinatra's "My Way."

Boomers

Boomers are so named because they entered the culture during the post-World War II baby boom of 1946 to 1964. The majority of *new* churches in the last two decades were focused on reaching this segment of the population. The style and governance of these churches look very different from the patterns of churches founded by Builders.

- Boomers are the first generation raised with absentee fathers.
- Boomers are the first generation whose grandparents had no significant input into their lives.
- Boomers are the most educated generation in history.
- Boomers were raised with extreme affluence and great opportunities.
- Boomers have less purchasing power than their parents at each stage of adulthood.
- Boomers were raised under the threat of nuclear war.
- Boomers were the first generation to be reared with television as a significant parenting tool.[6]

Elmer Towns, in his seminar "How to Reach the Baby Boomers," has explained that five things molded the Boomers: *birth* control, a *book*, *bucks*, the *boob* tube and the *bomb*.

The Boomers were the first group to have varied choices in birth control and family planning. This allowed two things. It allowed families to determine the number of children they would have. It also led to more promiscuity among men and women because *birth* control lowered the risk of becoming pregnant. This enabled the Boomers to be the first generation to be promiscuous without obvious consequence of pregnancy.

Dr. Benjamin Spock's baby *book* influenced an entire generation by influencing how North Americans raised their children. His permissive child-rearing methods led to the moral decline of the Boomer generation.

The Boomer experienced a tremendous influx of money: *bucks*. This generation wanted everything their parents had without having to save for it. This generation also accumulated a lot of credit card debt as it tried to "keep up with the Joneses" and worked hard to earn more and more.

The television *boob* tube had a great influence on this generation. Television brought with it advertisements, fads, and up-to-the-minute news and video coverage—something that radio was never able to do with just words. It has contributed to a unique North American culture.

The ever-present threat of the atomic *bomb* impacted the Boomer generation. The Boomers are the Cold War generation. From the dropping of the atomic bomb that ended World War II and through Korea, Vietnam, and the nuclear arms race, this is the first generation that has lived in fear of being destroyed by a nuclear bomb or war.

Boomers grew up with a team-oriented approach to organizations. The stereotypical heroes of the Boomer era appeared in the 1966 television serial *Star Trek*. The crew, though a team, did not always follow the captain's orders. This motif of individualism-within-teamwork both shaped and described the Boomer culture. Many Boomer-era musical stars were *groups* of individuals, more than individual stars performing as a group. For example, North Americans remember John, Paul, George, and Ringo more as the Beatles, rather than as individuals. This phenomenon describes the cultural shift from the strong individualism of the Builders that moved *toward* a team or a combination approach.

Boomers are psychotherapy-oriented and have an inclination toward self-revelation and seeking needed help. With the increasing availability of professionals practicing psychology and with psychotropic drug therapy advertised as the cure for all ills, the Boomers are more inclined to "treat" than to "do."

Planting Boomer Churches

Church planting consultant John Worcester has written an excellent article about planting Baby Boomer churches. This article is summarized below. The full article is available at www.churchplanting.net.

Why should we plant churches to reach Baby Boomers? Perhaps the best reason is the massive size of this generation. Boomers are the largest single segment of the population. While they are largely unreached by the church, they have shown that they are open to God.

Baby Boomers long for intimacy. They have a special need for small groups where they can get to know one another and communicate on an open, honest level. They want to experience God in their daily lives and to see his hand at work. But they have little interest in going to church just because "it's the thing to do." They don't like to be pressured to do something out of a sense of duty or obligation.

Certain forms of worship appeal especially to this generation. They are known as the "rock" generation, so they like contemporary music with a snappy beat. Casual dress is definitely the "in thing" with this group. They demand quality child care and enjoyable activities for their children during adult worship. They are especially open to sermons with humor that are communicated in a warm, conversational way. If you want to appeal to Boomers, don't do anything during the worship service that tends to put people on the spot.[7]

Baby Boomers need to be reached. Many resources are available that explain how to reach them, and most churches planted in the 1980s and 1990s were focused on Baby Boomers. In addition, models have sprung up across North America that provide successful paradigms to reach the Baby Boomers. Jacks Simms explains that churches reaching Baby Boomers tend to have certain common traits.

- They are open to a spiritual experience.
- Their Bible teaching emphasizes practical living.
- They place a healthy emphasis on relationships.
- They have fewer titles and less formality.
- They understand the new family in America.
- They share their faith by what they say and do.
- They recognize the ability of women.
- They place an emphasis on worship.
- They have a high tolerance for diversity.
- They are action-oriented.[8]

The 1980s and 1990s saw the growth of many Baby Boomer churches across North America. Many of these were church plants, but many others were established churches reinventing themselves to reach out. There have been fewer church growth success stories in postmodernism, which is where we will look next.

Resources for Further Study

McIntosh, Gary. *Three Generations*. Grand Rapids: Revell, 1995.

Murren, Doug. *The Baby Boomerang*. Ventura, Calif.: Regal Books, 1990.

Light, Paul. C. *The Baby Boomers*. New York: W. W. Norton & Co., 1988.

Jones, Landon. *Great Expectations: America and the Baby Boom Generation*. New York: Ballantine Books, 1986.

CHAPTER TEN

Emerging Postmodern Generations

Postmoderns have no universal worldview. They recognize a series of worldviews. It is an error to think that Gen-Xers can be neatly described like every subsequent generation or that Millennials all think one particular thing. This is actually a good time to set aside the idea that postmoderns can be neatly categorized. The concept of Baby Boomer was easily recognized if you were white and middle class. But just because one generation had some similarities does not mean that subsequent generations can be easily described.

Why Not Gen-Xers?

The transition between modernism and postmodernism took place in and among what has been commonly called "Generation X." Jimmy Long considers Generation X a case study for the transition into postmodernity because of the pace of the cultural change.[1] Celek and Zander point out that Busters (Gen-Xers) are the first generation raised and educated in postmodernity.[2] Yet this categorizing has been taken too far. Andy Couch explains:

> [After the Boomers began to age] it was clear that the generational shtick was too useful to be allowed to expire with the passing of the Boomers. So Madison Avenue must have breathed a huge collective sigh of relief when a young Canadian writer hit the best-seller charts with a self-deprecating novel of sorts called *Generation X: Tales for an Accelerated Culture.* Within a year, Douglas Coupland was being offered five-figure fees to speak to corporate marketers

about the new "generation" and how to "reach" them with their own brands—offers which fell on ears strangely deaf to commercial success.[3]

The stereotypes were primarily demographic flags placed on these age groups by Madison Avenue. The stereotypes about Gen-Xers changed so quickly it was hard to keep pace with the shifts. In the early 1990s there was a rash of new books describing Generation X. According to several authors, young adults who were unable to find meaningful work were often cynical and unconnected, and they experienced prolonged adolescence. Numerous books were written to describe how to reach such societal dropouts. Then came the "dot.com boom." Suddenly, Xers were affluent.

Church growth books in the late 1990s explained how to reach "up-and-out Generation X." They described the ways to reach the newly affluent with cutting-edge strategies. Then came the "dot.com bust," which changed the cultural landscape again.

This is enough to illustrate the danger of generationally focused ministry. Generational trends are, by their very nature, too trendy. Trends can change very quickly. Leonard Sweet is correct when he warns, "Beware of predictions."[4] Almost every Gen-X-focused book written in the early to mid-nineties considers economic pessimism central to the generation.[5] J. Walker Smith, a well-known demographic futurist, wrote of Generation X, "Their defining experience is the disappointment in the downsizing of the late 1982."[6] However, after a decade of unprecedented economic expansion, this "angst" had lost its edge. A Web page posting from the late 1990s is illustrative:

I've made a startling observation concerning my Xer friends and family: financially, they are all doing quite well (myself included)!

I remember having a very difficult time finding a job in the early 1990s, right after college graduation. Many of the people I knew had the same problem. We were forced to take jobs far beneath our educational levels because of the poor national economy at the time. Several of us had to move back home for a while just to survive.

How times have changed. Sometime in the mid-1990s we all found our intended career tracks and started to prosper. Now half are home-owners and the other half lives, if not lavishly then at least very comfortably. Many of us have also met or exceeded our parents' salaries.

Remember the observations made about the lack of opportunities for GenX, and how they could look forward to a life of diminished expectations compared to their parents. I'm not sure this (is) completely true anymore.

Can the stereotype of the overeducated, underpaid, GenX service-sector-employee be finally put to rest?[7]

Thus, Gen-X experts who predicted that this generation would be the first not to exceed the wealth of their parents apparently spoke too soon.[8]

It is good that the Gen-X, Buster, and Millennial terminologies have fallen into disfavor. Those who used the terms recognized that the groups they sought to describe were bound together more by attitude than by age.[9] These reasons should be enough to encourage us to quit using generational labels—but the most powerful reason is that postmoderns tend to resent labels.[10]

While the church needs to be careful not to focus too much attention on the oracles of the marketplace, we must admit that specialized ministries to Gen-X opened the door to a better understanding of ministry in a post-modern culture. There is no longer real value in using such labels. We need to dispose of them. It is never a good strategy to identify an age group, ana-lyze its current situation, and then make pronouncements of how to reach them. Economies are too unstable, and fads are too short-lived. Good mis-sionaries uncover the deeper issues—the underlying values, thought processes, and ideas of a culture or people group. Using this information, they develop a plan to reach them based on these deeper issues.

Reaching Postmoderns from a Modern Evangelicalism

The approach of established churches will be difficult to change; the North American church is deeply rooted in modernity.[11] Many churches are seeking to minister within the postmodern context. These churches are most likely to be church plants.

The church wants to reach and should reach postmoderns. But the church must not *adopt* postmodernism. Postmodernism comes up short; its basic presuppositions are actually antithetical to the gospel at times. We cannot "move with the times" and embrace postmodernity without strong discernment. So the modern church is not being successful with postmoderns in its current state, and the church cannot become postmodern. A middle course needs to be found.

Most of the authors who have discussed how to reach postmoderns have focused on how *we* can reach *them* by getting them to come to *us*. They miss the fact that the Christian church is no longer the first choice of those who are seeking a spiritual reality. We can no longer think of ourselves as the preferred source of truth.

Evangelicals need to adopt some new approaches—not just use the old ones over and over. What we are doing is not working—postmoderns don't get the picture. It is time to discover some new clues so we can connect with them. But we must not love our clues more than their needs. When responding to my survey of how evangelicals have responded, a pastor wrote the following:

> I'm not too sure about the evangelical's church as a whole, but I can say that within my contact with [my denomination], postmodernism is a "threat" that is being dealt with through ignoring it. Many people are running around with "The Sky Is Falling" banners, but no one is addressing all of the open doors that this shift is opening. Even in those churches that have "progressed" to the seeker level (which is a great step that should have happened about twenty years ago), there is a tendency to think that they have "arrived." The danger is the thinking that this is enough to reach postmoderns. One of the things that I have run into time and again is the idea that the only thing we need to do to "convert" postmoderns is to get them to understand that evolution is a lie and that they need to be forced to embrace absolutes. These same people completely miss the point, because they somehow see postmodernism as a break in the system. "If only we could get these people to

see things this way they would be better" is the mindset. Then it doesn't help that the only encounters they think they are having with postmodernism is the little they hear Chuck Colson talk about it, or even folks like Josh McDowell or Dobson. Who are all great folks, but when they are speaking on the evils of postmodernism and the need to fix it they are trying to force this thing into a modern mold by trying to create steps 1, 2 and 3 to convert a postmodern. Nothing repels us more than a system that is a quick fix. Mystery has been lost. Paradox is nonexistent. . . . I'm not quite sure the attitude of the rest of the Church, but in [the area I live], there seems to be a reluctance to embrace the incredible freedoms postmodernism opens for ministry.

Contrary to what some have written, postmodernism is not a cause for panic. We have been here before! The church has been in the midst of a pluralistic milieu, and it reached millions. The first century was much more pluralistic than North America is today, but the church remained faithful to its witness and saw great results.[12]

Though not a cause for panic, this is surely a cause to think differently. The church has waited for hundred of years for the world to come to it in repentance. Today, we must go to them. We are in a missionary location because North America is a mission field in the same way we once considered the undeveloped world the mission field.[13]

The Good News is that "just as God is a missionary God, so the church is to be a missionary church."[14] Jesus taught, "As the Father has sent me, I am sending you" (John 20:21). Our purpose, therefore, is to go to this new expression of life, culture, and values and to "face a fundamental challenge. That challenge is to learn to think about (our) culture in missional terms."[15] We need to think like missionaries to a postmodern tribe.

What Is Postmodernism?

Sometime in the last few years "it" became "the next big thing." Walter Truett Anderson has exclaimed that "reality isn't what it used to be"[16] and every professor and church growth guru soon had a PowerPoint presentation and a notebook with surefire methods to get these new post-moderns into the church.

Many new books hit the market. These described Gen-Xers, Busters, Millennials, and the generations that followed. Some were good, some were bad, and, to be honest, some were awful. But all of them represented attempts to address a fundamental issue—*these people are different and the church is not reaching them.*

Why Is Postmodernism Important?

Postmodernity is the water our people swim in, and the lenses they see the world through. They have, whether willing or unwilling, adopted a new epistemology. Therefore we are always challenged to look for the redemptive windows of this culture through which the gospel can shine.

—a church planter reaching postmoderns
in Portland, Oregon

Churches need to reach postmoderns because postmoderns are people. Starting a new Korean church is an obvious response to an influx of Koreans. The church would reach people who swim in the water of Korean culture. The same must be done for postmodern people, who are swimming in the new North American culture.

Evangelicals have struggled with responding to these new realities, finding reasons not to respond. *It is important to note that the shift to post-modernism has not happened everywhere.* The shifts have not yet impacted many in the church culture because the church culture acts as a protective shield, unmolested by a secular culture's music, literature, and values.

There are still large pockets in North America where people live out their lives in much the same manner as their parents before them. These people have more toys, but they still go to church (or at least feel guilty if they do not go), still have relatively stable family lives, and still espouse the "old values" of America. Most evangelicals live in these pockets and have been somewhat insulated from the societal changes. Still, television can't be avoided. In our fallen world, something seems to be wrong. These people see the shifts coming. While the societal shifts may not have impacted them yet, they see the changes reflected in their children's eyes. The chart below illustrates this point.

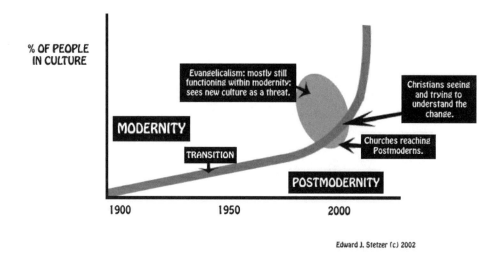

% OF PEOPLE IN CULTURE

Evangelicalism: mostly still functioning within modernity: sees new culture as a threat.

Christians seeing and trying to understand the change.

MODERNITY

Churches reaching Postmoderns.

TRANSITION

POSTMODERNITY

1900   1950   2000

Edward J. Stetzer (c) 2002

Evangelicals and Postmodernism

The evangelical subculture is still predominantly entrenched in the worldview of modernity. That is ironic in a way, since the church of the last two hundred years has struggled so adamantly against the advances of modernistic science. But the church needed to reach moderns, and modernism in turn has shaped our worldview. Meanwhile, a smaller number of evangelicals are struggling to understand the worldview of postmoderns and the philosophical backdrop of postmodernity. An even smaller number are actually living and ministering within that worldview—engaging and reaching postmoderns.

The chart might also help to explain that being a postmodern is not an age issue alone. The worldview that we identify today as "cultural postmodernity" is not new in academia, the art world, or even in many major cities. A sixty-year-old artist from San Francisco might be thoroughly entrenched in postmodernity while a twenty-four-year-old banker from Memphis might hold more modernist values. Perhaps most importantly, *many evangelicals have not engaged postmoderns because they do not want to have contact with the value systems of the postmodern world.* It is much easier to deny its power than to acknowledge its influence.

A recent evangelical journal focused on "confronting" postmodernism rather than "engaging" postmoderns. It is a common practice for the church to oppose cultural change rather than to change its methods to reach a new culture. It happened in the first century with "the Judaizers," and it has happened in every age since.

Many evangelicals will choose to sit out the changing culture and remain isolated. Many nonevangelical churches will adopt postmodern values and try to hitch their fading star to their value system. (Yes, that will be as embarrassing as it was when they tried to adopt the values of the 1960s, then the 1970s, etc.) Thankfully, some churches will choose to engage the culture in radically biblical ways—becoming missionaries to a culture they have not traveled to, but which has instead traveled to them.

How will the church respond to postmodernity? Consider a church planter's comments:

> Modern Evangelicalism has built much of its understanding and practice on modern assumptions. I hear this type of language a lot: "If we don't have absolutes we can't have Christianity; if you don't believe in objective truth, you can't believe in truth," etc. My response is: "Really? Do you really believe that?" This is the most important discussion for the church in the last 500 years. What will we do with a new set of assumptions to work with; how will we do evangelism with a new set of assumptions? How will we do theology with a new set of assumptions?
> —Church planter and pastor, Fort Worth, Texas

Churches will have to think differently if they want to reach this different kind of people. This will obviously be hard to do in established churches. Some churches are just now adopting the music of the 1970s (and consider this to be a radical change). To postmoderns, the debate about traditional versus contemporary music in churches is about as important as listening to dad and granddad fight over the television remote. The churches most likely to become missional will be new churches—churches founded for and primarily led by indigenous postmodern leaders. Their methods and media will be radically different from that of the present church, but their message will be deeply biblical. They will be missionaries to the majority North American culture.

Cultural or Philosophical Postmodernism?

One clear distinction needs to be made. We must distinguish the people whom I term "postmoderns" from the philosophy of postmodernism itself. Later, I will detail that philosophy in depth. It is important to understand that postmodernism is a worldview antithetical to the gospel. Because this is true, some people will read the phrase "postmodern churches" as an oxymoron—two opposing ideas that cannot be held in common. If this referred to postmodernism in churches, this would be true. The fact is that most postmoderns in our society have no clear understanding of post-modernism as such. Even if they did, they would refute it.

Our concern is with reaching postmodern *persons*—people who have been born into this postmodern-influenced world and are trying their best to make sense of it. It's really no different from any cross-cultural missions experience. If we seek to reach Buddhists who grew up in a Buddhist world, we must communicate with them where they are. Our relationship to the postmodern world must be one of communication, not compromise.

Understanding Modernism

Millard Erickson explains the bases of modernism:

- naturalism (reality is restricted to what can be observed or proved),
- humanism (humanity is the pinnacle of the universe),
- the scientific method (knowledge is inherently good and is attainable),
- reductionism (humans are highly developed animals),
- progress (because knowledge is good, its acquisition will lead to progress),
- nature (evolution—not a Creator—is responsible for life and its development),
- certainty (because knowledge is objective, we can know things for certain),
- determinism (the belief that things happened because of fixed causes),
- individualism (the supremacy of each individual and their ability to discern truth), and
- anti-authoritarianism (each person was the final arbiter of truth).[17]

There are many suggested dates for the beginning of modernity—from the invention of the printing press to the writings of Descartes. Oden defines this era as the time from the Bastille (1789) to the Berlin Wall (1989).[18] Grenz may be correct in identifying the first postmodern philosopher as Nietzsche,[19] who in the late nineteenth century[20] began the attack on modernity.[21]

The Enlightenment and its worldview of "empirical verifiability" defines the modern era.[22] The Enlightenment proclaimed the value of continuous progress; because of the inherent goodness of man and his rational processes, scientific progress would be continuous and "good." Just as the Enlightenment had overcome the dark ages of the medieval period, human reason would help overcome each obstacle in its path. The *New York Times* stated on January 1, 1901, that it was "optimistic enough to believe that the 20th century will meet and overcome all perils and prove to be the best this steadily improving planet has ever seen."[23] The modern era devalued the stories of earlier cultures as myths to be discarded.[24]

Some believe that evangelicalism itself was born out of reaction and response to the Enlightenment.[25] Evangelicalism honed its teeth by defending the faith against evolution and secularity, but it did so by appealing to science and the rationality of Christianity. In the process, evangelicals were influenced by modernity more than we might realize.[26] We developed a working, effective apologetic for the modern era by using the tools of modernity.

The system of modernity worked well and served the Western world for two hundred years. In the last few decades, the cracks in the wall of modernity have begun to show. David Wells says of modernity, "It had made extravagant promises about life, liberty, and happiness, but in the modern world it had become increasingly difficult to see where those promises were being realized."[27] In other words, at the end of the inevitable progress of the Enlightenment came mustard gas in World War I, Hitler in World War II, Mai Lai, Tuskegee, Oklahoma City, and the World Trade Center. The failure of the Enlightenment ideal has led to the new postmodern mood.

Wells writes: "As the nostrums of the therapeutic age supplant confession, and as preaching is psychologized, the meaning of the Christian faith becomes privatized. At a single stroke, confession is eviscerated and reflection reduced to mainly thought about one's self."[28]

Some historians identify 1968 as the transition point from modernity to postmodernity.[29] During that year, the North Vietnam Tet offensive foreshadowed the inability of a superpower nation to overcome a small revolution, Moscow crushed the "Prague Spring" by invading Czechoslovakia, Martin Luther King Jr. and Robert Kennedy were assassinated, and a young man in Paris gave up hope for Enlightenment ideas. Eleven years later in 1979, Jean-François Lyotard wrote *The Postmodern Condition*, which helped define the values of the emerging shift from modernity.

Understanding Postmodernity

Postmodernism means "that which comes after modernism." Much of what defines postmodernism is a reaction against modernism. Erickson provides some helpful categories. Postmodernism is based on:

- the denial of personal objectivity,
- the uncertainly of knowledge,
- the death of any all-inclusive explanation,
- the denial of the inherent goodness of knowledge,
- the rejection of progress,
- the supremacy of community-based knowledge, and
- the disbelief in objective inquiry.[30]

These philosophical values have been transferred into the common culture. Of course, the average person does not talk about "the denial of personal objectivity." Instead, he knows that "everybody has their own point of view and all are equally valid." Using Erickson's categories, we can see how these values play out every day in postmodern culture.

Erickson's Description	Cultural Expression
denial of personal objectivity	I do believe in God, but that is really the influence of my parents. Nobody can know for sure.
uncertainty of knowledge	The government says that the Atkins diet does not work, but who really knows if it is true.
death of any all-inclusive explanation	You know, things just don't fit into a nice, neat explanation.
denial of knowledge's inherent goodness	The more knowledge out there, the more dangerous the world is becoming.
rejection of progress	I have all this technology but am still not happy.
supremacy of community-based knowledge	It is arrogant to think that I, alone, have figured out spiritual truth.
disbelief in objective inquiry	Here is what I think that verse means, but I could be wrong. What is your interpretation?

While modernity and postmodernity hold some things in common, as a whole postmodernity tends to be more cynical. Maybe that is the point—modernism and its hopeful notions of progress seem quaint in a post-rational era.

I have tried to simplify with three overarching themes. They may help illustrate the shift toward postmodernism. Each section starts with a vignette from the church and then from the broader culture—illustrating how these philosophical shifts have impacted our thinking.

From Text to Interpretations

In the Church

Jim, a small group leader at Grace Church, sits with his small-group members. He wants them to value the Bible and to feel valued themselves. He reads the Bible verse and shares his best interpretation of it. Then he turns to his left and asks Valerie, "What is your opinion of what this verse means?"

By teaching in this manner, Jim is reflecting the value that every person has an opinion and every opinion is valid. Unfortunately, that approach creates a problem: the writers of Scripture had specific truths in mind when they wrote, and our job is to apply them—not just to get everyone's opinion on them.

In the Culture

"This right of privacy, whether it be founded in the Fourteenth Amendment's concept of personal liberty and restrictions upon state action, as we feel it is, or, as the District Court determined, in the Ninth Amendment's reservation of rights to the people, is broad enough to encompass a woman's decision whether or not to terminate her pregnancy."—Justice Blackman in *Roe v. Wade*

We often refer to our "right to privacy," but in fact there is no right to privacy in the same sense as the right of free speech or the right against unreasonable search and seizure. The U.S. Constitution is silent on privacy, although the First, Fourth, and Fifth amendments have been interpreted to include privacy rights.

Justice Blackman considered it perfectly acceptable to "find" a right to privacy (thus, abortion) in the constitution because it has become accepted legal practice to interpret the document based on the current court's interpretation and not that of the original text.

One of the foundational shifts in postmodernism is the move from texts to interpretations. For centuries the reader would ask, "What is this person trying to say?" Instead, today the reader asks, "What does this mean to me?" Jacques Derrida and Paul DeMan, two postmodern deconstructionists, explained that texts themselves have no meaning. The texts' only meaning is the meaning we bring to the texts.

Postmodernism reminds evangelical Christianity that there is no such thing as the disinterested observer[31] but that everyone reads everything through the lens of his or her own opinion. Thus, the Chiapas Indian will read the Bible differently than the Southern California businessperson.

Philosophical postmodernism, however, goes much further. In the postmodern world, all facts are interpreted facts.[32] Truth is not found in words, but it is found in the context in which the words are used.[33] Thus, any interpretation is valid. Therefore, if I want to have a homosexual, feminist, or atheist interpretation of the Bible, all are equally valid. There has been a shift from how we are to discover truth (epistemology) to how we interpret truth (hermeneutics).[34] Knowledge has been replaced by interpretation.[35]

So what is the big deal? If it is true that everyone has his or her own interpretation, why is that a problem? Explaining the views of Nietzsche, Stanley Grenz echoes the view of many postmoderns: "Because all knowledge is a matter of perspective, knowledge is really interpretation—and all interpretations are lies."[36]

Therefore, anyone who believes Truth (the capital *T* indicates God's Truth) and believes that Truth to be universal is a danger to the culture. He or she has bought into a lie and now seeks to spread that lie. The implications are staggering. How can we evangelize a generation that believes we are holding up the "truth" when they believe that anyone who says that is either a liar or has bought into a lie?

From Meta-narratives to Mini-narratives

In the Church
"Don't tell them all about the whole biblical story of Jesus. Tell them the story of what Jesus has done for you."
—from an evangelism training manual.

Though it is not a bad thing to tell of one's personal experience, the focus has moved from the big story of redemption to a personal story of redemption. As we will see later, this is both a good and a bad thing. However, the culture has shifted from the big stories (meta-narratives) to the small ones (mini-narratives).

In the Culture

"I don't buy into your comfortable suburban American dream," explained the man sitting at the airport lunch counter. "You tell me about God, but what it really seems is that you want me to fit into your standard of what I should be. My partner and I have found our own happiness. I don't buy your values."

The description is not uncommon. People do not want what they are "supposed" to want. People are "supposed" to want a nice white picket fence in the suburbs. That is the American dream—work hard, play by the rules, live in the suburbs, and retire in Florida. One problem—fewer and fewer people are committed to that "story." Instead, they set their own view of what an idyllic existence would include. They create their own story (mini-narrative) rather than buy into the grand story of the culture (meta-narrative).

The one thing all agree on about postmodernism is that it represents the death of a single, universal worldview.[37] Jean-François Lyotard, a well-known postmodern leader, defined postmodernism as disbelief toward universal worldviews. "Simplifying to the extreme, I define *postmodern* as incredulity toward meta-narratives."[38] He believed that the point of this new movement was to help liberate men and women from the idea that there was a universal point or reason for existence. These universal values, whether they are the American dream, Christianity, or capitalism, are called meta-narratives.

A meta-narrative is a unifying cultural value that explains and gives purpose to life, meaning, and existence. It is the reason people go to work and live their lives. Thus, in a sense, Christianity is a meta-narrative. It includes truth, meaning for life, and the purpose of our existence. However, capitalism is also a meta-narrative. It provides truth (profit is good), meaning (providing more for you, your family, and children), and existence (getting ahead is a key value).

It is important to note that individuals often hold to more than one meta-narrative. Or, more precisely, they hold one meta-narrative that is often a mix of different values. For example, the meta-narrative of most North American Christians would be a mix of Christianity, capitalism, and the American dream.

Philosophical postmodernism, often represented by the views of philosopher Michael Foucalt, explains that meta-narratives and all constructs of truth are used by those in power to control the disenfranchised. The mental pictures of how things are (or how they should be) are not "value-neutral."[39]

Christians would be mistaken to completely disregard the death of the meta-narrative. It is true that meta-narratives have been used to oppress throughout the ages. The meta-narrative of medieval Catholicism suppressed and persecuted heretic Protestants, the meta-narrative of Victorian Christianity kept women in their "right place," and the meta-narrative of the American dream tried to keep African-Americans in quiet submission. Good postmodernists not only resist such "categories" for themselves; they also must deconstruct them for others. They believe this is just the right thing to do.

Instead of finding grand, universal, and timeless truths, postmoderns find truth to be that which is expressed by a community of people. Truth is that which is agreed upon by the community to be beneficial to that community.[40] Only those within our group have the ability or right to comment upon or criticize "our" truth.[41]

If all the "big truths" are not true and are really there to control the people, where do we find the Truth? People are still looking for truth, meaning, and existence. However, now they are finding it in "little" stories that do not claim to be universal. For example, rather than proclaiming the universal value of the American dream, a postmodern might say, "I can instead find truth, meaning, and existence in the writings of Deepak Chopra, and I would not dare claim that this truth would be something that I would try to apply to you. It is my mini-narrative—my personal story that gives me personal peace."

This may help to explain partially the prominence of myth and legend as teachers in a culture that values these mini-narratives.[42] Consider this: "Native American spirituality can bring me peace, while my neighbor can find peace in Kabbalah (Jewish mysticism)." There is no "big story," so we each hold tightly to our own "little stories" that bring us peace and serenity.

The implications for ministry are important to grasp and may provide a window on our culture. It is unlikely that the average person on the street would say, "I think that this meta-narrative you are promoting is intended to oppress me." Nevertheless, this is exactly what many postmoderns think when we try to evangelize them. They see us attempting to impose a truth that we consider universal. This truth has been used to oppress women and slaves, and now we want to oppress *them*. Since they already have their own mini-narrative, we must be seeking to destroy it. In the minds of some people, evangelism is not just wrong; it is a hate crime.

From External to Internal Truth

In the Church

"But I love him," Rebecca explained to the pastor. The pastor continued to encourage her not to move in with Larry. He pointed out that the Bible taught that sex before marriage is wrong and living together would hurt their witness. But Rebecca had made up her mind and explained, "Larry and I have prayed about it and we are at peace with our decision."

When truth is "internal," it does not come from an outside source. Instead, it comes from one's best understanding of truth. In the case of Rebecca and Larry, their "internal truth" did not line up with the "external truth" they claimed to follow. Like most postmoderns, they chose to follow the internal truth over the external.

This can be seen today in the fact that Baptists have a higher divorce rate than average Americans and Catholics have abortions at the same pace as non-Catholics. They choose their internal truths over the external values they claim to hold.

In the Culture

We often hear, "You can't legislate morality." (Actually, we do it every day because we outlaw murder, rape, and theft.) Still, more and more persons are attempting to expand this claim to an increasing number of issues. They believe that no external truth (law) should touch their internal truths. Early on the issue was whether adultery should be illegal. Now it has progressed to issues such as pornography, homosexuality, alcohol use, and marriage.

One MIT staff member explained regarding teen out-of-wedlock pregnancy, "Certainly, teenagers shouldn't be getting pregnant on a regular basis. But to punish teen pregnancies just because it's 'wrong' for most individuals doesn't make sense, especially given the other things that are legal in our society."[43]

Postmodernists tend to reject external truth as "made truth" imposed by others. Richard Rorty, a radical postmodern philosopher, believes that all truth is *made* and not found. Thus, any value or moral belief is "made up" by the person or the group to which he or she belongs.

Deconstructionism, a common term in academic postmodernism, plays a large part in the process. In the postmodern world there are no valid truth claims—all must be deconstructed by the new postmodernist. This means that "wise" people make a point to "take apart" (deconstruct) false truth claims. Since all truth claims are false, that is a full-time job!

The valuing of internal truth is not new. The modern era was defined by the idea of the autonomous self. This remains. People still believe that "everyone has a right to his or her own opinion." Postmodern consciousness seeks for truth to be local, not just individual. This eliminates the need to prove oneself right and others wrong. Truth is expressed in groups without the need to exclude the truth of other groups.[44]

This internal truth is another challenge for evangelicals seeking to reach postmoderns. It is not just that postmoderns feel that they have their own internal truth but that they are suspicious of those who claim there is any external truth. Furthermore, savvy people also deconstruct the religious truth beliefs of others. (This may help to explain why the current sage religious celebrities go to great pain not to claim any external truth—just that this is right for them.)

There is a clear gulf between many philosophical postmodernists and the expression of postmodernism in contemporary culture (pop-postmodernism). One *does* influence the other. But it is worthwhile to understand the philosophical background. Books like *The Challenge of Postmodernism* (edited by David Dockery), *A Primer on Postmodernism* (Stanley Grenz), and *Telling the Truth* (D. A. Carson) will help you understand the philosophy. Postmodernism undergirds the culture even though the culture is not aware of such. Like a missionary learning the historical background of a tribal ritual, he or she understands how the formation of that ritual influences current practice—even though the tribe is unaware.

"Soft" or "cultural" postmodernism and its openness to spiritual things is partly good news to the evangelical. Hard philosophical postmodernism is not.[45] Cultural postmodernism is an emptying of so many of the lies of modernity—that happiness could be found in success, that peace would be found in progress, and that man was inherently good. One of the marks of postmodernism is pessimism.[46] Christians, like postmodernists, reject the inherent goodness of knowledge.[47] That pessimism helps people to see the need for God.

Conversely, hard philosophical postmodernism is about destroying truth claims, debunking all-inclusive explanations, and opposing systems of belief. This is why many people will resist the idea of a postmodern church. "Postmodern church is actually an oxymoron." But when you understand the cultural nature of postmodernism, a postmodern church is just as acceptable as an Arab church, a contemporary church, or an inner-city church. They are just different cultural expressions of biblically faithful churches.

The task is not easy, nor is it nice and neat. Some postmodern church leaders will go too far, and some will not go far enough. It may be messy, according to Newbigin:

> Everyone with the experience of cross-cultural missions
> knows that there are always two opposite dangers, the Scylla
> and Charybdis, between which one must steer. On the one
> side there is the danger that one finds no point of contact for

the message as the missionary preaches it, to the people of the local culture the message appears irrelevant and meaningless. On the other side is the danger that the point of contact determines entirely the way that the message is received, and the result is syncretism. Every missionary path has to find the way between these two dangers: irrelevance and syncretism. And if one is more afraid of one danger than the other, one will certainly fall into the opposite.[48]

In my attempt to be missiological, I draw not from my own knowledge but from the knowledge and experience of those who are on the cutting edge of ministry.

Churches that reach postmoderns have ten tendencies that distinguish them from successful churches of modernity. I discovered these ten characteristics of successful postmodern church plants through survey, and those ten qualities will be discussed in coming chapters.

Resources for Further Study

Dockery, David S., ed. *The Challenge of Postmodernism: An Evangelical Engagement.* Grand Rapids: Baker, 1995.

Gibbs, Eddie. *ChurchNext: Quantum Changes in How We Do Ministry.* Downers Grove, Ill.: InterVarsity Press, 2000.

Grenz, Stanley J. *A Primer on Postmodernism.* Grand Rapids: Eerdmans, 1996.

McLaren, Brian D. *Church on the Other Side.* Grand Rapids: Zondervan, 2000.

CHAPTER ELEVEN

Culturally Relevant Ministry in a Postmodern World

A fascinating movement has been born. Postmodern churches have begun to spring up across North America. They have been described in different terms—postmodern, Gen-X, even the overused "contemporary." Leonard Sweet refers to these as "Noah's Dove Churches"[1] because they are testing the waters of how to reach a postmodern North America.

They are predominately (though not exclusively) young, and their services are geared toward persons looking for different experiences. Spotty reports of these churches can be found on the Internet and in some limited magazines. But no large-scale study has been undertaken.

This is tricky; in a culture that thrives on diversity and disdains uniformity, there is no *right* way to plant a postmodern church. There is no single answer to reaching postmoderns because there is no one, stereotypical, North American postmodern.

Postmoderns do not fit into a nice little cultural box, but all people with a postmodern mind-set have this in common: They need to be reached with the gospel of Jesus Christ, and the current pattern of "church" isn't reaching them.

Despite the obvious difficulty of defining postmoderns, there are some similar patterns in their thinking and feeling. There are *almost* universal values held by *most* postmoderns (note the double caveat). Helping to plant an indigenous church is an art more than a science, but missionaries around the world do it every day. One thing is very clear: postmoderns are different from the people churches have reached successfully in the past. If we write them off as "beyond help"—as some churches seem inclined to do—we will ignore the Great Commission.

New congregations are effectively reaching postmoderns.[2] These may be new worship services within existing churches, intended to meet post-moderns' needs, or entirely new congregations. Styles of expression change between eras,[3] and new churches should reflect the change of style without any change of substance. Patterns are emerging that fit this changing yet unchanging paradigm.

Why Is It So Hard?

1. Postmodern seekers have *never* been to church (they're not 'coming back' like modern seekers.)

2. They've been educated in politically correct schools that Christianity is bigoted and small-minded.

3. I live in Silicon Valley, *not* Seattle, so flannel, incense and candles don't work here—our postmodern seekers make six figures, have retirement plans and families.

—Church Planter, Silicon Valley, California

Being a missionary is never easy, but when the culture change has taken place in one's own home, it is even more difficult. We are much like Anglos living near Eighth Street (Calle Ocho) in 1959, during the era when locals were overwhelmed by new immigrants. Anglos in south Miami had two choices—think like Cubans and understand how to function in their world or move. Most chose to move rather than engage the new cultural shift.

The church does not have such an option. Our job is to reach the lost world and bring greater glory to God. Yet, rather than engaging the new cultural change, the most prevalent Christian response is to pretend that there has been no shift.[4] The church continues to function as it always has—protecting its youth in summer camp, keeping its members listening to Christian music, and, as a whole, staying away from change.

This is the easiest approach, but it is not the way of Christ. Those who are trying to preserve the existing church unchanged have little time to think about what the future of the church should look like.[5] Most churches do not even have the vitality to be a healthy modern church, let alone to make the transition from a modern to a postmodern world.[6] Nash believes that the big story of the new millennium will be the death of thousands of local churches.[7] This die-off will not be surprising, considering the current trends.

It will not be a great surprise to even the casual observer that Christianity has been disestablished as the primary belief of North Americans. Being part of the clergy was once considered a position of prominence, often leading to invitations to serve on boards and commissions. Being part of the clergy is now a detriment to such involvement.[8] Self-described "spiritual" North Americans see uniting with a church as unnecessary.[9]

On the other hand, many Americans are still "churchgoing." The United States is second only to Ireland as the highest church-attending Western nation.[10] Unfortunately, though these statistics are still high, they are declining. More importantly, it is the social influence of Christianity that has declined.[11] Attending church does not necessarily indicate true belief and may no longer determine lifestyle.

There is a definite need for churches and church services geared toward postmoderns. Few Boomers or older adults would want to sit in a church service geared toward postmoderns. Why should we expect that postmoderns would wish to sit in a service geared toward older adults? Postmodern generations are turning away from institutional Christianity in a way not seen in several generations.[12] This is not because of the gospel—as many postmoderns respond eagerly to Jesus—but it is because of the traditional culture of the institutional church itself. Church planters who are committed to communicating Christ, who are immersed in the postmodern culture, and who do not feel constrained by the traditional patterns of the "old" church will be the best change agents.[13]

Where Are Postmoderns?

Two years ago, I was discussing mission strategy with church leaders in Kumasi, Ghana, West Africa. The mission was seeking to reach the primarily Muslim Walla people from Wa, in northwest Ghana. There were a few minutes of discussion about how best to go about the strategy. During this time, an insightful missionary and former Muslim asserted, "We must go to them." Everyone quickly agreed and started speaking of going to Wa. In the midst of the discussion, he interrupted and explained, "Yes, we must go to Wa and plant churches there, but they are here in Kumasi as well. Almost every man who carries lumber on his head to the market is Walla."

The result was a mission strategy for reaching Wa and another for the Walla. Missionaries went north to the town of Wa, and missionaries went into the lumber markets of Kumasi. Both were focused on the Walla people.

The same can be said for North American postmoderns. Churches need to be planted in Buckhead (metro Atlanta), Marin County (San Francisco), and at the University of Wisconsin. These are just a few of the "hometowns" for postmoderns. But the Walla are not just in Wa! Postmoderns also live in upstate New York, rural Alabama, and New Mexico. We must go to them everywhere.

Postmoderns, like the Walla, are not *a place*; they are *a people*. It is not correct to say that Seattle is postmodern—just that many postmoderns live in Seattle. Postmodernism spread quickly in the last decade of the twentieth century because it became the reigning philosophy of the popular media. Most adults thirty-five or under grew up learning morality on MTV, understanding marriage from TV talk shows, and learning about relationships from sitcoms. Postmoderns are everywhere; postmodern churches need to be everywhere.

Postmoderns do congregate in certain social centers, but they are different from community to community. According to the survey, the most common place where postmodern church planters build relationships is where most would expect—at the coffee shop. For that reason, a planter could assume that the coffee shop in the cultural district of any given town is a good place to find postmoderns—but that might not be true in every case.

Won't They Grow Out of It?

It is natural for church leaders to ask, "Haven't we seen youth cultures that have claimed to have a new way of thinking merge back into the greater culture? Won't they grow out of it?" The 1960s serve as a good example. Many people looked on the hippies with the idea that they would grow out of their values. People rightly assumed that slogans such as "never trust anyone over thirty-five" would not last beyond their thirty-fifth birthday. Most did assimilate into the broader culture, cutting their hair and putting on ties. But they also brought some of their values with them (consider the sexual revolution of the sixties and the sexual antics of Bill Clinton).

Perhaps this postmodern mind-set is a fad that will pass. But if the 1960s are to be used as a barometer, it should be noted that many of today's church leaders were touched by the Jesus Movement while they were still wearing beards and bellbottoms. At that time, they could not have been touched otherwise. The argument for moving aggressively into the postmodern culture—and not avoiding it—is strong. Postmodernism has only a few of the characteristics of an enduring value system (in that it is often described and defined more by what it is not than what it is), but mainstream popular culture has already embraced its values, or nonvalues. This compounds the problem.

The *Oprah Winfrey Show* is a good example of postmodernism expressed through popular media. The influence of the Oprah Winfrey Show is hard to understate. "Oprah 101" has become the cultural classroom of America. A guest will often talk about his or her alternative understanding of morality or spirituality. Oprah then asks the audience for questions where an individual might say, "Well, the Bible says," (We immediately throw up a quick prayer that Christians will not be embarrassed!) But the person continues, "The Bible says that God's best is found in a committed marriage."

Oprah will nod and smile, but say something like, "That may be true for you, but who are we to judge, as long as people are happy and are not hurting anyone else." That is postmodernism, that is media influence, and that is now the majority view of our culture.

Oprah might not know that she is influenced by a cultural system called postmodernity, but postmodern values are showcased on her show each day. She is not alone. Talk shows, "reality" programs, and even the news illustrate the values of postmodernism daily. Postmodernism is the reigning cultural paradigm in popular media. Postmodern values touch all those who are exposed to popular media—that is, everyone who watches television! This is virtually everyone.

Resources for Further Study

Hunsberger, George R. "The Newbigin Gauntlet." In *The Church Between Gospel & Culture,* ed. George R. Hunsberger and Craig Van Gelder. Grand Rapids: Eerdmans, 1996.

Guder, Darrel L. *Missional Church*. Grand Rapids: Eerdmans, 1998.

Sweet, Leonard I. *Soul Tsunami: Sink or Swim in New Millennium Culture*. Grand Rapids: Zondervan Publishing House, 1999.

Van Gelder, Craig, ed. *Confident Witness—Changing World*. Grand Rapids: Eerdmans, 1999.

CHAPTER TWELVE

Emerging Planting Models in a Postmodern World

*H*ow we plant churches is in many ways determined by the location and focus group (where and among whom we plant churches). Moreover, within a rapidly changing world, not all church plants will look the same. As a result, different models to reach the needs of this new culture are emerging. The models of the 1950s were focused on the Builder generation. The models of the 1980s and 1990s were focused on the Baby Boomers. Emerging generations will most likely be reached by new and yet to be discovered models. Though this whole book is about church planting in the postmodern age, this chapter focuses on models for reaching postmoderns.

Some interesting patterns become evident when examining existing models. Those models that are used most successfully in one generation often prove less effective in reaching the next. The reason seems obvious: those using one model see that it works and believe that if the church would just try it again, then it would work again. Members of the Builder generation often believe that a good radio ministry and a weeklong revival will get the church growing again. Baby Boomer Christians often think that if they can just make their service smoother and more professional, then they will be able to reach emerging postmodern generations. It is difficult to convince a person that what worked previously will not work any longer.

This is not to say that critics will not surface at every paradigm shift. There is a scathing critique of me and my thoughts on emerging models at http://www.cnview.com/archives/march_april_2001.htm. It makes the point. I keep a copy at www.newchurches.com to remind me that there will always be critics.

The details of how to plant a church are provided in the rest of this book. Every church plant will need to deal with the issues of child care, rental facilities, finances, etc. But there are some new characteristics rising to the surface within the emerging churches being planted in the post-modern culture.

Based on my observations, the ten most frequent traits of successful postmodern churches are expressed in their key values:

- Being unashamedly spiritual
- Promoting incarnational ministry
- Engaging in service
- Valuing experiential praise
- Preaching narrative expository messages
- Appreciating and participating in ancient patterns
- Visualizing worship
- Connecting with technology
- Living community
- Leading by transparency and team

Some of these characteristics were already present in the North American church fifty years ago; some old patterns are being revived. Other values are new and are challenging the manner in which the church does ministry. Most seminary trained pastors have been trained to minister in a modern world.[1] They do not think like postmoderns because they have been trained not to think that way. They have been taught a system of values and methods that do not match some of those listed above.

Being Unashamedly Spiritual

Churches that are reaching postmoderns have learned that postmoderns are open to the spiritual.[2] Douglas Coupland, who coined the term "Generation X," wrote in *Life After God*, "My secret is that I need God— that I am sick and can no longer make it alone."[3]

People have grown tired of the modern belief that everything can be answered by science and reason. They are open to something "mystical and spiritual."[4] A hunger for the spiritual runs rampant in postmodern pop culture. From Hollywood to politics, spirituality is at a popular high.

Postmoderns are unashamedly proud of their spiritual quests. Postmoderns hold beliefs in many things, including astrology, New Age, tarot cards, psychics, ESP, channeling spirits, reincarnation, witchcraft, palm reading, UFO and aliens, mother earth, crystal power, and Eastern or African spirituality.

Postmodern pop culture is unashamedly proud to throw spirituality at us. On your next trip to the video store, note the array of spirituality on the shelves. Movies such as *Signs, The Matrix,* and *City of Angels* are a few of the box office hits that illustrate this point.

Television is unashamedly spiritual in its content. Many shows are centered on the spiritual. Oprah Winfrey has included a daily segment in her talk show on remembering your spirit. After the 11 o'clock news on most channels, we are blasted with commercials for psychic friends and tarot readings. For three dollars a minute you can be told that wealth and love will be a part of your near future.

Music has been greatly influenced by postmodern pop culture. Postmodern music has confessed to the world that it is also unashamedly spiritual. Gregorian chants and other recordings of spiritual music are best-sellers in music stores around the continent.

If we are to reach these unashamedly spiritual postmoderns, we must take notice of their concepts and beliefs that do not fit within an evangelical worldview. At the beginning of this book, I explained Paul's approach to the Athenians. Remember that Paul did four things in his effort to be culturally relevant:

1. He understood the Athenian position on reality.
2. He understood an underlying spiritual interest.
3. He looked for positive points within their worldview.
4. He encouraged them to find true fulfillment in Christ.[5]

It may be difficult for many Christians to see the current emphasis on non-Christian spirituality as positive, but Paul emphasized that very thing. Though no reaction is recorded from other Christians, we can assume that not everyone appreciated Paul's praise of the Epicurean poets! Even fewer people will appreciate us looking for the underlying spiritual interest in Creed or Moby. Yet just like the philosophers Paul preached to, they are "already very religious."

There are some basic tenets that can describe the secular spirituality of postmodernity. First, it is widespread. In her recent book, Faith Popcorn argues, "We're all at the start of a great awakening, a time of spiritual and religious revival . . . What's different about this awaking is that there's very little agreement on who or what God is, what constitutes worship and what this outpouring means. . . . The need to anchor has found expression in all of the world's religions, whether they celebrate the Old and New Testament God, Buddha, Allah, Brahma, unnamed higher powers or self-discovery."[6]

Len Sweet states in *Soul Tsunami* that in the class of 2001, nine out of ten believe in God. This gives Christians great hope that they can introduce postmoderns to the true God of spirituality.

Second, postmoderns want a spirituality that is applicable to all areas of life. Postmoderns do not want spirituality that only lasts for two hours on a Sunday morning, but one that they can rely on all week. A spirituality that does not *work* (bring peace, make for better relationships, and improve our quality of life) does not matter. Thus, Christians without joy are an antievangelism strategy!

Third, most postmoderns want a spirituality that is authentic above all else. A true postmodern spirituality does not have to be perfect, but it must be genuinely and humbly held. The authenticity of the faith, and that it is sincerely held, is more important than the rational basis of the faith.

This thinking differs in some ways from the great "seeker sensitive" movement that grew in the 1980s and 1990s. Seeker-sensitive churches like Saddleback and seeker-driven churches like Willow Creek showed that the unchurched are willing to attend Christian church services. But many "seeker" churches have yet to recognize that seekers may wish to be more engaged than just as spectators.[7]

This is a change from the seeker-sensitive approach of the past two decades. Morganthaler correctly explains that when reaching seekers is the purpose of worship, it defines the church. Whatever the main worship service becomes, it becomes the main "point of reference."[8] Many postmodern churches are focusing on meaningful worship that allows non-Christian seekers to see Christians in genuine spiritual pursuits.

The most surprising news of postmodernity is that postmoderns are on a "spiritual search and not an intellectual quest."[9] They are willing at times to take that quest with Christians, if they are genuine and live a holistic faith. If their worship services and small groups embrace a participative spirituality, their participation might lead to a genuine faith experience.

Stiver believes that this news is not all bad for Christianity. He explains that being free from the confines of reason has "created a greater opportunity for reasoned dialogue between faith and the world."[10] I agree. Churches that will reach postmodern generations need to give evidence of biblical spirituality, drawing from the rich spiritual resources of the Bible and even church tradition.

Promoting Incarnational Ministry

Authenticity is essential, and authenticity only comes when we are real and present. That "presence" is what theologians call incarnation.[11] When referring to Jesus, it means that the "Word became flesh and made his dwelling among us" (John 1:14). When speaking of missions, it means that we become a part of the community we are seeking to reach.

Postmoderns are looking for persons who are genuine and transparent. They do not ask, "Is it true?" They ask, "Is it real?"[12] Such observations can come only when relationships are real and present. Postmoderns distrust authority and authority structures. They want to see Christ through persons who have earned their respect and trust.[13] As Ron Nash affirms, "Know that the fruit of this type of ministry comes only from considerable time spent listening and learning from postmoderns. Go to their hangouts and listen. Listen and learn, and be willing to wait."[14]

Many postmoderns feel as if they are entering an alien culture when encountering evangelical Christianity.[15] It is not the job of the unchurched postmodern to enter our culture. It is our job to invade theirs. We do that by recognizing this as mission work.

Mission work is the same in every place; the missionary must radically engage the culture. We must "live among them, learn their language, build relationships, and work to discover what kind of redemptive analogies we can adopt from their culture to communicate the message of Christ to them."[16]

Postmoderns are not responding to "sit and let them come to us" evangelism. Reaching postmoderns takes more than just a weekend outreach or a new program. Evangelism to postmoderns is a day-to-day effort. Postmoderns do not want to hear about Christianity; they want to see Christianity in action. A new evangelism paradigm must be used.

Evangelism must adopt "Jesus-type" methods. We must go to postmoderns in order to reach them. We must live in their neighborhoods, eat at their restaurants, drink coffee at their coffee shops, and shop at their stores. Living in Christ must become a daily reality. Being a Christian is not a label or a banner that is flown only on Sundays; it is a way a life.

This may force us to change our church planting strategies from those used in the 1980s and 1990s. In the last two decades of the twentieth century, mass outreaches were common and effective. Telemarketing campaigns could predict for every ten thousand phone calls, one hundred people would come to church. Direct mail generally had a predictable response. If you sent out twenty thousand mailers, one hundred people would come to the first service.

These methods still work (church planters are using them every day), but their effectiveness has been reduced. It is not only that people are more skeptical about advertisers, but it is also that they are less willing to respond to that which should be relational (spirituality and faith) but instead has been packaged in a slick way.

The formation of a Bible study group and eventually a core group will foster a sense of community in the church. Attendees will share a common living experience. They will know the same stores and shops of a particular area. Being involved in the local community will foster the creation of transformational communities.

Engaging in Service

The key to engaging the postmodern passion is service.[17] This relates not just to postmodern Christians engaging in service.[18] It also involves churches engaging in service as *part of* evangelism.

The postmodern generation is looking for an opportunity to serve. Volunteerism is at an all-time high as people have the desire to make a difference in their community and their world. Organizations such as Habitat for Humanity and the Peace Corps serve as outlets for postmoderns to make their mark on society. Postmoderns are looking for hands-on opportunities to get involved and be active. In his book *Postmodern Pilgrims,* Len Sweet addresses the issue of the postmoderns' desire to be actively involved: "Postmoderns don't give their undivided attention to much of anything without its being interactive. It is no longer enough to possess things or to enjoy positive events. One now has to be involved in bringing those events to pass or brokering those things into the home. People want to participate in the production of content, whatever it is . . . this is a cultural shift from passivity to interactivity."[19]

Churches can connect with postmodern Americans by offering them an outlet for their passion to serve. Genuine faith always expresses itself in ministry. As postmoderns see that faith produces service, the validity of the faith is proved. A wonderful outlet for this is to engage postmoderns in mission work. Mission work is not just service in international locations, and it is not limited to traditional ways of evangelizing those who do not know Christ. Downtown Community Fellowship in Athens, Georgia, takes advantage of their proximity to the local college campus. The pastor explains, "We hand out icy-pops and hot chocolate downtown and at the University of Georgia campus in order to meet people, share God's love and invite them to worship with us."[20] He adds:

> The concept of servant evangelism is nothing new. The Salvation Army and others have been doing it for years. However, what we're proposing involves some new twists. Steve Sjogren, pastor at the Vineyard Church in Cincinnati, Ohio, has been influential in our thinking in this regard. Steve has built his church from zero to more than five thousand simply by going out into the community and serving people . . . over the years, Steve and his congregation have touched more than a million people within the greater Cincinnati area by serving them in a variety of ways.[21]

Acts of service are not the only way to get postmoderns involved in reaching their own generation. When a group of young adults started meeting to plan a group vacation, they discovered that they wanted to take a vacation that would mean something for God's kingdom. Time spent in worship and prayer led them to the decision to plan a short-term mission trip rather than a vacation. They identified the following needs:

- Young adults want to test whether they have a genuine call to the mission field.
- Young adults want to build relationships with one another and with other peoples of the world.
- Christians need a challenge to be wise stewards of their time, money, and energy.
- The gospel needs to be shared.
- World poverty needs to be addressed.

Once the teams knew the needs that moved them, they could assess their values. Based on the above, they came up with the following core values:

- *Relationships.* Our ministry should focus on healthy relationships with other people and with God.
- *Discipline.* Our ministry should challenge members to grow in the spiritual disciplines of stewardship and service.
- *Evangelism.* Our ministry should teach people to be passionate about spreading the gospel and addressing human suffering.[22]

This group went on to make short-term, mid-term, and long-term goals. They assigned leaders to make sure that these goals were carried out, and they discovered other resources that allowed them to make the best use of the time and money available. In addition, fulfilling their goals would also benefit those they would be serving during their trip. The same kind of passion and ministry focus needs to be a part of the planning of a new church.

Service is a wonderful outlet to engage postmoderns in mission work.[23] New Horizons Fellowship[24] in Apex, North Carolina, uses Habitat for Humanity house-building projects as an evangelistic outreach. The church members invite their friends to serve the poor by building a house. In the process, they can see the Christ-centered service of believers and see the gospel in action. The church family is trained to share their faith as part of this mission work.

Valuing Experiential Praise

Worship is essential in every generation.[25] The large group gathering will still function in the church that reaches postmoderns. These large group meetings will "lower the drawbridge" to create opportunities for genuine community.[26] Still there is an "ecstasy deficit" in many churches.[27] Emerging postmodern churches are seeking to experience worship in a new way.

The typical Boomer church is big on technique. This makes sense in the modern world. Guder makes the point that such technique is both moving and expected in the contemporary worship service.[28] Boomers expect to be emotionally lifted by the music, lighting, and well-choreographed program. These seeker-sensitive services helped Boomers glorify God in a manner that was culturally appropriate for them.

One of the most significant changes over the last two decades was discovering what constituted a seeker-sensitive service. In many large Boomer churches, seeker-sensitivity always involved a high degree of anonymity. This may be changing in the postmodern culture. Being sensitive to the postmodern seeker may involve allowing him or her to be involved in the learning process. Postmoderns do not want to be spectators; they want to be contributors in the learning process.[29] "Postmoderns want a God that they can feel, taste, touch, hear, and smell."[30] According to Sweet, "Some new-style churches are finding that [postmoderns] respond to the counter-cultural nature of ancient worship; it's a far cry from the user-friendly contemporary worship predominant among baby boomers."[31]

A dynamic worshiping community becomes a powerful apologetic to a generation open to the spiritual yet unaware of how to connect with the Spirit.[32] We should not deny them such a life-changing experience.[33] Instead, we need to create deeply biblical worship services. Believers need to be focused on worshiping the ever-present God. At the same time unbelievers will see the joy that such worship brings. Unbelievers cannot experience true worship, but they can see the effect of genuine worship.

Postmodern spirituality believes that our rational abilities are unable to grasp the whole truth and unable to provide the whole story.[34] These "already religious" people can see true believers worshiping in spirit and truth. They will be attracted to this worship. Worship can be unintentionally evangelistic.

Postmodern worship is not antiliturgical. It may find its manifestation in liturgical expressions. Modern generation Christians have tended to focus on becoming "like" Christ. Instead, postmoderns may focus on "participating in the divine nature."[35]

An article in *Regeneration Quarterly*, a publication seeking to engage postmodernity, explained: "The worship of the Orthodox Church is meant to be nothing less than participation in the eternal Liturgy at the Throne of God in heaven. It is the earthly type, symbol, and image of the heavenly reality; and through these earthly types, by the Holy Spirit, we actually participate in the heavenly."[36] Beaudoin believes that churches reaching postmodern generations will evidence "a renewal of mystical practices or spiritual disciplines."[37]

In order for worship to promote evangelism, Morganthaler says it must include four elements: "nearness—an awareness of the presence of God; knowledge—worship that is centered on who Christ is; vulnerability—worship that involves opening up to God; and interaction—participating in the worship of God."[38] She is correct. Her book *Worship Evangelism* should be required reading for every church planter seeking to reach postmodern generations.

Music as art plays a vital role in experiential worship. Imago Dei Community[39] in Portland, Oregon, encourages creativity by using hymns and music mostly written by their community members. Their purpose is to show what biblical worship looks like contextualized in urban Portland. The Bridge Church[40] in Pontiac, Michigan, describes their music as "rock-in-roll guitar driven." The Water Community of Faith[41] in Las Vegas believes in using all types of music (or no music at all). Freeway Church[42] in Baton Rouge, Louisiana, best describes their music as "alternative." Freeway has a regular house band that plays praise and worship.

Preaching Narrative Expository Messages

One of the emerging trends in new churches among postmodern generations relates to preaching style. Postmoderns tend to prefer the Gospels to the Epistles because they value the power of story.[43] Eugene Peterson observes:

> We live in an age when story has been pushed from its
> biblical front-line prominence to a bench on the sidelines,
> condescended to as "illustration" or "testimony" or

"inspiration." Both inside and outside the church, we prefer information over story. We typically gather impersonal (pretentiously called "scientific" or "theological") information, whether doctrinal or philosophical or historical, in order to take things into our own hands and take charge of how we will live our lives. And we commonly consult outside experts to interpret the information for us.[44]

Jesus' life was not an essay, doctrine, or sermon. His life was a story.[45] Early church preaching was often story-focused. A return to narrative preaching is a good thing—as long as the focal narrative is the narrative of Scripture. Jesus frequently used narratives in his preaching. Often the story was the point. But we are told to preach the Word and not just tell meaningful stories. Preaching must be both narrative and biblical. To some people, narrative preaching is telling a contemporary story with biblical texts sprinkled in. This is not enough. New Testament churches still need to be biblical and to present Scripture as their text and focus.

Postmoderns are accustomed to stacked narratives—narratives that move in and out of varying stories. The typical television show provides three or four interwoven plot lines in one episode.[46] Some people have termed this narrative approach to preaching as a "collusion of narratives."[47]

As emerging new churches present the Word of God, they can build an effective message around a biblical narrative, surrounding it with contemporary illustrations and applications. I will give more information on narrative expository preaching in the chapter on worship.

Appreciating and Participating in Ancient Patterns

Postmodern leaders are spellbound by the ancient-future faith of the past.[48] Although postmodern generations tend to see the now as paramount, they will be attracted to a faith that is rooted in history.[49] There is a new interest in ancient things: Gregorian chants, Celtic Christianity, ancient art, etc.[50]

This postmodern generation "stays away from most congregations in droves but loves songs about God and Jesus, a generation that would score very low in any standard piety scale but at times seems almost obsessed with saints, visions, and icons of all shapes and sizes."[51]

For many Boomers, the trappings of traditional church bring back memories of negative childhood experiences. This is not true for many postmodern generations, who are often devoid of any church memories. For them, the symbols are new and meaningful.[52] Mark Sayers points out, "The dominance of the spoken word is diminishing as the modern world is eclipsed by the new millennium culture. The Protestant reformation saw a massive backlash against the opulent symbolism of the Catholic Church, however the baby was thrown out with the bath water and symbolism and full sensory worship was totally rejected instead of being re-invented."[53]

In many ways, the postmodern desire is to mimic the action of the Reformation but not its essence. A recovery of the experiential faith of the past with its sacred symbols and shared doxology unite individuals in a way that is unfamiliar to this individualistic society. In a transition to contemporary worship and seeker-sensitive services, there is a backlash among postmoderns to reach toward the stability of the past. "There are many among the Baby Boomers and especially among the Gen Xers, who are attracted to liturgical worship, represented by Roman Catholic, Eastern Orthodox, and Episcopal churches."[54]

Most postmodern thought is a reaction to the failures of modernism and its materialistic perspective, yet postmoderns revert to this same past as a place of stability. The church of the modern era failed to answer many of the questions postmoderns were asking, but the ancient traditions still hold the mystery of the transcendent and the experience of spirituality. The churches that are reaching the postmodern culture have reached them at this major intersection where the worldview of Christianity and the worldview of postmodernism collide. "The philosophical shift from reason to mystery provides an opening to the discussion of a supernatural view of the church connected with the work of Christ."[55]

The contact with the stability of the past, as well as multisensory worship, gives the postmodern seeker a place to start in his or her journey for truth. This is a generation of doubting Thomases. They will not believe Christ until they experience him in their lives. The candles, hymns, and other ancient forms of worship are a safe place for the postmodern seeker to enter into the meta-narratives that run so contrary to the subjectivity of the day.

Visualizing Worship

Many people look to the prevalence of MTV as the reason that churches should use multimedia if they want to reach postmoderns. But the fact that "video killed the radio star"[56] is not enough to elevate the visual above the spoken word. There is a place for both.

In the postmodern age, truth is also expressed in images.[57] The church that began in a preliterate culture must rediscover its values in a post-literate culture.[58] Postmoderns may best be reached by returning to pre-modern approaches.

Postmoderns are not looking to be entertained; they are seeking to be engaged.[59] A worship service held in a sterile auditorium, led by professional worship leaders without blemish, may not appeal to the typical postmodern.[60] Sweet points out:

> This is an experience economy. The primary cultural currency out there is basically images and experiences. When you have those two put together, the primary arena for accessing reality and truth is the arts. . . . In this way, the postmodern world is much more medieval. The church was a major patron of the arts. We forget this—there was a time up until the 19th century that some of your major art dealers and traders were clergy. Then, something happened. Right now is a major renaissance for the arts in the church as we make worship multi-sensory and experiential.[62]

This has been most obviously expressed through the introduction of video screens and PowerPoint presentations in new churches. But it is much more than that. Many emerging postmodern churches are discovering the value of banners and liturgies that connect them with biblical truth.

Connecting with Technology

Technology is no longer an option in this postmodern culture. It is part of the culture.[62] Technology may have assisted the rapid spread of postmodernism more than anything else.[63] It makes sense that new churches would also use technology to reach postmodern generations. Technology tends to be used in three settings: the worship service, evangelism, and community.

Worship services. Since technology has been a great influence on post-modern culture, it makes sense that any missions strategy to reach them must consider technology. New churches reaching emerging postmodern generations are using technology in many ways. Cornerstone Church[64] in San Francisco uses light gels to transform their worship into a liturgical church—projecting stained glass where there is none. Their Web site explains:

> The Cornerstone Experience is unique. This is a place
> were music, media, and the message converge together to cre-
> ate a powerful, multi-sensory worship experience. At the core
> of this experience is the life changing reality of Jesus Christ.
> Because He lives we live also and Cornerstone has dedicated
> itself to sharing the Good News of Jesus Christ in a highly
> creative and unique fashion.[65]

Evangelism. Cyberspace has had a leveling effect on postmodern generations, presenting a myriad of religious options at the fingertips of the average postmodern.[66] Most postmoderns who are interested in spiritual things will do some research first—and most of that will be on-line.

There are hundreds of thousands of sites for exploring spirituality on the Internet. Most of them present ideas and proposals that are not biblical Christianity. The church must be more widely represented in the cyber world. Churches that take this new frontier seriously will be more likely to thrive in the postmodern world.

Ginghamsburg Church[67] is a good example of a church that is using technology, particularly the Internet, for evangelism. They actually have a staff member for cyberministry. Many churches place extensive information about Christianity on their site so spiritual seekers can do research in private before asking questions about the community. There is more information on how to link to sites appropriate for evangelism in a postmodern age. Visit the links page at www.newchurches.com.

Community. Some churches are exploring the use of technology to foster community. Most churches using the Internet for community are not doing so in place of personal interaction; they are doing it to enhance interpersonal interaction. Internet churches without meaningful community beyond chat rooms are just occasional anomalies. Steer clear of them.

Living Community

"Before the church is called to do or say anything, it is called and sent to be the unique community of those who live under the reign of God . . . a form of companionship and wholeness that humanity craves."[68] Both evangelism and discipleship seem to be an individual endeavor in modern Christianity.[69] These were things that we did alone in our prayer closet. That is still true, but it is not the whole story.[70]

Community is a central value in most churches that are reaching postmoderns. Community will be a central value in all postmodern communities, whether secular or sacred. This is good news for the church because community is central to its mission. With a culture anxious for genuine community, the church of Christ can offer community with man and with God. In the new church of the postmoderns, spiritual growth does not take place outside of community.[71]

Postmodern generations are searching for the security provided by relationships.[72] The popularity of the television show *Friends* is illustrative of a generation creating family bonds from friendships. To many, this is a new type of family, connected by friendships and not kinship.[73]

Groups seeking to build relationships among postmoderns will not be short-term study groups. These groups will sometimes meet for two or more years before becoming true communities.[74] This is not a limitation on new participants. On the contrary, true communities will welcome new people because they are communities.[75] In such small group communities, there is no time constraint on the journey.[76]

The key to evangelizing postmoderns is the presence of Christian community.[77] In a world where Christianity is not the establishment religion, it must provide the strength of community to reinforce its message.[78] Notice the connection between community and proclamation: "All the believers were one in heart and mind. No one claimed that any of his possessions was his own, but they shared everything they had. With great power the apostles continued to testify to the resurrection of the Lord Jesus, and much grace was upon them all" (Acts 4:32–33).

Evangelism among a relational people group needs to be relationship-oriented: "We can't stress enough that connecting to others in relationships and building a sense of community are driving forces for (the postmodern generations). It's a *we*-centered spiritual approach, not a *me*-centered approach. This is a generation that longs to belong."[79]

The Christian church was intended to be a faith community. It has more frequently been seen as a building rather than a community. Christianity revolutionized the perception of religion because it was not "temple-based."[80] Relationship with God and others is the foundation of the Christian faith. There is no church without community. We are rediscovering that truth today.

There is always a danger in building relationships. We must not just build them with people like us. Postmodern churches must not just become churches of "cool people." Instead, they need to be places where all are welcome in the community—the old, the young, the sick, the well, the rich, the poor, the postmodern, and yes, even the modern.

> Certainly, behind some "contemporary services" or new church plants are thoughtful evangelists who are contextualizing this scandalous gospel. Equally certainly, behind some others are self-absorbed young people who just want to run something all by themselves, No Grownups Allowed. But behind the majority of segmented ministries, I suspect, is a failure to welcome the stranger.[81]

Emerging postmodern churches are reaching out by inviting people into their community. They are allowing the spiritual journey to begin before conversion. Spiritual seekers are invited to participate in the faith community before they share the faith. Allowing someone to belong does not mean that he or she is incorporated into the body of Christ.[82] It means they are seeking in a safe place. As Grenz observes, "Members of the next generation are often unimpressed by our verbal presentation of the gospel. What they want to see is people who live out the gospel in wholesome, authentic and healing relationships."[83]

You can't buy community; you can't program community. Community is a result of one relationship plus other relationships. Community only delivers the safety that is longed for when enough people know who you are, and they accept you for who you are. Community does not mean the acceptance of all ideas and lifestyles; it does mean loving people despite their ideas or lifestyles. The devout atheist and the homosexual will not come to Christ until the love of Christ annihilates the worldview upon which they depend.

Community is the love of God manifesting itself in and through the people of God. That is the advantage the church has in this postmodern society. You can't fake community; it is the reality of the relationships that makes Christ believable to an unbelieving society. "Postmodern preachers don't populate the pews; they connect people to the living Christ. Postmodern evangelism doesn't say to the world, 'Come to the church.' Rather, it says to the church, 'Go to the world.'"[84] Community will break out of the walls of the church building and break down the misconceptions that society has about Christendom—the misconceptions that Christendom has created for itself through its misrepresentation of the true Christ.

Community is the lightning rod that attracts postmoderns to participation in the meta-narrative. Community is the living, breathing answer to the question of "Is this real?" Postmoderns use many questions to keep truth questions at a distance. Through community seekers will be able to ask questions in a safe place. In this safe community, the seeker may remain long enough to receive the answers. To many postmoderns, Christ is best expressed through community.

Leading by Transparency and Team

Leadership in the postmodern context tends to be dramatically different.[85] In the modern context, the leader was penalized for transparency. Leaders who shared their struggles frequently regretted it later as it became an example in future arguments. In the postmodern era, struggle has more value. Thus, the "wounded healer" is a well-accepted leadership approach.[86] According to Long:

> Paul was not afraid to be transparent. He admitted that he often found himself doing the things that he shouldn't be doing, while neglecting to do the things that he should be doing (Rom. 7:15). Paul understood what it meant to be real with his audience. Paul personified being a sinner saved by grace. Ministers that tend to forget their past mistakes and to be accountable for the ones they make daily are not being true to Christ. Paul was not afraid to show his thorns. Paul

refused to be placed above others. He preferred a level play-
ing ground. A "thorn" was placed in his side to keep him
from being exalted above others.[87]

The Scripture text clearly calls for such transparency. But this has not
been practiced in our churches. Professional ministers have learned to guard
against being transparent in order to protect their ministries. The Scriptures
tell a different story:

For to be sure, he was crucified in weakness, yet he lives
by God's power. Likewise, we are weak in him, yet by God's
power we will live with him to serve you (2 Cor. 13:4).

Praise be to the God and Father of our Lord Jesus Christ,
the Father of compassion and the God of all comfort, who
comforts us in all our troubles, so that we can comfort those
in any trouble with the comfort we ourselves have received
from God (2 Cor. 1:3–4).

Team. Leaders in the postmodern context prefer a team-oriented
approach to leadership. Many postmodern leaders will struggle when they
are asked to take solitary leadership.[88] It is not their way. Instead, they are
seeking a community of leadership.

Visions of success are important in every culture. In the modern culture,
perhaps influenced by Machiavelli's *The Prince,* the value is to get ahead.
This is not so in much of postmodern culture. Seeing the consequence of
unbridled competition, some postmoderns are often more concerned with
getting along than getting ahead.[89] Baby Boomer evangelicals have talked
the talk of team leadership but have failed to develop true teams. For postmoderns, team leadership is a much more natural approach.[90]

The process is often more important than the product. Postmoderns
tend to ask of the decision making process: "Was it fair? Was it just? Did
it make sense? Was I valued?"[91] These process-oriented questions must be
considered in depth in the postmodern leadership paradigm. This will
probably challenge a world where 70 percent of pastors say they do not
have a single friend.[92]

New attitudes. As the church moves into the twenty-first century and
begins reaching the postmodern generation with the gospel of Jesus Christ,
new attitudes toward leadership must be embraced. Leadership in the post-

modern context tends to be different than it has been in other models. This new trend in leadership is most commonly referred to as team-based leadership—the concept by which a group makes decisions and implements new ideas, rather than have one leader making all the decisions and trying to lead a group without the input of others.

According to Len Sweet, "Postmodern culture is a choice culture."[93] He presents the postmodern culture as having shifted from representative to participatory by giving the following examples:

A representative culture is based on certain beliefs:

- People want and need to be controlled and have decisions made for them.
- The task of leadership is to administer guidance and regulations.
- People do only the things they are rewarded for doing.
- People cannot be trusted to use their personal freedom in service to the society or organization.

A participatory culture is based on just the opposite beliefs:

- People want to make their own decisions and have multiple choices.
- Leadership is emboldening and empowering others to lead.
- People will make sacrifices for the good of the whole.
- Human systems are self-organizing, and people can be trusted to invest wisely of their resources and time.[94]

Team-based ministry allows those involved to make decisions to accomplish their common goals. Rich Hurst discusses the importance of involving everyone in ministry decisions. Instead of getting together a group of people and telling them, "Here's what we are going to do," a group can be pulled together and asked, "What would you like to do to reach people like yourselves?" The door then is open wide for endless possibilities as ownership of the ministry is created. Hurst goes on to say, "Relational ministry encourages group members to determine their own ministry direction. . . . If you don't learn to empower people to create, you will find yourself driven to do everything yourself. You'll have an endless need for more volunteers, and eventually become the preoccupied shopkeeper."[95]

According to Hurst, the new goal of leadership is to use the "I'll do it with you" model: "Many young adults simply don't respond to authoritative leadership that barks out orders, demands results, and micro-manages tasks. While young adults need direction, they prefer guidance within the context of a relationship. Therefore, in order to lead today's young adults, we must continue moving toward a more relational style of leadership."[96]

Eddie Gibbs in his book *ChurchNext* discusses teaching seminary students the importance of team building and team-based ministry. Otherwise, "a lone pastor all too easily becomes a lonely pastor."[97]

(With the) emphasis in education on individualism, self-reliance, and individual performance . . . the church leaders of tomorrow have been trained in a competitive environment where private study is at the heart of the learning experience—a habit that is hard to break.[98]

I cannot say it better than Wayne Cordeiro, pastor of New Hope Christian Fellowship in Honolulu, Hawaii. He explains: "Doing church as a team is a whole new mind-set for our churches today. But if we are going to be the church of the twenty-first century, there's just no other way! The days of the lone ranger are over. Often in the Bible, God refers to us as the body of Christ. The better we understand this metaphor, the more we will be able to cooperate with God's design for the church."[99]

For my article on church planting through multi-cultural teams, go to www.new-churches.com/ research

Talking about team is not enough. Teams are messy, painful, difficult, and rewarding all at the same time. We are all fallen creatures with fallen motives. Some recommend the development of covenants—written or verbal agreements regarding how to deal with conflicts when they occur.[100] Regardless of how these challenges are handled, they need to be recognized and addressed. Ultimately, the work is worth the reward. The covenanted leadership team models Christian community to the whole church. The church, in turn, models community to the world.

Conclusion

Not all churches that reach emerging postmodern generations will give evidence of all of these traits. Some of them are my own interpretations. But most of these traits will be evident to some degree. Perhaps by being aware of them early, postmodern church planters will reach their communities effectively today—rather than struggling and waiting five years for these trends to become commonplace. Moreover, within the next five years new methods and strategies will most likely develop to either replace or compliment existing strategies. What an exciting future of change we have before us in reaching postmoderns!

Resources for Further Reading

Gibbs, Eddie. *ChurchNext: Quantum Changes in How We Do Ministry.* Downers Grove, Ill.: InterVarsity, 2000.

Shenk, David W., and Ervin R. Stutzman. *Creating Communities of the Kingdom: New Testament Models of Church Planting.* Scottdale, Pa.: Herald Press, 1988.

Sweet, Leonard. *Aqua Church: Essential Leadership Arts for Piloting Your Church in Today's Fluid Culture.* Loveland, Colo.: Group, 1999.

Webber, Robert E. *Ancient-Future Faith: Rethinking Evangelicalism for a Postmodern World.* Grand Rapids: Baker, 1999.

CHAPTER THIRTEEN

African-American and Ethnic Church Planting

*A*nother aspect of culture that must be understood is ethnicity. Churches are not just being planted among Anglo populations. In most denominational settings, the *majority* of church planting is African-American or ethnic.

African-American Church Planting

One out of every six churches in North America is African-American, yet the number of unchurched African-Americans is constantly rising. The need for planting new churches in African-American communities intensifies every year, especially in light of the gradual erosion of interest in traditional worship styles among African-American young adults.

There are three helpful resources produced by African-Americans that can assist African-American planters in starting new churches in their communities. The first of these works is the 1989 book *Church Planting in the Black Community,* edited by Sid Smith. The second publication is the 1993 collaboration by Joe Ratliff and Michael Cox, *Church Planting in the African-American Community.*

The most recent work, *Church Planting in the African-American Context,* is by Hozell Francis. The author focuses on the sociological factors that are not covered as thoroughly in the other works. A careful reading of all three of these works will sensitize the student to crucial cultural and methodological issues in planting churches in African-American communities.

African-American pastors Joe Ratliff and Michael Cox speculate that pastoral leadership in an African-American church plant is even more important than in an Anglo church plant.[1] There are differences in leadership expectations and style from Anglo to African-American churches. According to Hozell C. Francis, an African-American pastor must carefully balance the demands of "social, political, and spiritual" needs to be effective.[2]

One area of difference with church planting in this community is that some new African-American churches will never be financially self-supporting, particularly if being self-supporting is defined as having a full-time salaried pastor. African-American churches need to be started in upper-middle-class communities, middle-class neighborhoods, in ghettos, and housing projects. A diversity of strategies and pastoral leadership styles is needed.[3]

Ratliff and Cox believe that a theology and a strategy for church planting and growth in a black community must differ from that in a predominantly Anglo community for three reasons.

1. Lack of intentionality in church starting in traditional African-American church starts.
2. The number of unchurched blacks.
3. Lack of resources on the topic.[4]

There is generally little divergence between the religious views of African-Americans and the religious view of the remainder of the population. There are a few exceptions. For example: 51 percent of African-Americans as compared to 40 percent of whites and Hispanics are concerned about social justice issues being addressed in the church. In addition, 60 percent of Hispanics and 54 percent of whites agreed with the statement, "One church is as good as another." But 70 percent of African-Americans agreed with that statement.[5] These issues will impact the church planting strategy.

Ratliff and Cox describe the African-American planter in terminology similar to the planter described earlier by Charles Ridley: "Selling a vision is generally couched in the personality of the church planter. However, this does not necessarily mean the church planter has to have a vibrant, slap on the back gregarious personality. Rather, the church planter must have a communicating personality, a listening personality, a people personality. The church planter must be serious and sincere about the vision."[6]

Ratliff and Cox consider sponsorship a unique challenge. Most church plants will be sponsored by another church. In any type of church plant, there is already the tendency to see if the new church has a "baby."[7] Frequently, African-American churches are sponsored by churches of a different ethnic group, usually Anglo churches.[8] Any cross-cultural sponsorship will have its difficulties. It is important that cultural differences be recognized and addressed up front. For example, the sponsor church may agree to provide resources. This may mean money to the new church but literature to the sponsoring church. In any cross-cultural partnership, a good amount of time should be given to details, definitions, and everything necessary to make sure the sponsoring relationship is clear.[9]

I hesitate to write more about African-American church planting since I am not African-American and have not served in that context. The best resources are listed above. Consult them if you plan to start an African-American church. This book shares principles, but the listed books offer context and cultural discernment.

Ethnic Church Planting

Although most growth in church planting in recent years has occurred among ethnic groups, comparatively little has been written on the subject. Noteworthy exceptions are Oscar Romo's *American Mosaic* and a series of church-starting guides, focusing on various ethnic groups, published by the Home Mission Board of the Southern Baptist Convention in the early 1990s.

The Internet is the best source for up-to-date information about ethnic church planting. The Ethnic Harvest Web site (www.ethnicharvest.com) is a must for those planting ethnic churches. In addition, the Southern Baptist North American Mission Board provides all its "Working With" brochures on-line (http://www.namb.net/cp/About_CPG/brochures.asp).

Up-to-date ethnic church planting links are found at www.new-churches.com/ethnic.

From its beginning, America has not been the mythical melting pot, but instead has been marked by its diversity.[10] Today, more than 10 percent of the population of the United States were born outside of the country. Canada has always valued diversity and has always been a multicultural nation as well.

Most Anglo North Americans know very little of the ethnic journey. For example:

- The dialects of Native Americans, representing 497 tribes and speaking 250 different languages and dialects, are found more frequently in urban cities than on tribal reservations.[11]
- Toronto is the world's most ethnically diverse city.[12]
- The Japanese have experienced more prejudice and discrimination than any other immigrant ethnic group in America.[13]
- There are more than five hundred different ethnic groups in America.[14]
- All the following have distinctive cultural identities: Mexican-Americans, who live primarily in the American Southwest; Puerto Ricans, who reside primarily in the Northeast; Cubans, who are found primarily in New York City, California, and Miami; and Central and South Americans, who are scattered across America.[15]
- French Canadians are the largest unreached group on the continent.
- Seventy-eight percent of Los Angeles residents are ethnics.
- More Jews live in New York City than in Israel.
- Chicago is the second largest Polish city anywhere. [16]

Reaching people living within a culture requires a missions commitment. Bible translators act on the premise that people will never be effectively reached for the gospel until the gospel is in the language of their souls.[17] Planting churches in the heart language of the people groups of North America is an essential strategy if we are to reach North America.

A major component of this continued growth is the emergence of cultural (indigenous) leaders among ethnic groups. When an ethnic church sponsors a new ethnic church, 98 percent of the pastors come from that ethnic group. When leaders encourage indigenous leaders to arise within ethnic population groups, the growth of churches of that ethnic segment often doubles.[18]

In Phoenix, Arizona, the United Methodist Church is currently trying to start more ethnic and African-American churches. Tim Butcher, director of congregational development at the United Methodist Center, knows the importance of training new indigenous leaders. Their churches do not have corporate worship until there are at least twelve small groups of twelve people meeting weekly. Even though they use the first year to develop small groups, leaders need to multiply quickly.

Ethnic Church Planting Models

The Nazarene Church publishes an excellent research Web site that includes a study of types of ethnic church sponsorship.[19]

Models of Ethnic Church Planting from the Nazarene Church

Natural birth. A church decides to plant an ethnic church in a neighborhood geographically removed from the planting church.

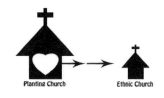

Adoption. A sponsoring church finds an existing church in another neighborhood and adopts it to help in its development.

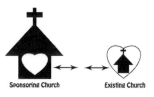

Implantation. A sponsoring church begins an ethnic mission in its buildings, realizing that it will eventually need to be transplanted to a neighborhood where it can grow.

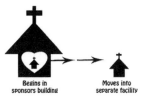

More Than One Organized Church Meeting in the Same Building

All congregations work in a continuing fellowship to build unity. All expenses associated with the use of the building facilities are shared proportionately by each group. Each group is equally accountable to the district or state church organization.

Natural birth. A church plants another church within its facilities with the intention of keeping it there.

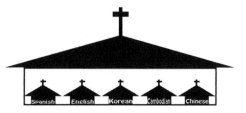

Adoption. A church reaches out to an existing church in its neighborhood and "adopts" them into the church family. The churches share facilities but exist as two separate organizations.

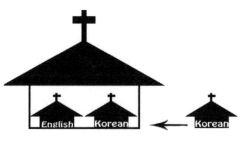

Transition. When a neighborhood changes, a new church is formed to take over the facility as the existing culture dies out.

More Than One Culture in One Church Organization

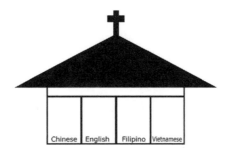

Multiworship service. When more than one worship service is held in the same facility, the service may be cultural but is usually language-based.

Multilanguage classes. Many new immigrants who need to learn in their own language are moving in. Bible studies are changed to help meet their needs.

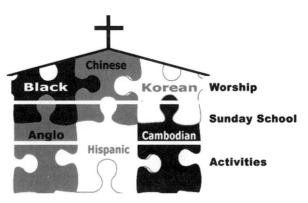

Multicultural. A church designs its church services for a variety of cultural groups.

Planting ethnic churches is an essential part of any strategy. There is an emerging trend that needs to be encouraged—multicultural leadership teams planting multicultural churches.

Ethnic church planting may also be a good place for an established church to get involved. An established church could sponsor a language church plant without much controversy and with churchwide involvement.

Conclusion

Planting predominantly African-American or ethnic churches is not the same as planting a predominantly Anglo church. Yet the postmodern world appropriately values the mosaic of cultures. The cultures *are* different from the Anglo majority culture. If you want a deeper understanding, I encourage you to check the books mentioned or contact planters in the appropriate culture group. If you are an ethnic or African-American church planter, please go beyond this book in the research you conduct on this subject.

Resources for Further Reading

Francis, Hozell C. *Church Planting in the African American Context.* Grand Rapids: Zondervan Publishing House, 2000.

Hesselgrave, David J. *Planting Churches Cross-Culturally: A Guide for Home and Foreign Missions.* Grand Rapids: Baker Book House, 1980.

Ratliff, Joe S., and Michael J. Cox. *Church Planting in the African-American Community.* Nashville: Broadman Press, 1993.

Romo, Oscar I. *American Mosaic: Church Planting in Ethnic America.* Nashville: Broadman Press, 1993.

http://www.ethnicharvest.org/

CHAPTER FOURTEEN

House Churches

Significant interest in the house church exists among postmodern church leaders, even though there are only a few successes to report. House churches have been an intriguing, though limited, experiment among Christians in the West. House churches are known best in China, where somewhere between fifty and eighty million Christians meet regularly in house churches. China has unique characteristics that make the house church work in that context. They have not worked everywhere.

The House Church phenomenon has caught the attention of even the *New York Times*:

> A growing number of Christians across the country are choosing a do-it-yourself worship experience in what they call a "house church." Although numbers for such an intentionally decentralized religious phenomenon are hard to pin down, as many as 1,600 groups in all 50 states are listed on house church Web sites.[1]

Assuming two thousand such house churches at twenty people in each, at least forty thousand Christians are involved in these congregations. Though two thousand churches may seem small, the number is growing—and new churches are being planted in homes across North America.

House Churches by Choice

Throughout history, Christians have tended to meet in larger and larger groups under more highly trained leaders when they have the freedom and ability to do so. When the government restricts the use of large buildings, the church thrives in homes as it has in China. When church buildings are out of the question due to economic factors, the church can thrive by meeting under trees in a village. When it has been possible to gather in larger groups, Christians have historically done so.

For many years, some Christians have promoted the house church as a viable alternative for the Christian church. For example, one book written in 1972 explained, "It was after this first year as a congregation that some of us discovered, to our surprise, that groups elsewhere called themselves House Churches. Through our reading we were discovering, too, that the House Church had appeared in the early life of the church. The importance of its historical roots and its contemporary emergence slowly dawned upon us."[2]

Some people are calling for the "third reformation" that will lead to a restoration of New Testament structure for the church:

> In rediscovering the gospel of salvation by faith and grace
> alone, Luther started to reform the Church through a reforma-
> tion of theology. In the 18th century through movements like
> the Moravians there was a recovery of a new intimacy with
> God, which led to a reformation of spirituality, the Second
> Reformation. Now God is touching the wineskins themselves,
> initiating a Third Reformation, a reformation of structure.[3]

There is a genuine feeling that this expression of church will lead to a great move of the Holy Spirit: "A new wind is stirring in the land! A mere zephyr, but we expect it to become a hurricane which will alter the landscape of Christendom. The wind is the Spirit, who in our time is again doing new things. He is bringing renewal and transformation to the individual and corporate lives of His people, His church."[4]

Many people have advocated that the church abandon its buildings and embrace the relational nature of the house church, but this has not caught on in the North American church world. House-church adherents may consider it a failure of the church, but Christians generally have not chosen to worship in small house churches.

To download some of these elec- tronic resources, go to www.new- churches.com/ house.

Many have claimed that this expression of church structure is the future, and they have been, thus far, wrong. Observers of church growth have heard this in the Jesus Movement of the 1960s, the charismatic movement of the 1980s, and the house church networks of the 1990s. All have failed to provide a long-term viable model of church structure. When their vision-ary leaders passed, they dissolved or became more common models.

The culture shift into postmodernity may have the escape velocity that the other movements lacked. This remains to be seen. There have been a few models but not great successes. Yet we cannot deny that the potential for house churches is great in a culture that values intimate relationships, shared leadership, transparency, and teamwork.

I personally long for this model to become the norm. I pray that Christians might gather in missional house communities, practicing solid New Testament church structure, and reaching out to their neighbors. I have seen a few such examples. This encourages me that more are possible.

What Is a House Church?

A significant amount of literature on house churches has emerged. Since the newest emphasis on the house church started in the late 1990s, much of the literature is available on the Internet. I have assembled some of this information at www.newchurches.com/house. I will not attempt to duplicate these materials here; you can find them at the Web site. Instead, I will focus on what house churches may look like in an emerging post-modern world.

Not Home Cells

A basic understanding of the difference between house church and home cells might be helpful. A home cell is a part of a larger church and supports the ministry of that church. Most churches planted in the last few years have had a large celebration service for worship accompanied by meeting in homes for small group care.

The house church is different in that it is not a part of the church, it *is* the church. The house church performs all of the functions of the church—baptism, Lord's Supper, study, giving, etc. It is a church.

Not a Temporary Arrangement

House churches do not start in a home and then move to a larger rented or permanent facility. The home is their permanent facility. The church is a church in a home.

I recently trained church planters in Romania. Their church planting strategy involved building a "mission house" or a "house church" where the missionary church planter would live. The missionary would reach out to the people of the village and invite members to meet with him in his home—which included an extended living room with benches. As the church grew, it would then build its own building.

The same pattern is very common in North American church planting today. The vast majority of new churches start as churches meeting in a home. But they do not stay there. Eventually they move to a larger facility.

The house church is different. Fundamental to its design is the idea that it will remain a *house* church. As it grows, it will *multiply,* not *enlarge.*

Not Always a Sect

Most readers have had some contact with house churches—either by personal experience or by reputation. It is difficult to define the house church because it has so many expressions. Frank Viola wrote an article that described the streams of the house church movement.

Stream 1. Those influenced by Gene Edwards. This stream is often referred to as the "radical wing" of the House Church movement. These groups tend to be anti-formalist to the extent that they claim no leadership, no order, no structure, no organization, and other traditional elements.

Stream 2. Those influenced by Watchman Nee and/or Stephen Kaung. These groups are typically centered around Christ, His eternal purpose, and the Scriptures. Most follow the teaching (some loosely, others strictly) outlined in Watchman Nee's "The Normal Christian Church Life. . . ." Deeper life themes are often stressed in these groups.

Stream 3. Those influenced by T. Austin-Sparks. These groups tend to be virtually identical to the above, but are inclined to stress the heavenly and spiritual nature of the church more than the practical and earthly side.

Stream 4. Those influenced by Witness Lee (Living Stream Ministry). This camp is ardent in its belief that Lee now has the "Divine baton" and is the vessel that God is presently using to recover His purpose and the truth about "the local church." These groups were more militant in the 1970s (often "taking over" other weaker home fellowships) than they are now; yet many still regard them as exclusive and divisive.

Stream 5. Those who are fundamentalist in their orientation. This strand of House Church tends to rigidly stress a specific pattern for meeting, regarding it as the pattern to follow. Most hold to Reformation theology right down the line and/or party-line fundamentalist themes.

Stream 6. Those who are neo-evangelical (or post-evangelical) in their orientation. These House Churches tend to color their interpretation of Scripture with modern biblical scholarship and often contribute fresh insights to old questions. They are highly relational.

Stream 7. Those associated with Word-faith teaching. Although few in number, these House Churches (as well as a network directed by C. Alan Martin) are built around the prosperity-faith teachings of Kenneth Hagin, Kenneth Copeland, Fred Price, Charles Capps, and similar personalities.

Stream 8. Those influenced by the Sonship teachings of the Latter Rain. Sam Fife and/or George Warnock are often regarded as the fathers of this camp. Many of these groups meet in intentional communities, are self-sufficient, and often act as refuges for people who need extreme help and can't make it in the streets. They are Pentecostal in nature, adventist in outlook, and place a heavy emphasis on the preparation of God's end-time remnant for the time when the "sons of God are manifested."

Stream 9. Those who circle their lives around the 3 H's (home church, home school, and home birth). Many are influenced by the teachings of Bill Gothard and believe that God wants virtually all Christians to raise large families which are home schooled. According to some, these groups have often become their own subculture, wholly disconnecting themselves from the larger culture (including Christian) and from anything that is conventional. Some House Churches of this ilk have a penchant for keeping the Jewish customs.

Stream 10. This stream has known little or no human influence (consequently, folks who swim here have probably never heard of any of the above streams). These groups are characterized by a sovereign leading of God's Spirit to meet according to New Testament principles.

Stream 11. The eclectic types. These are those who swim in two or more of the above streams.[5]

The focus of this chapter will be on the streams described in numbers six and ten. These are not fringe groups or sects but New Testament Christians trying to be the church God called them to be.

There are committed believers meeting across North America (and the world), worshipping in biblically balanced and theologically faithful house churches. Unfortunately, many people lump all house churches in the same category. This is an unfair stereotype.

Often Not a Solo Enterprise

House churches often exist in networks. They are not solitary groups of Christians, but they are related to other churches in a given region. These house churches may meet together for fellowship with other house churches, but it is usually not weekly and it is not seen as "real church." Real church takes place every time the church meets.

An Emerging Interest among Emerging Generations

There is growing interest in house churches among many postmodern Christians, particularly in the major cities. The way this occurs will vary from place to place, but a key focus is the idea of authentic relationships. Instead of focusing on the idea of the location, "house church" is not the "best term to use because it gives the impression that anyone meeting anywhere other than in a 'home' isn't doing it right . . . A better term . . . would be relational church."[6]

A relational church stays relational by staying small. House churches usually multiply into smaller groups before reaching thirty people. It makes sense that emerging postmodern generations, with strong interest in authentic relationships, would be attracted to churches that are built upon relationships.

How Does It Work?

How does the house church work? There is no one answer. Some people say the house church should "keep it simple—no corporation, no name, no statement of faith, no property, no titles, no salaries, etc.—just believers gathering simply, in His Name."[7] Others say house churches need some of these things. But they all agree on one thing—house churches do not need a building. It is fundamental to the new house church that it meets in a residential setting. As it grows in size, it multiplies into other houses—but not to a church building.

The house church is a *church,* and it should function as one. The Bible teaches that churches have pastor-elders and other leaders. Biblical churches covenant with one another. These churches participate in the Lord's Supper and baptism. All characteristics of a New Testament church need to be present in a house church. This should not be too difficult; we have a model in the New Testament.

Charles Brock, well-known church planter and trainer, explained: "Many years have passed since I wrote *The Principles and Practice of Indigenous Church Planting.* In that book I said there are four absolute essentials in church planting, the Seed, Spirit, Sower, and Soil. Today I am more convinced than ever that these are the four essentials which are indispensable. Caution must be observed when adding anything beyond these four essentials. Anything additional may be detrimental to healthy church planting."[8]

Brock goes on to explain, "We must answer clearly what a church *is* before we can think of objectives and strategies. . . . I believe a perverted and tarnished view of what a church is constitutes one of the greatest hurdles faced by church planters."[9]

In the New Testament, "the word 'church' was applied to a group of believers at any level, ranging from a very small group meeting in a private home all the way to the group of all true believers in the universal church."[10]

Almost all of these references are to local house churches (1 Thess. 1:1, the church of the Thessalonians; Rev. 2:1, church at Ephesus, and others).

These things became confused over time. Soon people began to "go to" church instead of *being* the church. Church began to be recognized as a place instead of a way of life. This struggle was most pronounced on mission fields of the nineteenth century. Missionaries struggled to determine what made a church a church. Roland Allen sought to teach that what was needed was only what the Bible required: "[believers] were members one of another in virtue of their baptism. Each was united to every other Christian everywhere, by the closest of spiritual ties, communion in the one Spirit. Each was united to all by common rites, participation in the same sacraments. Each was united to all by common dangers and common hopes."[11] It was simple, it was biblical, and it did not require a building or a budget.

Floyd Tidsworth gives several items that a church should possess before it constitutes as an autonomous church. In *Life Cycle of a New Congregation*, he asks, "Does the mission have enough members to do basic work without help from the outside? Do the members have enough money to carry the financial responsibility of the congregation? Is the mission mature and stable in its biblical beliefs?"[12] All of these can be answered *yes* in many house churches, but they would not possess the typical outward signs of church structure.

What Next?

My attraction to the house church springs from its simplicity and faith. I have been a part of larger and larger church starts. My last three had 234, 244, and 261 in attendance at their opening services. Each involved more and more money. In my heart, I often feel that church planting should be simpler. I like this definition of a church: "A New Testament church of the Lord Jesus Christ is . . . an autonomous local congregation of baptized believers, associated by covenant in the faith and fellowship of the gospel; observing the two ordinances of Christ, governed by His laws, exercising the gifts, rights, and privileges invested in them by His Word, and seeking to extend the gospel to the ends of the earth."[13]

Others may prefer this older definition of the church: "Unto this catholic visible Church, Christ hath given the ministry, oracles, and ordinances of God, for the gathering and perfecting of the saints, in this life, to the end of the world: and doth, by His own presence and Spirit, according to His promise, make them effectual thereunto."[14]

A New Testament church exists when its people function as a church and see themselves as a church. A house church of ten is a church if it functions as a church and sees itself as a church, while the mega-church-size Bible study, Breakaway,[15] at Texas A&M is not.

House church planting also includes an important focus on planting churches in multihousing communities. For more information about multihousing church planting, go to www.newchurches.com/multihousing.

If you want to plant a house church, you can use some of the principles in this book. Many of the patterns in this book would be applicable in the house church setting. Some would not be as appropriate, particularly issues related to the "large launch" and facilities.

Several excellent resources are available at www.newchurches.com/house. These include *Houses that Change the World* by Wolfgang Simpson and *Planting House Churches in Networks* by Dick Scoggins.

Resources for Further Reading

Allen, Donald R. *Barefoot in the Church*. Richmond: John Knox, 1972.

Banks, Robert. *Paul's Idea of Community: The Early House Churches in Their Historical Setting*. Grand Rapids: Eerdmans, 1980.

Banks, Robert J. and Julia Banks. The *Church Comes Home*. Hendrickson Publishers, Inc., 1998.

Barrett, Lois. *Building the House Church*. Scottdale, Pa.: Herald Press. 1986.

Birkey, Del. *The House Church–A Model for Renewing the Church*. Scottsdale, Pa.: Herald Press, 1988.

Bunch, David T., Harvey J. Kneisel, and Barbara L. Oden. *Multihousing Congregations: How to Start and Grow Christian Congregations in Multihousing Communities*. Atlanta: Smith Publishing, 1991.

Felicity, Dale. *Getting Started: A Practical Guide to House Church Planting*. House2House Ministries, 2002.

Hadaway, C. Kirk, Francis M. DuBose, and Stuart A. Wright. *Home Cell Groups and House Churches*. Nashville: Broadman Press, 1987.

Kreider, Larry and C. Peter Wagner. *House Church Networks: A Church for a New Generation*. House to House Press, 2002.

Simpson, Wolfgang. *Houses that Change the World*. Authentic Media, 2001.

Viola, Frank. *Rethinking the Wineskin: The Practice of the New Testament Church*, 3rd ed. Present Testimony Ministry, 2001.

http://www.homechurch.com/

http://www.housechurch.ca/

http://www.home-church.org/

http://www.fcpt.org/

http://www.house2house.tv/

Part 4

Church Planting Nuts and Bolts

CHAPTER FIFTEEN

Choosing a Focus Group

*O*ne of the earliest decisions the church planter must make is how to select the group that the church will reach. Such choices are termed "focusing." Focusing is commonplace in international missions. Missionaries talk of focusing on taxi drivers in Calcutta or farmers in Mexico. But focusing is more unusual in North America. Let us consider how people group segmentation or focusing works.

Some people object to the idea of focusing on a particular people group in a church plant. Their concern is that planters need to focus on everyone. The problem in their mind is that focusing is perceived to be an exclusionary process. A better description is that planters are *open* to everyone, but the new church is *focused* on a certain people group.

If you object to the terminology, let me challenge you. If you choose contemporary music, are you not focusing on those who listen to contemporary music? Would you not be excluding some senior adults who will not like that music? If you are a Hmong church using the White Hmong language, are you likely to reach Kurdish immigrants?

Focusing is an acknowledgment of the fact that people generally prefer to come to Christ without crossing social, racial, or economic boundaries.[1] Every international missionary is aware of this and focuses on a selected receptive group of people. When I was in Malaysia training church planters, I had Indians, Malaysian-born Chinese, other Chinese, Iban aboriginal people, Westerners, and a few others. I did not have to explain to them that Iban are more likely to reach Iban. They would use traditional Iban music and expressions of worship, even though they might speak the same language as the others in the class. There was not an attitude of division or segmentation, just a mature recognition that Iban people would be more likely to come to Christ in an Iban church.

The good news is that they also understood that an "Iban church" would be incomplete. Their *evangelism* was not their *fellowship*. The evangelism was focused on reaching the Iban. But the church fellowship believed it should be representative of every tongue, tribe, and nation.[2] So, although the music was Iban, the church also included those from other ethnic groups who enjoyed the Iban expression of worship.

Developing a Focus Group

Following are some guidelines to help you develop a focus group.

Who lives here? Different types of people live and earn their income in every geographical area. The first step toward intentionally focusing upon a specific people group in a particular area is to ask, What are the people here like? or, Who lives here?

Example of focusing. Saddleback Church (California) is probably the church best known for focusing in the North American context. It has developed a profile of "Saddleback Sam," a composite image of their ministry focus. This composite image describes Sam's values, income, education, and lifestyle preferences. Saddleback Sam is well-educated, enjoys his work, likes where he lives, listens to contemporary music, prioritizes fitness, and is skeptical of organized religious expression.[3] Saddleback Church's process for profiling (not their profile, *per se*) provides a model for planters in North America.

The central question. The question that every church planter must ask is how to proclaim the gospel to focus the audience in a manner that is effective and life-changing and fits within the context of the culture. The answer to this question materializes when they understand the people group that God has called them to reach. According to the New Testament, Paul spoke differently to Jews than he did to Greek philosophers. He considered their different lifestyles and backgrounds (1 Cor. 9:19–23). Church planters need to follow his model.

Begin with data. Research is a good way to begin developing a focus group plan. This process involves using census data, economic profiles, and other databases for gathering information. That information would include demographic, socioeconomic, cultural, ecclesiographic, and spiritual data on the focus group. The effective planter must reach persons in the focus group in ways appropriate to their cultural settings. Effective missions and church planting methodologies are contextual and indigenous.[4]

The fallacy of the average. Information such as age, household size, educational level, median income, housing type, and ethnicity can help to refine the strategy for reaching the new church's focus group. But the planter must be careful when using demographics because the "fallacy of the average" may skew the application.

For example, a community made up largely of two age groups, one in their late sixties and the other in their early twenties, may present its *median*[5] age as early forties, but few middle-aged adults may actually live in that community. Thus, if a significant number of people, people who do *not* resemble the church's focus group—live in the geographical focus area, demographic data may present averages that do not exist in reality.

Census tracts, not zip or postal codes. Researchers may be able to avoid this problem by focusing on census tract studies (available at public libraries) instead of larger, potentially more diverse zip code-focused studies. Even so, there is no guarantee. All data must be tested by other research. "Soft data" surveys with community leaders, local people-helping agencies, and other sources of information will help provide valuable data verification.

Fishing and focusing. Saddleback Church pastor, Rick Warren, has developed several analogies that help in the pursuit of accurate demographic focusing. His first analogy argues that the church planter should know for whom he is fishing. The identity of the "fish" will largely determine the approach the planter uses. Planting tools that work effectively in one culture may not work as well in another.

Second, according to Warren, the planter should "go where the fish are biting," where people respond positively. This analogy suggests that finding those people who are receptive is necessary. Another way to describe Warren's advice is to go where God is at work; determine where people are interested in spiritual things.

Third, the planter should "learn to think like a fish." As a teenager living near a lake in Florida, I learned that some fish like to hide among the weeds that grew along the bank. I found such information difficult to understand because *I* did not like to hide in weeds. I grew up in New York

City, far from reed-filled marshes. I could not reason why fish would like to hide among the weeds. I had not learned that fish think differently from the way I think. I disliked fishing among the weeds because my line consistently became tangled. When reaching the lost, we may find ourselves tangled up in matters that we do not enjoy because we have not learned to appreciate their way of thinking.

Fourth, the angler must catch fish on the fish's terms. We should offer bait that meets the needs of the fish. This advice means that we must address people's *felt* needs with the gospel. Eventually the planter will, after having established relationships and trust, address the *real* needs of the unchurched. This will be considered in greater detail in the following pages.

Finally, the planter should seriously consider using more than one "hook." Different methods reach different kinds of people. In utilizing multiple approaches, the planter increases the likelihood of reaching larger numbers of people.

Christ for the Whole World

The church planter's *ultimate* focus is nothing less than the whole world for Christ. But such a huge focus can frustrate and overwhelm the planter. The journey of a thousand miles begins with a single step. One way for the planter to manage the *global* focus is to begin with an *immediate focus*—the people group that God has placed on the planter's heart—and then expand to other people groups.

Multiplied efforts. A key feature of this strategy for expansion is not only to reach a particular subgroup of the unchurched, but also to teach those first converts to focus on and reach yet other unchurched focus groups. This approach reinforces the first converts' journey toward faith and allows the church to reach others who may be different from that first generation of converts. Planters must focus on and reach lost people. But their task is not finished until they have influenced their converts to reach others as well.

If the planter does not fit the context. Occasionally in the course of researching and focusing, a planter may see a mismatch with the focal people group. If the planter discovers there is no match with any of the subgroups in the community, a choice must be made. The planter can change the planned church's location (to a group where there *is* a fit) or "missionize" that location cross-culturally.

For example, an African-American church planter believes that God has called him to reach Hispanics in Des Moines, Iowa. Although this task may not be easy, this calling means that God has not only called him to church planting but also to *cross-cultural missions*. In the process of fulfilling his call, the planter must answer not the *secondary* question, Can I reach this subgroup? but the primary question, Is God calling me to missionize this subgroup?

If God is calling the planter to missionize cross-culturally, then the answer to the second question lies in the answer to the first: "*Since* I am called, I *can* reach them." The African-American church planter then starts to teach new Hispanic Christians to become the primary evangelists in the Hispanic community. The cross-cultural church planter becomes a discipler, teacher, and mentor for the next generation of leaders.

Missionizing the Unchurched

Church planters *can* missionize the unchurched, even cross-culturally, if they are able to reach receptive persons, to understand lost persons, to understand felt needs, and to overcome resistance to church relationships.

Identifying receptive people. Who are the receptive people in a given area? Generally, they are people in a major life transition or under pressure. Life transitions—relocation, forced employment change, divorce, marriage, childbirth, or the illness or death of a loved one—create unique circumstances where people may respond more positively to the Good News. At least for a period of time, these people are likely to be the most receptive to a gospel presentation. An example would be an area where new subdivisions are being built. As people move into new homes, they are more likely to consider a new church.

Talking through resistance. Many unchurched people resist connecting with a church for several reasons—both real and imagined. One way to break through such resistance is to find out what they think about church. The planter should probe the focus group for their perceptions of church and denominations, perhaps through in-home discussion groups or coffee shop conversations.

When all else fails, ask. One way—perhaps the best and most affirming way—to find out how unchurched people think or what they need is to ask them. The list of such discernible needs is limited only to the number of people the planter can engage to answer questions and talk about their felt needs. Focus groups are an excellent way to discover this desired information and to build relationships.

Felt needs exposed for what they are. While building relationships, the church planter may discover opportunities to offer support for meeting group members' felt needs, such as a class focused on Parenting by Grace or First Place for weight loss. Through these studies, parents may discover that resolving their marital struggles and overcoming selfishness between mates is the greatest need in the family. The dieter may find that low self-esteem prompts overeating and inappropriate self-nurture with food. In addition, high-trust relationships will afford the planter opportunities to introduce group members to the answer for their deepest need—a lasting relationship with Christ as their personal Lord and Savior.

What is that music they hear? Worship style is another barrier to church involvement for many unchurched people. Musical taste often lies at the center of this issue. The planter may approach focus group members with questions about musical taste. Some church planters may simply identify Arbitron's five highest-rated music radio stations in the area. In all likelihood, focus group members are tuned in—stylistically, as well as literally—to those stations.

Styles and values. Patterns of time management and type of recreation can also shape church planting strategy. The planter's awareness of patterns of recreational, political, and other social activities can help the planter develop a strategy that will fit the needs of the focus group.

From Felt Needs to Real Needs

Many unchurched persons feel no need for a savior. They may conclude that they need *something*, but they do not know what that something is. Moving an unbeliever from concern about *felt* needs to concern about *real* needs happens as a result of applying a relevant strategy. An effective strategy will help unbelievers identify the true nature of their needs.

The process to real needs. Moving from felt needs to real needs is a process. Every spring and fall Millcreek Community Church presented topics related to felt needs because most of our focus group initially attended during those seasons. During the winter and summer months, we focused on moving the people to deeper spiritual needs.

Church planters cannot afford to remain at a felt-needs level. We may begin with felt needs in order to gain a hearing, but life change will only occur with a systematic process of moving from felt needs to real spiritual needs.

Strategizing by discovery. The wise church planter strategizes to meet real needs by discovering the longings of the focus group he or she wants to reach. Thus, although we commit ourselves to the principle that the Bible determines our message, our focus group's needs must determine when, where, and how we communicate the unchanging message.

Strategizing by repeated analysis. As planters strategize, they should determine the focus group's needs and what methods may work most effectively to meet those needs. Beyond an immediate plan, however, effective strategizing must also include maintaining a network of resource persons who are able to provide information updates. This new data should enable the planter to address the ever-changing needs of the focus group.

Crucial questions. In *Reconnecting God's Story to Ministry,* Tom Steffen encourages his readers to ask crucial questions when engaging a new culture.[6] First, what is the *worldview* of the focus audience? Whether the focus is a tribe in Pakistan or a group of postmoderns in Seattle, one must understand their worldview.

Second, the church planter must identify the focus group members' *decision-making patterns.* This will help isolate the redemptive analogies that best describe the culture. This process also demands that the planter seek to identify what this culture group believes about the basic components of the gospel. Other questions may include the following: Is this focus group a "shame" or a "guilt" culture? How will this culture understand Christian rituals? What is the best delivery system for exposing these people to the gospel?

Materials relevant to the focus. The church planter must also develop relevant materials to connect effectively with the focus audience. One church planter discovered that many people in his focus group believed sermons were boring. The church was careful to affirm, in an early informational letter, that many sermons *are* boring. The same letter also promised that there would be no boring sermons at the new church.

Different context; different concerns. In studying our region of the northeastern United States, Millcreek Community Church and its daughter churches found its focus group had different concerns. We were planting a church among primarily nominal Roman Catholics who wondered whether we were a non-Christian cult because we did not own a church building. They worried that we would hold long worship services in which people would act in bizarre ways. Many of our focus audience came from a background of what they termed "the great Catholic guilt machine." They expected us to beat them down verbally with guilt-laden preaching or to emphasize legalism. Our focus group had other worries than boring sermons.

You can download the Millcreek mailers and the mailers of one hundred other churches at www.new-churches.com/examples.

In order to address our focus group's concerns, we provided direct mail pieces that described us as being "rooted in historic Christianity." I often reassured prospects that our service would begin at 9:35 and end by 10:30 and that no one would pressure them or attempt to make them feel guilty.

By designing materials that addressed the concerns apparent among our focus group, we alleviated some of the focus group's fears. We were also able to present the gospel to them in a nonthreatening environment.

Objections to Focusing

Some people resist the concept of demographic focusing as a vital part of the church-starting process. They give several reasons to explain their reaction.

Focusing as exclusivism. Some persons regard focusing as a form of racism or classism. Donald McGavran's Homogenous Unit Principle[7] identifies the reality that people generally prefer to come to Christ without crossing social, racial, or economic boundaries.

Even though the reality of this principle is obvious, some planters fear that the Homogenous Unit Principle will be used as an excuse for racism or as a means for excluding others from new church starts. In the same way, some planters fear that focusing may become a means for excluding persons whom members find "undesirable."

More and more church planters seem to target the upwardly mobile middle class suburbanite. It appears that God has had a special burden for new churches in places with hundreds of new homes as compared to the inner city with thousands of old homes. That may be an abuse of the focusing principle.

Regardless of the focus, new churches more readily attract those from the lower socioeconomic strata than from the higher. Upper-income families are generally less religious and less interested in spiritual concerns. The planter who targets Rich Roger might need to consider targeting Average Al instead. The greatest mission fields in North America are those often abandoned by others, including the inner cities.[8]

In spite of these misgivings and the potential for abuses, planters need to consider demographic focusing. Although God's Spirit *can* defy sociological realities such as the Homogeneous Unit Principle, the Spirit seems historically to have used such truths in reaching people and starting congregations. We would do well to learn from international church planters. They have been experiencing success in reaching people groups that North Americans have not. People need to be reached in a manner consistent with their culture—but without compromising the gospel in any way.[9]

Focusing and moving outward. Focusing is essential because it enables the congregation to *focus* its light. Such focus enables accomplishments and successes in a way that diffusion of light cannot. Focusing is not exclusivism. Rather, it enables the congregation to concentrate on reaching increasing numbers of unchurched persons with the Good News of Jesus Christ by beginning with one group—the focus group—in order to expand its influence to many other groups.

Reaching the unchurched with the Good News of Jesus Christ can be summed up in one word—*evangelism.* Next we will explore how evangelism and church planting are interdependent.

Resources for Further Reading

Apeh, John E. *Social Structure and Church Planting.* Shippensburg, Pa.: Companion Press, 1989.

Brock, Charles. *The Principles and Practice of Indigenous Church Planting.* Neosho, Mo.: Church Growth International, 1981.

McGavran, Donald A. *Effective Evangelism: A Theological Mandate.* Phillipsburg, N.J.: Presbyterian and Reformed, 1988.

McGavran, Donald A. *How Churches Grow.* New York: Friendship Press, 1959.

Wagner, C. Peter. *Church Planting for a Greater Harvest.* Ventura, Calif.: Regal Books, 1990.

Evangelism in a Postmodern World

*D*oes it seem odd to include a chapter about evangelism in a book on church planting? Unfortunately, recent technological developments in church planting—direct mail, Web pages, and such—have undercut evangelism as the basis of the birth of new churches.

The development of an evangelistic plan for a church plant is a crucial issue. It may surprise many that starting a church without evangelistic effort is actually possible. In fact, it is much easier to start a church by drawing together Christians from other churches than to win new disciples from among the lost persons of the community. The process of developing an evangelistic strategy takes effort.

Evangelizing postmoderns requires a different kind of strategy than those used in the past. Remember, the gospel remains the same, but the methods change from culture to culture. This chapter will address the need for a postmodern evangelistic strategy and how new churches can reach the emerging generations.

Authentic church planting—planting a church that reaches unbelievers—requires what we might call "the soil of lostness." The church planter must be intentional about developing an evangelism strategy for a new church.

We must act with intentionality and reach the lost instead of just rearranging church members in a given community. First, the planter should recognize that evangelism must be *intentional*. Without intentionality, evangelism remains undone. Intentionality causes the planter to plan for personal evangelism and leads to the creation of a strategy that is characterized by a high level of commitment to reach the unchurched. The staff members at many new churches hold one another accountable for building relationships with the unchurched.

Second, intentionality means having a *system* of organizing evangelistic prospects. Many computer programs provide tracking software for prospects that can be very useful. If the planter is not high-tech, a simple index card system may suffice. The idea of keeping a prospect list may seem a little contrived to many postmoderns, but it is essential. People are never just names on a card. You must show that you have concern for those you are seeking to reach and that you care enough to remember them and keep in contact with them.

Third, intentionality means developing a *plan*. The planter's first goal should be to design an evangelistic plan. Such a plan might include training lay ministers to share their testimonies, sharing the simple plan of salvation as the worship hour begins, or including it in the order of worship. Every service should include instructions on how to turn to Christ, but this plan does not require a weekly ten-minute evangelistic sermon.

Rock Springs Church[1] explains that their strategy, borrowed from North Point Church in Alpharetta, Georgia, is to "invest and invite." They encourage the church family to invest in the lives of their unbelieving friends; they do this by spending time together, serving others, encouraging them, etc. After this is done, they are encouraged to invite them to church. Pastor Chris Brewer explains, "We partner with our people. If they will invest their lives in the unchurched and then bring them to church, we will have activities to help lead them to Christ."[2]

Evangelism as a Process and Event

Authentic evangelism is progressive, not just a one-time event. "Nobody goes from atheism to faith during a sermon. . . . Salvation is not a process, but coming to faith is."[3] Each step to faith in Christ is part of a journey and not a destination. There is a point where each person must have his or her name written in "the Lamb's book of life" (Rev. 21:27). Conversion is an event, but evangelism is helping people on a journey to conversion and then on to maturity.

Imagine a missionary who has traveled around the globe to a tribe that has never heard the gospel, never seen a Bible, or never heard the name of Jesus. Imagine that the missionary preaches immediately upon arrival, "All you need to do is repent of your sins, believe the Bible, and ask Jesus into your heart." Only blank stares would follow. The church planter *cannot* assume that people understand who Jesus is or what sin has done to their lives, even in North America.

The Engel Scale

One helpful tool for helping the planter understand people's spiritual awareness is the Engel Scale. This linear scale,[4] which resembles a number line, depicts a series of steps from complete unawareness and ignorance of the gospel to a maturing commitment to Christianity.

The Engel Scale classifies awareness in a range of steps from -8 to +3, as follows:

-8: Awareness of a supreme being but no effective knowledge of the gospel

-7: Initial awareness of the gospel

-6: Awareness of the fundamentals of the gospel

-5: Grasp of implications of the gospel

-4: Positive attitude toward the gospel

-3: Counting the cost

-2: Decision to act

-1: Repentance and faith in Christ

REGENERATION

+1: Post-decision evaluation

+2: Incorporation into the body

+3: A lifetime of growth in Christ—discipleship and service

Negative one, repentance and faith in Christ, is the crucial step, but not necessarily an isolated event. Reaching this point demands a process. God can make repentance and faith in Christ an instantaneous event, but it is usually a *process* that leads to this event.[5] Following conversion or regeneration, the new believer begins to evaluate the decision, is incorporated into a fellowship of believers, and becomes a person who actively shares the gospel. The church planter's task is to partner with God in order to move people toward understanding the gospel—toward the point of repentance and faith in Christ. The effective evangelist-planter will learn to recognize that people are at different stages on this scale when they attend worship services.

In this partnership process, the planter may meet a person who seems to stand at −6. The wise Christian will not rush into the reasons the Bible says we need Christ. Such an approach assumes that person believes in the authority of Scripture and its personal application to his or her life. A better approach might be to share biblical passages that can help the non-Christian understand more about Christianity. Before a person can make an intelligent choice for the gospel, he or she must know what the gospel *means*. Jesus encouraged men and women to "count the cost."

Again, we must recognize that people are at different stages in their spiritual development. For instance, one young woman in a former pastorate came to church and was crying by the end of worship. Speaking with me after the service, she said, "I know I need to receive Christ into my heart because I'm separated from him." She stood at the point of conversion. All I had to do was offer her assistance in taking the step of faith. On the other hand, when I served a Chinese church, I encountered many people who had no awareness of Christianity. I began evangelizing them by teaching the existence of God as displayed in the Scriptures.

Culture has changed in North America. At the dawn of the twenty-first century, we live in a post-Christian culture in which many people are "further back" on the Engel Scale than their parents were.

The Gray Matrix

The Engel Scale has two problems. It tends to be linear when most people are not. It also does not take into account that people can misunderstand or reject parts of the truth. The Gray Matrix[6] is a modification of the Engel Scale that may help people better understand the evangelism process:

- Anything which moves people from left to right across the scale is "evangelistic." This might include acts of service and friendship, mom and baby clubs, medical and development work—many things which are not apparently "preaching." Yet in fact, the word Jesus used when he told us to "preach the gospel" has a much wider meaning than speech. It refers to communication.

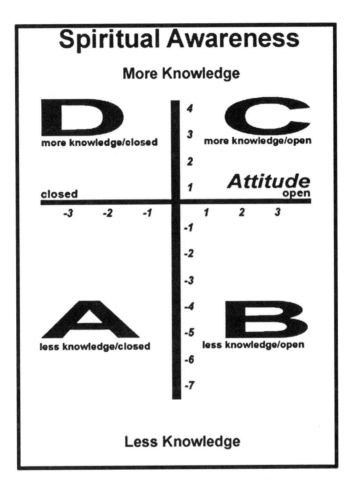

- If we can understand roughly where a single person or target group of people is situated on the scale, we can choose an appropriate approach to reach them.

- If people are near the bottom of the scale, we must not use Christian language and ideas which will mean nothing to them. We must assess our message through their eyes, not ours. It may also be inappropriate to give a heavy "preach for a decision" at this point.

- Pressures of society and culture, and the strategies of Satan, will tend to pull people down toward the bottom left-hand of the scale. God's purpose is to draw people to the top right-hand side by his Spirit, through the witness of his people.[7]

An Alternative Evangelism Process in a Postmodern World

Evangelism is more than a scale, and it is not complete with the matrix. I believe that evangelism is a *journey* involving stages or steps. Thus, Engel is right. But Gray is also right because evangelism is more than a neat linear process. I suggest a new idea—the Stetzer Evangelism Journey. It is a combination and revision of the ideas of Engel and Gray with some additional clarification of the journey taken from Darrell Guder's *The Missional Church*.

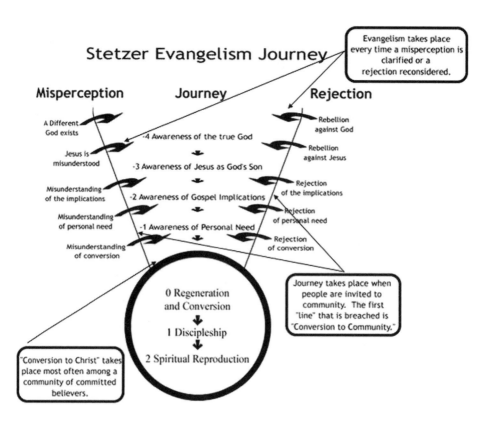

There are two conversions—one temporal and one eternal. The first conversion is the *conversion to community.* With few exceptions, people come to Christ after they have journeyed with other Christians—examining them and considering their claims. They can come into community at any point. Thus, the funnel-shaped lines (representing community) stretch all the way to the top of the diagram. At any point, a person can decide to begin a spiritual journey toward Christ.

The circle represents the church. Church and Christian community must not be the same thing. Unbelievers can and should be invited into the community, but they cannot be part of the church. A church is a body of believers (more on that later). A person becomes part of the church with the second and eternal conversion, *the conversion to Christ.*

Each curved arrow is representative of evangelism. For example, a person who has rejected God and who is living in rebellion can be challenged to live a different kind of life by a committed believer. In this context, lost people can decide to consider the validity of a just God in conversation with Christian friends. They may begin to believe that God is real and may then consider the claims of Christ. At some point, they begin to consider these things in community with believers.

The journey is not intended to be the same for each people group, worldview, or culture. The central line remains the same—it is the universal journey of evangelistic discovery. For each culture, the misperceptions and reasons for rejection are different. The only thing that is constant is the center column. The sides depend on the people involved. For example, among Muslims the chart might look something like this:

Muslim Evangelism Journey

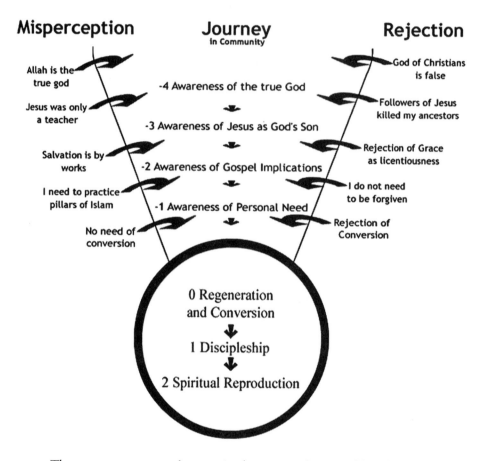

Misperception

- Allah is the true god
- Jesus was only a teacher
- Salvation is by works
- I need to practice pillars of Islam
- No need of conversion

Journey
In Community

- -4 Awareness of the true God
- -3 Awareness of Jesus as God's Son
- -2 Awareness of Gospel Implications
- -1 Awareness of Personal Need

0 Regeneration and Conversion
↓
1 Discipleship
↓
2 Spiritual Reproduction

Rejection

- God of Christians is false
- Followers of Jesus killed my ancestors
- Rejection of Grace as licentiousness
- I do not need to be forgiven
- Rejection of Conversion

The same process can be seen in the postmodern world. Of course, in a postmodern community in the predominately ex-Catholic Northeast, the journey will look different than in the eco-pagan Northwest or multicultural Canada. Here is an example of a postmodern evangelism journey in New York City's lower East Side.

Each church planter should consider making a diagram of his or her people group's worldview. In this way, when sharing about faith the church

Postmodern Evangelism Journey
(Lower East Side of Manhattan)

Misperception	Journey	Rejection
	in Community	

Misperception

God is a positive force

Jesus was a good teacher

All good people go to heaven

If I am good to others, I am Christian

No need of conversion

Journey *in Community*

-4 Awareness of the true God

-3 Awareness of Jesus as God's Son

-2 Awareness of Gospel Implications

-1 Awareness of Personal Need

Rejection

God is about guilt & control

Followers of Jesus are all hypocrites

Not interested in changing lifestyle

Reject need of personal response

Rejection of Conversion

0 Regeneration and Conversion
⬇
1 Discipleship
⬇
2 Spiritual Reproduction

planter will know the needs of those being reached. When sharing Christ with Muslims, we need to explain that grace is not an excuse to indulge the flesh even though they watch television from "Christian America" and see that very thing. Postmodern people in New York may see no need for grace. Their concern is not licentiousness but need; in their mind, they are already good enough.

As mentioned in chapter 2, culturally appropriate evangelism answers the actual questions that are being asked by the culture rather than those that the church believes the target culture should ask. "But in your hearts set apart Christ as Lord. Always be prepared to give an answer to everyone who asks you to give the reason for the hope that you have. But do this with gentleness and respect" (1 Pet. 3:15). The process is:

- Understand the issues in the worldview.
- Address those issues (misperceptions or rejections) with redemptive witnessing opportunities based on where the listener is.
- Encourage the listener to consider the truth claims of Christ.
- Invite the listener to journey with the faith community as they live out the truth claims (invite "conversion to community").
- Invite the listener to make a faith commitment (invite "conversion to Christ").

Losing Evangelistic Focus

I have asserted that it is possible to plant a church without evangelistic emphasis, but even when churches begin with a heart for evangelism, they may later lose that focus. This tragedy occurs because two typical problems arise—large-group panic and vision hijacking.

Large-Group Panic

This challenge arises when significant numbers of unchurched people come to Christ quickly. The new church can feel overwhelmed, and some people may think that even the church needs a break from evangelism.

At Millcreek Community Church, one committed believer approached me about slowing down our outreach in order to disciple the large number of new believers. Rather than agreeing, I responded to this with a request that he take on the discipling ministry as his primary concern while others continued with the outreach emphasis. The plan worked.

If the church planter is not intentional in evangelism, the planter—and very soon, the new church—will lose its evangelistic zeal. A reduced evangelistic focus foreshadows the long-term loss of evangelistic zeal. Missional churches need to model Christian community and to invite others to join the journey of faith while practicing intentional evangelism.

Vision Hijacking

The second problem that often kills new church evangelism and zeal might be termed "vision hijacking." In nearly every new church, a portion of the core group makes the attempt to redirect—to hijack—the original vision shared by the church planter and the core group (more about this in chapter 27).

The stress and difficulty involved in reaching the unchurched often prompt attempts to hijack. These attempts often involve the loss of evangelistic passion. Reaching other believers is much easier than doing evangelism. The offerings of believers are greater, their children behave a bit more calmly in worship, and they have skills for leading church programs. The fact is that tension *will* exist whenever a church planter or planting team reaches lost people. The planter must be prepared to deal with this tension.

Use Sound Evangelistic Methods

Following are some sound evangelistic methods that can be used in all church planting efforts.

Meeting and Engaging Unchurched People

It is essential to build relationships with the unchurched. We do not just build these relationships so they can be "prospects." We build relationships because we genuinely care about people. Building relationships is not a difficult thing to do, but the church planter must be intentional in this task.

Relationship Building

Intentional relationship building begins with meeting community leaders. Planters often meet leaders by becoming a team or club chaplain, by becoming involved in a community organization, or by personally contacting the mayor and other government leaders.

If a church planter intentionally builds relationships, people begin to know who he is and why he is there. Some may even come to the new church. Intentional relationship building with community leaders adds credibility to your church.

Howard McNamara, a church planter in Princeton, New Jersey, serves as a good example. He signed up for a ten-week course entitled "Start Your Own Business" at the local rotary club. Each week three prominent business leaders made presentations. Each week they all concluded their presentation with, "If there is anything we can do, give us a call." Howard was able to meet thirty business owners, a few of whom became prospects for his church.

Marketplace Farming

Marketplace farming is the process of consistently making contacts with friends or neighbors—building relationships leading to an opportunity to share Christ. Church planters should know their neighbors. The planter cannot afford to spend all of his time with church people. Rather, the planter should become acquainted with the unchurched people who live nearby. This process of marketplace farming is also an intentional process.

When moving to a new area, you can move your bank account into that community, purchase your gasoline and meals and groceries from local businesses, and become acquainted with the clerks and servers by name. We *must be intentional* about meeting people.

Marketplace farming guides the planter into an intentional routine. For instance, I bought my gas at the same establishment for three years. That is the price one must pay to build marketplace relationships. Our culture relentlessly leads us toward isolation. We can order groceries and all of our books over the Internet. We no longer *have to* meet real people to purchase the items we want. Such options are not open to church planters. We *must be intentional* about meeting people.

Prospect Cards

Bob Logan developed marketplace farming as an intentional process for meeting people on a regular basis. According to Logan, the planter must meet people six times before a relationship can be established.[8] Prospect cards are one way to keep up with these contacts. Following each visit or telephone conversation, the planter should record the time and nature of the visit.

Allow your first prospects to be those people in transition or under tension. Contact persons who have recently relocated into your area. As a planter, you can order the names and addresses of newcomers to your city from LifeWay Prospect Services.[9] Other options for prospecting include contacting the newly married and new parents in the area. A simple card of congratulations on a marriage or on the birth of a child is an excellent way to contact prospects. The planter can provide an even more direct and positive witness by adding a reminder on the importance of spiritual things.

Existing Relationships

Ministering through relationships is paramount. Your church people already have a circle of friends. In one pastorate, I challenged the church family to reach their own "seeker seven," seven people they were praying would come to Christ. The Billy Graham Evangelistic Association's Operation Andrew, which is now called Friend to Friend, pro-

For sample new mover, new parent, and new married letters, see www.new-churches.com/ examples.

vides a simple format to teach intentional friendship evangelism.

Every person knew seven people who would be particularly open to a gospel witness. After the believers wrote their prayer lists, we helped those members work toward inviting the important family members and acquaintances on their lists to a Friend Day event.

Three-Minute Rule

Preparing the congregation for the arrival of guests is essential. One step of preparation is teaching members the "three-minute rule." The concept is simple: Members talk only to guests during the first three minutes following a worship service.

Our human inclination is to fellowship with persons we know. This communicates an unfriendliness we do not intend. Evangelistically speaking, attention spent on one another would be better spent on guests—for the first three minutes after the service.

Every-Sunday Registration

The use of a churchwide registration every Sunday is an excellent way to track guests without causing them to feel uncomfortable. This process, usually completed at the end of the worship hour, often uses a registration clipboard that attendees complete and pass toward the end of the aisle.

Welcome Cards

For the purpose of anonymity and, perhaps, more candid communication of personal needs, the use of cards may be a better option. In this process, *everyone* in attendance each week (not just visitors) completes a card at the end of the worship service. Regular attendees need to complete only their name and any prayer requests they would like to include. They should wait until the *very end* of the service to complete the card, along with guests and visitors. In this way, guests will not feel self-conscious or "spotlighted."

Guest Follow-up

The next step in this process is obvious—follow up quickly by making a personal contact with guests. Although anonymity is clearly a value for many guests, they give you permission to contact them if they have communicated their name, address, and phone number. Even the unchurched will know that submitting a card will prompt contacts from the church.

The first contact should be made immediately by a layperson over the phone. Initial contact could also be made by a personal visit *if* the person has given his or her address. This contact should be made first by a layperson.

One study revealed that "clergy" follow-up reduced the effectiveness of follow-up by one-half (compared to laypersons doing the same).

> No other single factor makes a greater difference . . . than an immediate visit to the home of first-time worshippers. . . . When lay persons make fifteen-minute visits to the homes of first-time worship visitors within thirty-six hours, 85 percent of them return the following week. Make this home visit within seventy-two hours, and 60 percent of them return. Make it seven days later, and 15 percent will return.

The pastor making this call, rather than lay persons, cuts each result in half.[10]

Although I prefer a phone call to a house visit, the key is the involvement of the lay people of the church in guest follow-up.

Door-to-Door Survey Through Mission Teams

Normal people do not like a door-to-door survey even though it is a good and time-tested method. In spite of most people's misgivings and even my personal dislike (although I have planted several churches), I understand that door-to-door visitation is part of the overall prospect development process. One of the best ways to address this challenge is to get someone else to make door-to-door contacts with you or for you. Prepared and trained mission teams are an excellent resource for this task.

Contact the team. When contacting mission teams, the planter must ensure that the mission team understands the needs of the church plant: door-to-door survey work in order to develop prospects.

Agree on the tasks ahead of time. Many mission teams want to perform activities that are irrelevant to church planting. For the sake of outreach needs and congregational protection, the church planter should insist on a simple rule: no mission team may serve the field unless they agree to *at least* twelve hours of survey work during their visit (typically less than a week for out-of-town teams).

Prepare for the team. The church planter must prepare for the mission team. Prepare precise maps of the area to be surveyed, including drop-off locations. Plan to send the team into at least four distinct areas. Give them enough houses to contact so they do not waste time doing nothing. Most teams can survey twenty houses in one hour. Plan to drop off the teams, give them time to work, and return to pick them up at an appointed time.

Train the team. Train the team to do outreach. A mission team can be an invaluable resource if they know what to do. Underutilized teams get frustrated.

The church planter must be prepared and organized for the arrival of the mission team. Mission teams can lead to "the best of times" or "the worst of times." Using mission teams is productive and satisfying, *if* the planter prepares for and trains the team, and *if* the team has agreed to the church planter's goals and agenda for their visit. If there are no teams available, the church planter must do door-to-door alone.

Conclusion

The church planter must become intentionally evangelistic. This commitment includes developing a pool of unchurched people to reach. Evangelizing lost persons does not happen by accident. The mature church planter will not expect unchurched persons to show up for church services just because a new church has arrived.

The planter should use every available means to contact and invite unchurched and lost persons. Mission teams, door-to-door visitation, prospect listing, telemarketing, and follow-up are good tools for evangelism. But a church planter's most effective resources for evangelism and eventually for developing a core group are commitment, hard work, and Spirit-led prayer.

Resources for Further Reading

Arn, Win. *The Master's Plan for Making Disciples: Every Christian an Effective Witness through an Enabling Church.* Grand Rapids: Baker Books, 1998.

Long, Jimmy. *Generating Hope: A Strategy for Reaching the Postmodern Generation.* Downers Grove, Ill.: InterVarsity Press, 1997.

Terry, John Mark. *Church Evangelism: Basic Principles, Diverse Models.* Nashville: Broadman & Holman Publishers, 1997.

White, James Emery. *Rethinking the Church: A Challenge to Creative Redesign in an Age of Transition.* Grand Rapids: Baker Books, 1997.

http://www.namb.net/root/evangelism/thenet/default.asp

CHAPTER SEVENTEEN

Developing a Core Group

*T*he most difficult phase of church planting may be the early stages, when the church planter is attempting to attract a core group of people. At this stage the planter can offer no relationships, no meeting place, no programs, and no music. People have difficulty committing themselves to a dream that they cannot see. Recruiting a core group is a challenging phase, but it is an essential stage in new church development. During this period, the planter lays the foundation for the birth of the new church.

The prenatal stage of new church development is similar in many ways to the prenatal stage of human development. An unborn child must develop several different biological systems to enable it to function effectively after birth. These systems must be in place when birth takes place for proper development to continue. The same observation holds true for a new church. Certain key systems must operate in the new congregation. If they do not, the church cannot be successful after it is born.

You will recall from chapter 8 that five indispensable systems must function at the time of a congregational launch, according to Bob Logan.[1]

1. Assimilation process
2. Evangelism network
3. Program to mobilize spiritual gifts
4. Children's ministry team
5. Worship team and a plan for early worship services.

The heart of the church start is the core group that ultimately helps birth the new church and provides the ministry muscle for these systems. These ministries will not exist without core member volunteers.

Core Size

The size of the core group is important. Walsh Hughes, former director of missions for the Capital City Association in Columbus, Ohio, recommended engaging what he termed the "frontier four"—four families who would devote themselves to help birth a new church. They made themselves available "to teach, and tithe, and tarry." In this methodology, public worship began with the appearance of those faithful four families.[2]

Today, most planters wait longer to begin public worship. For core groups, Malphurs explains that bigger *is* better.[3] Moreover, the size of the core group should be determined, for the most part, by the kind of church being planted. Churches starting with large first services should have one person in the core group for every ten people they hope to attract to the first service (core to crowd ratio of 1 to 10).

Finding Core Members

The process of gathering a core group is not an easy task. With the right training, almost anyone can plan the launch, mail appropriate advertising, and prepare for people to come on the launch day. But molding an effective core group is another story.

Members of the sponsoring church. One possible source for core group members is a sponsoring church. The supporting church appeals for volunteer families to help in a new church start (sometimes also called "extension members"). Families that leave the sponsoring church become an "extension" of that congregation, helping to start the new work.

This type of core group development presents both positives and negatives. A strong positive is that the planter has a core group almost overnight; the length of start-up time decreases considerably. The church can begin services while developing one-on-one relationships. In addition, the planter usually finds that these volunteer families are solid believers who can assist immediately in the development process.

On the negative side, these "experienced" believers may have strong feelings about the form of worship, leadership style, and other matters. Such convictions, if different from the vision of the church planter, can create significant conflicts in the early development of the congregation. These conflicts may quickly put at risk the continuation of financial support from the sponsoring church. Using this recruiting method for core group development is recommended only if the sponsoring congregation is highly similar in philosophy and style to the new church and the planter and the context of the new start is similar to the context of the sponsoring church.

Developing a SWAT team. In settings where extension members are unavailable or their use would be unwise, several other means for recruitment are possible. One alternative has been termed a SWAT team. The acronym, SWAT, stands for Servants, Willing and Temporary.

SWAT team members commit themselves to the new church for a short period of time, usually about six months. These volunteers staff the nursery, teach small groups, serve on set-up teams, or fill any other role for which they are needed in the first several months following the launch of the new church. Mark Burks of Crossroads Church in Columbus, Ohio, used SWAT teams to launch his church. Ten people from the sponsor church (only fifteen minutes away) committed to work in the nursery and run the sound system for the first two months of Crossroads' services. Despite their initial short-term commitment, some SWAT volunteers often become permanent members of the church when their short-term commitment has ended.

Leadership on loan. Christians from nearby churches who want to become part of a new church are a third source for core development. For the sake of trust and in order to preserve a reputation of integrity, however, the planter *must* ask permission of the pastors of these churches before approaching their members. These people must be genuinely committed to planting the kind of church the planter has envisioned.

Advertise. Another means for recruitment is the purchase of Christian radio and television advertisements. Posting notices in Christian bookstores may also help locate volunteers.

Know the risks. These common methodologies for recruitment present their own risks. Christians often envision helping birth a "perfect" church. They may anticipate that their involvement will help them realize their vision. Difficulties quickly arise when "borrowed" or volunteer core members' ideas conflict with the planter's vision for the new church.

The planter *must* ensure that these volunteers understand and agree with his vision. If they do not agree, the planter faces the unpleasant task of asking such workers to find another place for involvement. Even though it may seem unpleasant, this confrontation is better done sooner than later. When you choose core members, choose carefully!

Even though it often seems best to have an existing core group, the reality is that the presence of that group does not make much of a difference as the church grows. It helps in the beginning, but this impact seems to become less important by the third and fourth years.

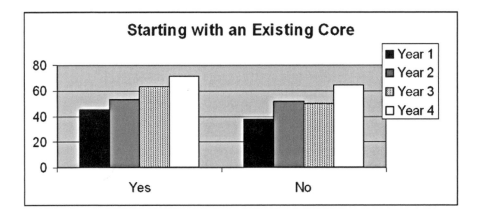

Core Development from the Unchurched

Although recruiting core members from outside sources may be helpful, it is better to find non-Christian evangelistic prospects and recruit them for the core group. One of the best ways to recruit the unchurched is through intentional relationship building. This is done in three ways: strategic contacts, door-to-door surveying, and phone outreach.

Many church planters argue that they prefer to recruit by direct mail and telemarketing. But the fact remains that even those prospects may not come without personal contact of some kind. Kevin Sullivan at Highpointe Church[4] in Seattle knocked on fifteen thousand doors to build his core group. Six months later he launched his new church with five hundred first-time attendees. By going door-to-door, he built a core group and established goodwill within the community that helped attract people for the launch service. This approach complemented the use of direct mail.

Core Development Through Relationships

One of my favorite new churches is Sojourn in Louisville, Kentucky. The church planter is one of my former students, Daniel Montgomery. He decided that he did not want to use any "artificial" forms of relationship building. Instead, he made a point of hanging out in coffee shops, music venues, and festivals in the Highlands area of Old Louisville.

As he built relationships in this artsy postmodern community, he decided he needed an intentional strategy to build prospects from the community. He rented, renovated, and transformed a building into an art gallery before the church ever held public worship. This became a place where he and the core group built relationships (and gained credibility) with the postmodern community.

Core Development by Using the Phone

Although personal visits ultimately follow, several methods can help the church planter jump-start the core development process. In the first weeks following my arrival in Erie, Pennsylvania, we placed five thousand phone calls. These core development calls are not to be confused with telemarketing for the launch. The conversations went like this:

"Hi, this is Ed Stetzer calling from the new Millcreek Community Church that will be opening this fall. If you are willing, may I ask you three quick questions?

"First, are you actively involved in a local church at this time?" (If the respondent said "yes," I thanked her for her time and ended the call. If the answer was negative, I continued.)

"Well, great. We're starting a new church, and we have Bible studies going in the area. Would you be interested in more information?"

Keep in mind that my purpose at this point was finding core group members. If the person indicated interest, I asked permission to mail her information and followed up with another phone call (this was the "third" question). This is a different strategy than telemarketing for the first service launch. At the time of this call, I was seeking only those persons who were immediately interested in being a part of our core development Bible study.

Core Development by Using the Core Development Mailer

Another way to jump-start the process of core development is to use a mailer. This piece enables simultaneous contact with large numbers of people that the planter would not normally be able to contact. Keep in mind that mailers just make the initial contact. People are reached most effectively through relationships.

This core development mailer asks for a response different from the prelaunch advertisement. The grand opening mailer is designed to convince the recipient to attend a public gathering. As such, it answers objections, calms fears, and announces the event.

On the other hand, a core development mailer is designed to convince interested, receptive people to respond by completing a postage-paid return address card. Although overall response to business reply cards is low (our experience was less than one-half of one percent), people who do respond often demonstrate high motivation and interest.[5]

See www.new-churches.com/ examples for examples of core development mailers and grand opening mailers.

One recommendation for the core mailer is a trifold brochure or letter design. It should include basic information about the church, some biographical information of the planter, and a business reply card to return. The message of such a mailer is simple: it should communicate the start of a great new church and that the leaders of the new church invite the recipient to be part of the new church start.

The core development mailer does not need to be expensive. You can utilize a strategy called Operation Epistle. This strategy involves volunteers

Operation Epistle information can be found at www.new-churches.com/ examples.

hand-addressing and applying first-class postage stamps to the mailers. These volunteers generally come from sponsoring churches around the country. In the end, the new church pays only printing costs and the start-up fee to open the BRMAS (Business Reply Mailing Automation System) account. Established church members are often enthusiastic about participating in mission activities such as this.

Filtering the Prospects

Building a core group may attract unbelievers, backslidden believers, new believers, and even mature believers. It may also attract people who are disenchanted, hurt, or power hungry. Such people may be difficult to assimilate. Knowing this ahead of time will allow the planter to use caution and wisdom in building a core group from these respondents.

Two weeks after I arrived in Erie, Pennsylvania, a family asked to become part of our new church. During our conversation, I learned that their church had recently closed. They tithed regularly, longed to be a part of ministry, and wanted good Bible teaching. Though they sounded great, they were not an appropriate match for the new church. They demonstrated strong convictions about what a church should be, and they seemed unwilling to accept the direction that our new church would take.

Although reasons may vary with every new start, the planter will have to turn away some people who want to be included in the core group. This becomes easier when the vision statement, mission statement, and core values of the new start are in place. These tools help to provide direction and protection for the new church. The core group should be asked to "sign on" to these values as a prerequisite for becoming a core member.

Conclusion

Core development is hard, labor-intensive work. After telephone and mailing campaigns, the planter faces the difficult task of filtering out persons who will not mesh with the new core group. But if these efforts net a few dozen appropriate, interested people, then the work should be well under way.

Developing a core group is indispensable to the long-term life and vitality of the new congregation. Great effort, time, and money should be invested in developing strategies that will help form a solid core group that will ultimately determine the future of the congregation. Use whatever methods are necessary—visitation, mailings, telemarketing—to achieve this task. Time and money spent at this stage of the development of a new church will be well spent.

Resources for Further Reading

Arnold, Jeffrey. The *Big Book on Small Groups*. Downers Grove, Ill.: InterVarsity Press, 1992.

George, Carl F. *Prepare Your Church for the Future*. Tarrytown, N.Y.: Revell, 1991

Long, Jimmy, and others. *Small Group Leaders' Handbook: The Next Generation*. Downers Grove, Ill.: InterVarsity Press, 1995.

McIntosh, Gary, and Glen Martin. *Finding Them, Keeping Them: Effective Strategies for Evangelism and Assimilation in the Local Church*. Nashville: Broadman & Holman Publishers, 1992.

Neighbour, Ralph. *Where Do We Go from Here? A Guide for the Cell Group Church*. Houston, Tex.: Touch Publications, 1990.

Small Groups

Small-group ministry is essential to the health of any church. Small-group organizations include cell groups, home groups, Sunday school classes, and other gatherings that promote relationships in the family of faith.

Each healthy church with more than fifty in attendance must develop a multiplying network of small groups. Although these groups may take different forms, they must accomplish the objective of binding a church together.

George Gallup found that 70 percent of Americans say that the church is not meeting their needs. When asked what these needs were, there were six common responses:

1. To believe life is meaningful and has purpose.
2. To have a sense of community and deeper relationships.
3. To be appreciated and respected.
4. To be listened to and heard.
5. To grow in faith.
6. To receive practical help in developing a mature faith.[1]

These needs can be met in a variety of settings, but they can be met best in a nurturing small group. This may help explain the rise of small groups in both secular and church settings in modern society.

The cultivative home group is a Bible study of a different kind. It does not exist only to display facts that the church planter learned in Bible college. The planter uses this home group to cultivate the unchurched person's relationship with Christ and to develop the new leaders' maturity in Christ.

Acts 2:42–47 describes the activities of the early church:

They devoted themselves to the apostles' teaching and to the fellowship, to the breaking of bread and to prayer. Everyone was filled with awe, and many wonders and miraculous signs were done by the apostles. All the believers were together and had everything in common. Selling their possessions and goods, they gave to anyone as he had need. Every day they continued to meet together in the temple courts. They broke bread in their homes and ate together with glad and sincere hearts, praising God and enjoying the favor of all the people. And the Lord added to their number daily those who were being saved.

Notice the frequency with which the disciples met in homes. The text says they met in the temple, but Luke was careful to describe the home meetings that took place on a regular basis.

Verse 42 tells us that the disciples "devoted themselves to the apostles' teaching." That teaching-learning process became a central part of their growth in discipleship. The text also points out that fellowship took place. Note that the disciples broke bread; this may be an indication that they took the Lord's Supper together in homes.

These Jerusalem believers also prayed; they *devoted* themselves to prayer. Signs and wonders took place, presumably on a regular basis. God was performing miraculous deeds. These people, who loved God, also loved others and cared for their needs.

Verse 46 indicates that they worshiped together at the temple and met in homes for the Lord's Supper and other matters. Small-group ministry involves people in worship. Praise and significant numerical growth followed the early church's ministry through home groups that ministered in a variety of ways. We would be wise to consider using small groups to achieve all of these purposes. The effective cultivative small group should feature worship, prayer, study, and fellowship.

Worship

The small group typically begins with worship. In the past, it was difficult for non-musicians to lead worship. But modern compact discs (CDs), computer midi files, and other tools have largely solved this problem. These resources enable a gathering of five to sound like a chorus.

Worship through music should be a part of every kind of small group except one: gatherings of fewer than four people. Groups of this size seem uncomfortable with singing—particularly if they are not used to singing in the presence of others.

Prayer

Prayer generally follows and grows out of worship through music. This time can bind group members and empower their growth. The planter should recognize that small group prayer often becomes a time of high anxiety for people who are not used to praying. Encourage people to pray at their level of comfort and with the type of words they use every day.

Bible Study

Worship motivates prayer, and prayer prepares the group for Bible study. Cultivative studies are student-focused and Bible-centered, not teacher-dominated. Thus, *study* must not mean "lecture." Nevertheless, a *cultivative* Bible study assumes little biblical knowledge on the part of the learner.

The best and most effective cultivative studies avoid "church" language. These studies do not begin with references to being "washed in the blood of the Lamb" and countless other phrases familiar to traditional church members. A *cultivative* Bible study should lead the learner to conclude that Christ is the answer. The cultivative study should be Christ-magnifying. Here are some fundamentals for leading a cultivative Bible study.

Start with a discussion, not a lecture. The leader guides the discussion and summarizes regularly.

Prepare leading questions. Such leading questions call on the learner to think, to feel emotions, and to probe a passage for God's hope or expectations. Leading questions enable the learner to draw personal conclusions based upon the study content. The leader should avoid yes-no questions, or those that are easily answered with one word.

Stay focused. The cultivative Bible study leader should involve every participant, eliciting comments from each one, but should stay focused. The study should not evolve into an opportunity for unknowledgeable group members to share their confusion about certain issues. Instead of teaching on the differing views of the end times, a cultivative Bible study could focus on how to make Christ the center of one's home.

Avoid sidetracks. Some group members will attempt to sidetrack the discussion toward side issues. Sometimes these arise because the student has real questions that need to be answered, but the cultivative study is not the time or the place for this. Sometimes those who lead the group astray are attempting to steal the leadership role from the facilitator or to thwart the Christ-centered purpose of the study. Christians often present great difficulties for the unbeliever or new believer through discussions of things like the fate of those who have never heard the gospel, different views regarding end times, or charismatic gifts. These matters *are* important, but the cultivative study is not the time to discuss them.

Use the same Bible text. Everyone in the group should use the same translation. Most unchurched persons have no idea where to find Matthew (to say nothing of Habakkuk). Providing students with the exact same Bible as your Bible allows you to list page numbers and other details in notes which students receive. Another option, especially when finances are tight, is to print text passages for each study by using one of the several CD-ROM Bible programs now available.

Make the points. The points, generally three to five bullet-point truths from the passage, outline the "meat" of the study. These points may have individual headings (e.g., 1. The Need of Humanity; 2. The Provision of God; 3. The Response of Faith; etc.). But the more important concern is the questions under each point that should spur reflection on and conclusions about Jesus Christ.

Formulate questions carefully. These questions make the cultivative Bible study different from other types of small-group studies. Good questions help to ensure a good cultivative Bible study. The best questions do not lead to yes-or-no answers. In addition, they should not be "interpretation" questions. It is a common mistake, but leaders often go around the room asking, "What's your interpretation of this passage?"

Dozens of cultivative Bible studies written by my students can be found at www.new-churches.com/examples.

An effective Bible study does not ask unchurched persons to determine what a passage means. Instead, one assumes that the text *has* a meaning. The task of the study leader is to guide participants in a discussion to unearth the meaning for themselves.

SMALL GROUPS | 215

Use the power of silence. Silence usually terrifies the new leader. Refuse to be afraid of participant silence. The best questions should provoke enough thought that most students will *not* be capable of answering—at least intelligently—at once. The leader must not consistently answer his or her own questions. If students know the leader always answers, they will feel no need to give an answer for themselves.

As students become accustomed to the process of the study, they will feel comfortable in answering questions. Reassure participants—and be consistent in helping them believe—that wrong answers are acceptable.

Draw the conclusions. The closing segment of the cultivative Bible study should be application. The application asks, What should the learner do, be, and feel, as a result of this study? From the application, participants should conclude how to allow the Bible text to reshape their lives.

Fellowship

The final element of the cultivative Bible study is a time for fellowship. Although the other segments of the study develop *spiritual* understandings, the fellowship period develops congregational *social* relationships. Before the church begins Sunday worship, the cultivative Bible study may be the congregation's only opportunity to encourage many attendees toward spiritual maturity.

The cultivative Bible study often brings about another vital, though secondary, effect. Intended primarily to win lost persons and weave believers into the body, effective groups also elicit gifted leaders and train them to lead future groups. The most effective church planters usually delegate Bible study leadership to maturing lay leaders when the time is right. The cultivative study serves as a training ground for discovering and equipping leaders who will eventually direct other cultivative studies or church cell groups.

The Importance of Small Groups

Thirty years ago many church planters started new churches by using small group Bible studies. From that stage, the progress followed uniformly and logically: Bible studies became chapels, then missions, and then finally, constituted churches. In the new millennium, most new churches no longer emerge through such a neat progression.

Most modern planters develop people in a cultivative Bible study, out of which emerges a core group. During this time, the planter trains leaders, and then the church goes public (an event usually called the launch). But the launch cannot replace congregational core development. The congregational leadership must be solidly in place at the time of the launch event. Some planters have attempted to start churches with a large crowd and without a core group. These rarely succeed because the congregation has no hub at the center of the wheel to bear the weight and carry the load.

The cultivative Bible study serves as the best building block to prepare for congregational and organizational maturity prior to the launch. Despite the effectiveness of direct mail, Internet communication, advertising, and telemarketing, nothing can replace small groups, and specifically the cultivative small group.

Small-Group Ministries

In *Prepare Your Church for the Future*,[2] Carl George establishes a strategy for church growth by dividing a congregation into small groups. He describes this type of fellowship as a "metachurch."[3] He uses this term instead of "megachurch." According to George, metachurches can be any size.

Though a metachurch uses cell groups, pure cell-based churches differ from metachurches in that a pure cell-based church is a congregation *of* small groups, not a church *with* small groups (metachurch). Thus, a cell-based church usually focuses on large-group weekly worship, but gathers in homes (or other sites) during the week. Aside from Sunday worship all church life takes place in home cell groups.

A metachurch can take various forms. It may be a pure cell-based congregation, or it may be a Sunday school-based church that offers care and ministry through small groups. It may be an intentionally Bible study-centered gathering in which attendees break into small groups on Sundays or on Wednesday nights. In this case, the church does not typically meet in homes at all.

The eighteenth chapter of Exodus poses one of the best examples of small-group ministry found in the Scriptures. In this passage, the father-in-law of Moses, a man named Jethro, recommended a means by which to avoid exhaustion because Moses was overworking himself and failing to delegate tasks to others.

It came about the next day that Moses sat to judge the people, and the people stood about Moses from the morning until the evening. Now when Moses' father-in-law saw all that he was doing for the people, he said, "What is this thing that you are doing for the people? Why do you alone sit as judge and all the people stand about you from morning until evening?" And Moses said to his father-in-law, "Because the people come to me to inquire of God. When they have a dispute, it comes to me, and I judge between a man and his neighbor and make known the statutes of God and His laws." And Moses' father-in-law said to him, "The thing that you are doing is not good. You will surely wear out, both yourself and these people who are with you, for the task is too heavy for you; you cannot do it alone. Now listen to me: I shall give you counsel, and God be with you. You be the people's representative before God, and you bring the disputes to God, then teach them the statutes and the laws, and make known to them the way in which they are to walk, and the work they are to do. Furthermore, you shall select out of all the people able men who fear God, men of truth, those who hate dishonest gain; and you shall place these over them, as leaders of thousands, of hundreds, of fifties and of tens. And let them judge the people at all times; and let it be that every major dispute they will bring to you, but every minor dispute they themselves will judge. So it will be easier for you, and they will bear the burden with you. If you do this thing and God so commands you, then you will be able to endure, and all these people also will go to their place in peace" (Exod. 18:13–23, NASB).

A planter-pastor who desires for church members to feel satisfied and loved by their church should encourage a strategy in which members receive love from leaders other than the pastor. Planters will never find the time and energy to express sufficient love to meet the congregation's needs.

A small group can meet such needs because they can build relationships that make a difference. A brief study of the Exodus passage above helps us understand the effective contribution of small-group ministry.

Jethro's suggestion to Moses outlined an administrative system for Moses to follow. For the church planter, the principles are clear. The planter must begin dividing the people into small groups from the beginning of the new church. The people must learn from the outset that the planter is not the sole caregiver in the church.

Christ the King Anglican Church[4] in Monument, Colorado, applied the Jethro administrative system to its church organization. They began by designating a lay leader for every ten families. The lay leader leds the small group in "four components of historical/biblical Christianity: 'They devoted themselves to the apostles' teaching, and to fellowship, to the breaking of bread and to prayer (Acts 2:42).'"[5]

That leader's specific task was to nurture those ten small-group families. An advantage to this approach is that a leader is not asked to oversee a large group. Ten is not too many to feel overwhelmed. Also, the size allows more contact from the leader. Since they only have ten families, they could contact those ten on a weekly basis.

In Carl George's system every small-group leader with ten people also supported an apprentice leader who served as an understudy to the group leader for a period of time. Many expect each small group to multiply itself within a year. The original group would spin off a second small group that the apprentice would oversee. If the group failed to reproduce itself within a year, some churches close the group and would fold members into small groups that demonstrated greater success in reproduction. Incorporating the less successful members into more productive groups enabled those members to catch a vision for multiplication.

While planting and pastoring, we expected two noteworthy individuals within every group. Carl George calls the first individual the EGR (Extra Grace Required). It seems that every group attracts at least one particularly needy person who wants to be the center of attention and to have the group obsess on his or her problems at every gathering.

The second noteworthy individual for every small group was the "seeker," one who was hungry for true relationship with God—a non-Christian "seeking" to know Christ. During our small group meetings, we insisted upon leaving a vacant chair to represent a seeker. Every week we prayed for that additional person, that God would fill that chair with his chosen one to whom we should minister.

The church planter should decide whether small-group membership should be required of all church members. Regardless of whether participation is *required*, a recommended goal is having 60 percent of Sunday attendance involved in small groups.

If the congregation decides to use Sunday school units instead of cell groups, it is best not to attempt pastoral care through the Sunday school organization. The reasoning for this recommendation is simple: Sunday school classes often grow beyond a size in which pastoral care remains manageable.

If the church still wants to conduct pastoral care through the Sunday school structure, two recommendations are appropriate. First, classes should be limited to approximately ten people. This size commends a healthy mix of comfort with accountability. Second, classes should not spend their entire hour on Bible teaching. Groups must devote a significant period of time to people's needs. Time should be set aside for pastoral concerns, especially since pastoral care will be carried out in the Bible study organization.

My friend Jeff Clark shared this example from a church he planted in Tennessee: "The Sunday school teacher I recruited for the young adults was 75 years old! He spent a great amount of time at the beginning of his class taking prayer requests, listening to members' week, and listening to the class talk. I found this frustrating. At the end of two years this man had started three other classes that went from 3 members to over 60 attending. I learned that the number one task of the teacher was to care for the class. People will gladly listen once they know you care."[6]

No matter what form these small groups take, every healthy church needs a multiplying network of small groups that aid in binding the church together. A church without small groups will often struggle to connect the members of the church with one another.

Resources for Further Reading

McBride, Neal F. *How to Lead Small Groups.* Colorado Springs, Colo.: NavPress, 1990.

Donahue, Bill. *Leading Life-Changing Small Groups.* Grand Rapids: Zondervan Publishing House, 1996.

Corrigan, Thom and the Pilgrimage Training Team. *How to Build Community Through Small Groups.* Littleton, Colo.: Pilgrimage NavPress, 1998.

CHAPTER NINETEEN

Finding and Handling Finances

*O*ne of the most frequent questions I am asked is, "How do I get the money to start a new church?" The subject of this chapter is funding and financing church starts. We will examine the funding of church plants led by paid staff and funding that involves partnerships with denominational systems. This chapter addresses sources of funding, start-up costs, the handling of funds, and missions giving.

Bob Logan and Steve Ogne do an excellent job in *Churches Planting Churches*. They spell out what a church planting proposal needs to contain if it is to be effective.[1]

Church Planting Proposal Contents

Why start a new church?

- Demonstrate a clear calling.
- Communicate an exciting vision.
- Identify reasons for good church planting.
- Demonstrate an understanding of the need for new churches.

Several examples of church planting proposals can be found at www.new-churches.com/examples.

Who is the ministry focus group?

- Describe the ministry focus group.
- Show understanding of the community's needs.
- Include appropriate demographics.
- Identify the proposed location.

What kind of church are we trying to plant?

- Clearly state your core values.

- State and expand your mission statement.
- Describe the church's ministry style.
- Define a ministry model.
- Include a ministry flow chart.

With whom will this church be planted?

- Describe the proposed launch team.
- Include a profile of any confirmed ministry partners.
- Define the specific roles to fill.
- Clearly identify team members needed.

How and when will this church be planted?

- Outline a comprehensive strategic plan.
- Include a detailed timeline for the first eighteen to thirty-six months.
- Provide a detailed explanation of how the core group will be gathered.

Sources of Funds

A new church requires a regular flow of money. While it is possible to start a new church successfully with a completely unsupported bivocational planter, most of the time the congregation will still need additional support for a meeting place, program, or other costs. In addition, there are times in the life of many church plants that require a special infusion of funds—launch activities, outreach projects, sound and video equipment, and gathering events, and the like.

Various denominational entities, congregations, and individuals have joined efforts and provided resources to underwrite new church starts across North America. However, it seems that church planters and their denominations often struggle with how to define the relationship.

Ralph Moore, founder of the Hope Chapel movement, has an excellent section on "How Can a Denomination Help?" in his new book. He explained: "You will soon find that your denominational support comes with strings attached. If you receive this support, you will be required to participate in denominational functions. This can be frustrating. Officials will busy themselves with programs that focus on the forest while you try to nurture a single small tree."[2]

Many new churches are planting churches that are dissimilar in worship style to the majority of their denomination. However, if God has called you to be a part of a denomination, then it is the church planter's job to reach across that divide (and others). When denominations help fund church planters it is an integrity issue. Church planters that receive denominational funding should have the integrity not to be ashamed of those that made their ministry possible. This does not necessarily mean they need the denomination in their church name, but they should have the denomination in their values.

Generally, there are denominational policies regarding fundraising that planters should get from their denominational leaders. If there are no restrictions, some of the ideas below may help.

Build networks. During my final year with Millcreek Community Church, we succeeded in gathering $200,000 for church planting and growth—money that we could not have generated by ourselves. By building various relationships and partnerships, we found resources to start two daughter churches on the same day—with over two hundred at the first service for each new church. Our denomination helped, we were given an empty church building (which we sold), and we raised funds. Some church planters find themselves underfunded because they function as "Lone Rangers." They refuse to take the time to build relationships and maintain strategic partnerships.

Get others involved. Other persons and churches may become involved as contributors in a variety of ways. Many church planters report that they have found Christian businesspeople to be open to supporting a new church. At InChrist Community Church,[3] businessman Fred Wehba helped underwrite a large portion of the new church costs (in partnership with several others).[4]

Talk their budget language. Donors have different pockets or line items from which they resource others. While established churches or other denominational entities are often willing to give, if the planter asks for church planting money (which they do not have) instead of ministry or evangelism money (which they do have), the planter may be disappointed. Doing some research ahead of time to determine how a congregation or donor has given in the past may help the church planter find valuable resources when he approaches others to establish relationships and request funding.

Talk their heart language. In addition, different churches and individuals operate out of different passions; they put their money where their heart is. Before you request help, learn about a potential donor's or congregation's passion. Some respond to need, but most respond to vision.

"Soft needs," or brick and mortar? One of my colleagues prefers to donate gifts to his college alma mater in the form of student scholarships. On the other hand, many people prefer to purchase "brick and mortar" gifts for new buildings or renovations. This is to say that some donors contribute to people projects or needs while others want to help with tangible projects. Knowing a donor's preferences can be helpful in your church's presentation of needs.

A hand up, not a hand out. Other supporters prefer contributing hands-on involvement more than monetary support. The "$32 Launch Day Project,"[5] in which churches commit to hand-address envelopes and pay for one hundred stamps, is a popular proposal with partner churches. The supporter's primary contribution is the time to address one hundred envelopes, not the payment for a roll of stamps. One of our sister congregations recruited two hundred people to participate in this project with us. In the end, this sister church spent over six thousand dollars for a special project, but they probably would not have given us six thousand dollars in cash.

In many cases, multiple churches may be involved as sponsors. Steve Allen, church planter strategist for the Frontier Baptist Association[6] in western New York, explains his strategy as 9–3–1–3:

9–3–1–3 Partnership Networking Strategy

9 Remote/Distant/External Partners

3 Local/Native/Indigenous Partners* supplying: *Money* (all 3 local partners contributing), *Mentoring* (most qualified individual available), *Manpower* (SWAT teams / hunting licenses).

1 Planting Team/Project

3 Year Covenant Relationship

   *One local congregation serves as primary sponsor.

Individual Donors

Individuals also contribute financial resources for new churches. The church planter may begin tapping such resources by developing a fund-raising brochure, a fund-raising letter, and a fund-raising conversation. In this approach, the planter should prepare the promotional letter and brochure, including a cover letter of commendation for the new church from a respected, well-known leader in the denomination. This brochure should be mailed to potential donors, especially to persons who have demonstrated interest in new work before.

After a few days, the planter should follow up with a telephone call to answer questions, using the information outlined in the fund-raising conversation. As needed, the planter may volunteer to pay a personal visit to the prospective donor. A concise, well-designed PowerPoint presentation given at the time of that visit may help the donor catch the vision for the future of the new church.

Fund-Raising Principles

Understanding fund-raising begins with understanding basic principles and the many pockets in which one may find resources. Psalm 50:10 describes God as owning "the cattle on a thousand hills." The real problem in fund-raising is not divine resources or believers' unwillingness to give resources. Church planters have not because they ask not or because they ask wrongly (see James 4:2–3). This is the first principle in fund-raising.

Another principle is that people give to vision, not to need. Begging donors probably will not generate a great response. But communicating one's story in a convincing, spiritual way can touch donors deeply. When God's people understand that the planter's life investment is worthy of their support and financial investment, they will become involved.

The Local Congregation

If the new congregation begins to think that they must rely on outside sources for pastoral support, they will never develop maturity in giving. Church planters can mention tithing in Sunday messages, but new churches should not do a stewardship series. Instead, the planter should address tithing whenever it comes up naturally in preaching and should leave the in-depth stewardship study for a more committed group.

A setting even better than the sermon for discussing new church finances is a class on spiritual maturity. This should be aimed at a more select group of believers at various levels of maturity and offered at various times during the year.

We followed a similar strategy for promoting tithing in our Millcreek start. In our "Life Class 201," we devoted thirty minutes to the doctrine of tithing and what tithing means. At the conclusion of the class, we asked participants to sign the members' covenant, which contained a commitment to begin tithing. We decided that we could afford to be aggressive in the area of tithing with people who claimed they wanted to move toward spiritual maturity. Our aggressiveness paid off, both for the congregation and for the believers who studied and made commitments.

Get a Job

A secular job can also supply funding for the church planter. Just because the denomination cannot fund the planter's church start does not mean that the planter cannot plant a church. If God has called a planter to begin a church, the planter must go forward in faith. Congregations and individuals must remember that denominations do not call church planters; *God* calls church planters. If God has called but finances do not follow as expected, the planter cannot argue that God has closed the door. Finances are not the determining factor in God's will; *God* is the determining factor in God's will. If God expresses a call, the planter must help make a way where there is no other way—by working at bivocational employment, at least for a period of time until the church has grown to support the pastor.

In their excellent new church planting book *Community of Kindness*, Steve Sjogren and Rob Lewin advise church planters to work outside the church until their congregation reaches two hundred in weekend attendance, even if those who have the financial backing to dedicate their full time to the congregation. They point out five advantages you will gain in bivocational work:

1. You will meet people to invite while on the job.

2. You will help "destroy the sacred-secular conflict . . . By that we mean the natural inclination of most already-converted people who think working in the church is more valuable than working in the marketplace—that it's more valued by God . . . ."

3. You will continue to send the message that you aren't trying to live off of other people . . . . Be sure to give substantially from the money you can earn outside the church to the church. Great leaders are always one of the top givers in their church."

4. You will be required "not to be available and allow for your congregation to work out their issues on their own on occasion . . . . Taking an outside job creates an understanding in the church that you aren't there as their free therapist."

5. You will be forced "to interact with the people in the marketplace," and they will see you "functioning in the role of a 'normal' person outside the rank of pastor."[7]

There are some jobs that are well suited for bivocational ministry. Dan Ramsey, author of *101 Best Weekend Businesses,* suggests the following as good jobs for bivocational church planters:[8]

Antique restoration service	Apartment preparation service	Auto detail service
Baking service	Bookkeeping service	Caregiver
Carpet-cleaning service	Catering service	Child care
Chimney sweep	Collection service	Companion to the elderly
Computer instructor	Computer maintenance	Construction cleanup service
Cooking instructor	Crafts business	Desktop publisher
Driveway repair service	Food-delivery service	Fund-raiser
Furniture refinishing	Handy-person service	Housecleaning service
House-painting service	Importer	Income tax preparation service
Information broker	Kitchen utensil-sharpening service	Mail-order sales
Masonry service	Newsletter publisher	Newspaper stringer
Personal consultant	Photography service	Picture-framing service
Plant-care service	Pool cleaning	Rental preparation
Research service	Resume writer	Reunion planner
Word processing	Security service	Small appliance repair
Teaching your skills	Telephone survey service	Translation services
Tree-trimming service	Tutoring service	Used car sales
Video-copying service	Wallpaper service	Wedding planner
Window-cleaning service	Woodworking	Writer

There are always cautions in bivocational ministry. For some people, being bivocational is a permanent ministry choice. For others, it will be a step into full-time ministry service. Both approaches are valid. For those who are working bivocationally with plans for full-time ministry, Steve Sjogren writes:

> If you are bi-vocational in the launching stage of your plant, don't forget why you are doing all of this—to launch a church. You did not move there to build a career in the secular workforce. If your job is robbing you of energy and enthusiasm beyond reason, find a new job. The ideal arrangement is a job [that] looks something like this:
> - pays an hourly rate
> - daytime hours so your evenings are freed up to build leaders and launch small groups
> - doesn't overly drain you emotionally or physically
> - puts you in touch with a good cross section of your city.
>
> I have found that jobs in sales or education tend to be ill-suited for planters.[9]

Many people already have a career. Others will find a job for the purpose of establishing the church. Regardless, bivocational and lay church plants are time-tested and biblical methods that every church planter should consider.

When I was unable to find adequate funding at my first church plant, I took a job insulating houses. I could start early in the morning and supervise several crews from my car and mobile phone. At the same time, I could do visits on my own time if I was in the area. My employer was flexible and gave me the freedom to clock in and out as needed. The job served as a good place for connections and ministry. It also helped pay the bills when the new church could not.

The Nuts and Bolts of Finances

Some of the typical *start-up costs* for a church include outreach, facility rental, and purchasing sound and video equipment. These purchases and expenditures are typical of the initial costs of doing kingdom business.

The first concern for the new congregation is to *develop a start-up budget*. Many new churches must start with nothing more than a guitar and an overhead projector. Some mission agencies no longer support pastoral income needs, but they will give one-time start-up grants for new churches to enable the best worship service from the very beginning. Although pastoral support amounts or duration may be reduced if some money goes to start-up, a few denominations actually offer both pastoral support and start-up money.

Safeguarding funds is a fundamental issue of reputation and integrity. The number of church starts that become tainted by mishandling (or mere *appearance* of impropriety) is significant.

In order to *avoid any appearance of wrongdoing,* the church planter should not set up an account tied to the planter. Even if the account is in the church's name, do not use your Social Security number. If you do, all money deposited to this account is taxable income. It is easy to get an Employer Identification Number from the IRS. In fact, you can get it by calling the IRS on their toll-free phone number. With that number it is possible to set up a checking account for the church.

The church should hold no account in its own name until significant safeguards have been put in place. Until a treasurer and a financial secretary have emerged and have been bonded, the account should not be opened. If the need for paying bills is great, then the treasurer of the mother church, a designated "treasurer" from among the sponsoring church missions team, or a qualified individual from the denomination may act as a temporary manager of the new church's funds.

The treasurer should not handle offerings *and* write checks. By having different persons functioning in these roles, the church will hold both the treasurer and the counter of money accountable to the congregation.

Some local or regional governments even require separate persons to handle the separate functions. No matter how the state feels about it, allowing one person to handle all the financial tasks for the church is risky. One individual should not be given so much responsibility. This is both a great temptation and a poor witness to the world.

A third group to appropriate the handling of the finances consists of counters for offerings and other receipts. They should always count at least in teams of two persons. The counters are responsible for counting the money; the financial secretary should deposit the money; the treasurer should write checks for disbursing the money. Expenditures should always be made by using written checks so there is a record of money management.

Two unrelated persons, neither of whom is the church planter, should sign all checks for the church. The planter must be protected by remaining at arm's length from monetary matters. Our culture already thinks that pastors have problems with finances. The planter must give no reason or excuse for anyone to point a finger of accusation.

A treasurer must be equally above board with all the finances in how reports are given. Reports should be regular (monthly), readable and straightforward, and reputable in their accounting for all funds and accounts. The more detailed, the better such reports are. With the evolution of computer bookkeeping programs, the church should have little trouble with money management and reporting.

From the first day of its life, the new congregation should begin to give to missions from its undesignated receipts. By giving to support missions in North America and around the world, the new church is immediately "giving back." Even the smallest new church can be a part of worldwide missions.

I recommend that each new church "tithe" to missions. Although I am not seeking to make a theological statement that the local church needs to tithe, the new church can model sacrificial giving from the start. This enables the church to demonstrate tithing to its own congregational members.[10]

The pastor and overseers of the church (however church polity is organized) should ensure that the church does not give *to* the mission fund *from* mission funds. For example, if the new start receives $12,000 per year through partnership funding, the treasurer must not send 10 percent ($100) of that income each month to missions. In effect, that money is a "designated" receipt—mission funds intended specifically for starting a new mission.

Some local givers earmark money beyond their tithe and offering to go for some specific issue such as a building fund, hunger fund, and so on. These monies are also "designated" offerings. But at least one-tenth of the rest of the church's income should be sent away for the purposes of missions support.

The total amount of money may seem insignificant to the congregation at first (almost a "why bother?" issue), but learning to establish a percentage, to maintain it, and to increase that amount over time will mean that many other church plants and other missions endeavors may go forward because of the young church's gifts. I personally recommend that the congregation begin by giving 12 percent of every local, undesignated dollar to missions.[11] At the very least, this attitude of generosity teaches by example that congregation members should give their tithe, and beyond.

Conclusion

When one examines the entire financial picture, "There's gold," as John Maxwell puts it, "in them thar' pews." This statement sounds a bit crass, but God's people—whether great foundations, wealthy donors, wealthy churches, or individual, typical believers—want to become involved in kingdom enterprises that are worthy of their gifts. The planter and the new congregation should be faithful and ethical in handling financial matters and also in how they approach donors and partners for money. May the planter be wise, and may God resource the church plant so miraculously and marvelously that both the planter and the planted congregation exult and proclaim in praise, "We couldn't have done it on our own, but God brought in the resources; now, we want to give back so that others might have a miraculous new church experience of their own."

Resources for Further Reading

Callahan, Kennon L. *Effective Church Finances: Fund-Raising and Budgeting for Church Leaders.* San Francisco: Harper and Row, 1992.

Mission Service Corps Support Development School, http://www.namb.net/beonmission/volunteers/msc/msc_orientation.asp

Powers, Bruce P., ed. *Church Administration Handbook.* Rev. ed. Nashville: Broadman & Holman, 1997.

CHAPTER TWENTY

Choosing a Name and A Logo

*C*hoosing a name is a significant action when beginning a new life or a new congregation. In planting a new work, the church's name and logo play a vital role. These symbols leave "first impressions" (and maybe, "last impressions") with the community about the new church.

Names for new churches in the twenty-first century should be meaningful and contemporary. Exceptions always exist, of course, but logic urges that contemporary names are more likely to attract contemporary people.

What's in a Name?

I discourage the use of some types of names—some of which were "contemporary" yesterday but are not today. The church should not be called a "mission." The term can evoke pictures of a skid-row rescue ministry, or perhaps, a Roman Catholic ministry in the southwestern United States.

Neither is the word *chapel* a good idea. Many denominations frequently used this term in naming new churches during the 1970s. By now, the term has come to suggest a site used specifically for weddings, or worse, for funerals.

Even the term *fellowship* may no longer serve the best interests of a new body of believers. It is best that the planter and congregation call themselves what they are—a church.

It is also wise to avoid names that are street specific. For example, Walnut Street Baptist Church would obviously identify the location of a church on Walnut Street. But there is no Walnut Street in Louisville—at least not any longer. The city changed the name to Mohammad Ali

Boulevard to honor the hometown boxer. The church was not enthusiastic about changing its name to that of a convert to Islam. The name has no meaning to those who are not familiar with the former street name.

The word *church* still has significance for our culture. Although most people may not understand the lofty theological implications of the term, they at least know that "church" is strongly related to the Christian faith and that it is a "place" where Christians go.

There is a trend today among many emerging postmodern churches to use a single name: Sojourn, Journey, Ekklesia, and the like. This is not necessarily a bad practice since the names have meaning, but they are not as easily identified as Christian churches.

Some church planters at the dawn of the twenty-first century choose generic names. Examples of generic names might be Community Church, Christian Church, or Bible Church. Planters have used generic names to attract people beyond their own denominational boundaries, to appeal to anti-denominational Baby Boomers, or to identify with a specific area.

Peter Wagner cautioned the church planter to "think twice before using the name of your denomination. . . . Not that these names should never be used, but ask yourself what they mean to the *unchurched* public."[1] On the other hand, Elmer Towns believes that if your denomination (in his case Baptist) has a bad name in the community, the church planter should work to make it a good name since people will attend a church because "of what it is doing, not because of its name."[2] Most new churches being planted today do not identify their denomination in their names.

A church planter who decides not to include the denominational label in the name of the church needs a well-thought-out explanation for the choice. Simply following a behavior commonplace among church planters is insufficient. A church planter needs to have a solid understanding of the issue and must be prepared to explain his reasoning to the denomination if asked.

If the church planter should decide to develop a church name that is free of denominational labels, that name *must* make a good impression on the target community. The name should convey reliability, theological meaning, and the church's commitment to reach and serve the unchurched community. Therefore, ask. Ask denominational leaders, the core group, and your focus group what name they prefer. Most importantly, following efforts in asking leaders, the core group, and the target group, the church planter must pray through the name issue. Since the planter is likely to feel pressure from every direction during the process, listening with an open mind and then quietly seeking the Lord's counsel seems a wise process for sound decision making.

In the debate about church names, a new church is different from an established church. I chose neutral names for every church that I planted because I thought it was the best decision for the location where I was planting. When I have pastored established churches (in two cases, revitalizing struggling or dying churches), I have recommended that the church not use a neutral name because they already have an identity in the community.

George Barna has done some excellent research on the subject. Below is one graph from his presentation analyzing the views of the unchurched toward major denominations.[3] This graph deals with the attitudes of the unchurched. It describes their perceptions of major denominations. One interesting note: he found that pastors thought that the unchurched had a more negative opinion of the denomination than the unchurched people actually did. The average unchurched person is simply not aware of most denominations. A small percentage have negative views. The vast majority have positive views toward or have no awareness of most major denominations.

Views of the Unchurched Toward Major Denominations

Some have said that the name of the church makes no difference to the unchurched. However, that conclusion cannot be applied when speaking of *new* churches. If the *only* thing that people know about a new church is the name, the name certainly makes more of a difference. (Go to www.new-churches.com/research for further information on the topic.)

No one would argue that a new church named "Landmark Presbyterian Tabernacle" will be more likely to attract the unchurched who receive information in the mail. Names *do* make a difference and can hurt the new church. The only question is if *any* denominational identification hurts a new church.

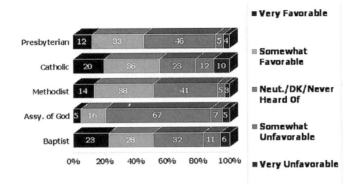

Developing an Effective Logo

Pictures—and logos—are worth a thousand words. The community surrounding a new congregation will form their initial impression of the church from its logo. Since that impression can be either positive or negative, the planter and church should exercise great care in designing the church's logo. Every image, whether a rugged cross or a brilliant sunburst, summons powerful emotional and intellectual responses from the community. Images that appeal to believers may not only fail to appeal to unchurched people but may also repel them.

The meaning of a logo should be clear. A church using an image cannot assume that the unchurched people who see it will understand what the congregation thinks it says. For example, one cannot immediately discern whether an image of the sun on the horizon conveys day*break* or the day's *end*. Does it signal the *dawn* of hope or the *end* of hope? Birth or the end of life? Dawning light or impending darkness?

We must ask ourselves what our visual images—buildings and logos—say to our community. The church's visual images—such as logos, signs, and facilities—communicate messages about the church's values, attitudes, and morale. The design of any visual image *must* communicate the messages that the congregation wants to communicate.

Technical Considerations

Manlove Church Marketing[4] is a marketing company that provides excellent logo service. They provide several technical recommendations that the church planter should keep in mind when designing a logo:

- A logo should quickly communicate the identity of a company or organization.
- The logo should reproduce well in various sizes.
- A logo should look great in gray scale. Often times a logo looks great in four-color but when it is rendered in gray scale it is unrecognizable or loses all its impact. The best approach to logo design is to establish that the logo is great in gray scale and then to add the complementary colors.[5]

Thinking through a Logo

A congregation's name and logo should "give permission" to the unchurched to visit and become acquainted with the new congregation. "Churched" people forget how timid and anxious unchurched people are in beginning a relationship with a church. The church's logo, signage, and other public displays should attract and comfort potential members. A trained artist can suggest colors that transmit warmth and welcome.

The message of the logo must be consistent across the spectrum of church communication. Stationery that welcomes and invites must be complemented by other visual images. Although church signage may proclaim, "Alive and Warm Toward Visitors," those words painted in gray and black, sitting in a yard without grass, and surrounded by an eight-foot chain-link fence topped with barbed wire hardly convey an inviting image. Passersby must be able to look at a building, signage, the lawn, and the logo and experience comfort, warmth, and welcome.

Chances are that nothing will help unbelievers say, "This church looks *really good*," but at the very least they should be thinking, "It doesn't look *that* bad." The church must remember that unchurched people are already "scared to death" about coming to church. The name and logo make it easier for them to take the next step.

Resources for Further Reading

http://www.1800mylogo.com/
http://www.churchlogogallery.com/
http://www.outreachmarketing.com/

Part 5

Starting Off Right

CHAPTER TWENTY-ONE

Finding a Meeting Place

*E*very new congregation must have a place for corporate worship. This is true, no matter the place or the size of the new, growing church—from the smallest house church to the largest megachurch start. By their nature, house churches do not need an external facility. All congregations, with the exception of house churches, require a facility—temporary or permanent. This chapter addresses the facility needs of both new and growing churches.[1]

Finding the Right Location at the Beginning

The new church's location is like a hospital—it is where the birth of the new church "happens." The location of your congregation will determine the available facilities. A few months ago, I attended a new church on the Upper West Side of Manhattan. Journey[2] is a new church meeting in the Triad Theater, a trendy community theatre. They meet in the theatre because it was available and it connected with their focus group.

Their "foyer," where they hand out coffee and church programs, is on the West 72nd Street sidewalk. Attendees have to walk to the second floor to be seated (above the bar). There is no room for child care, but there is little need. People who live in the Upper West Side have dogs, not children. Journey found a facility that met their needs. Every church needs to find a facility that connects with their people group. There are common trends and general guidelines for finding the right facility, but these must be applied in your individual context.

Save money; rent facilities. The young congregation probably can save money—probably a great deal of money in the long run—by renting facilities in the beginning of its life. New churches with no credit history are often unable to get mortgages for the purchase of land or a building. Building purchases demand closing costs and a host of other expenditures.

Fast-growing new churches may be wise to save for a significant period of time before they buy or build permanent facilities. This allows the congregation to actualize its membership potential *before* building, in order to concentrate on internal relational matters, to continue defining and refining its mission and purpose, and to save money for a later purchase.

Choosing a temporary facility means that the congregation must develop a "portable approach" to ministry. One excellent source for portable equipment is Portable Church Industries.[3] With the new church's specific needs before them, this company can design and arrange portable church furnishings and supplies to allow the congregation to hold public events in temporary settings without looking temporary.

The most common place that new churches meet is inside other churches. That is a tried-and-true practice. Many ethnic churches will meet within another part of a church's facilities, sharing the building with the mother church. Outside of other churches, the most common meeting place is in public schools.

Court decisions on school rental. Any congregation which desires to rent school facilities in the United States needs to be aware of Lamb's Chapel. The U.S. Supreme Court ruled that school districts could not discriminate against churches seeking to rent facilities on the basis of speech or the message of the renting group. This ruling was clarified even further in 2001 with *Good News Club v. Milton Central School.* In this case, the court ruled that evangelism and discipleship were allowed in a school building if other non-school groups used the facilities for their purposes.

Schools that rent to other nonschool groups must also rent to you whether you are showing Christian films, doing Bible clubs, or even having worship. But with this privilege come some limitations. If the school district believes that weekly worship would "excessively entangle" the state with the church, they can decline use of their facility. Eventually, this specific case will need to be heard and settled by the Supreme Court.[4] Until then, have your facts and ask (or act) wisely. Do not force your way in—you might regret it later.

In Canada, the legal issues are not as problematic, but renting from schools is still a challenge. One Canadian church planter (and seminary professor) explained:

Churches are on their own to negotiate as they can. Many school systems use a broker to negotiate for the entire system. We were refused, but there are at least four others who are in schools, usually because they have relationship with someone in the administrative system. Community Centres are happy to rent to churches but there is no rental protection (at least not in Alberta) so the church is often victim of the whims of the community council. Again when the church demonstrates that it is involved in the community, doing things that matter to the community, things (including rental) go much better. There are also a few church plants who have found good deals in hotels: conference rooms, set-up, and coffee all provided . . . one church pays only a dollar a head for their rental agreement.[5]

There is much litigation about churches using schools today. Since this may change, you can find up to date articles about U.S. and Canadian laws at www.new-churches.com/legal. Also, you can find a sample letter that explains the law to school administrators.

Other rental site options. Another common location for new congregational rental is a day care center. Although centers which consist of small meeting rooms may not serve as good locations, many day care centers have large, open rooms that can be adapted as a worship area.

Restaurants and meeting halls. Restaurants and meeting halls provide another type of location for new church meeting places. One of my former congregations met for a time in an American Legion hall that contained a restaurant and a large dance hall.

Other alternatives. Depending on the community, fire department meeting halls may offer a great choice for rental space. Many volunteer fire departments have a large room that they use for fund-raising or other events. Some Roman Catholic churches rent their fellowship halls to other organizations and even churches. Seventh-day Adventist churches, which worship on Saturday, often provide space for congregations that worship on Sunday.

Make your geographical selection wisely. The planter and congregation must be careful in choosing not only their building but their meeting area as well. Familiarity with community needs, history, and feelings will help the church avoid poor choices. In some communities certain buildings have a bad reputation, are in an unsafe location, or have some other problem which may turn prospects away.

Facility Needs

A large launch is likely to demand a large auditorium (more about that later). Many more options exist for smaller new churches.

Consider a garage or basement. A church in Florida met for some time in a two-car garage. They cleaned the facility each week in order to set up a lectern, a portable piano, and sufficient seating for the congregation and guests. A basement can also work if it is large, clean, and otherwise pleasant. If the congregation is relationally oriented and if the setting does not induce feelings of claustrophobia, such a location may work well. (Keep in mind that after you reach a certain size, you must meet certain building codes for your public assemblies.)

Other options. New churches have exercised several other options. The smaller new church may consider a recreation room in an apartment or condominium complex, a large living room, the back room of a restaurant, a school cafeteria or gymnasium, or vacant retail space in a mall. Sometimes older congregations are pleased to rent unused space in their building. Wherever the congregation meets, the space must be affordable, pleasant, logistically manageable (see the next section), and culturally suitable for the focus group. The needs of the focus group—*not* the cost—should serve as the determining factor. A low-cost facility that turns off the focus group is not a good choice.

Rental Fatigue

New churches normally rent facilities for a limited period of time. At first, they usually rent for Sunday morning worship only. These rented facilities are dramatically different from traditional church buildings whose furnishings remain in place from service to service. When renting space, "rental fatigue" develops. This describes the weariness experienced by the core group from having to set up and tear down week in and week out over a long period of time. This challenge may not *sound* ominous, but finding volunteers willing to get up at 5:00 or 6:00 *every* Sunday morning for two to three hours of setup wears people out quickly. Unless specific church members sense such activity as their calling and receive great satisfaction from doing it, fatigue can erode enthusiasm quickly.

Value of portability. Overcoming rental fatigue is challenging but not impossible. The planter's first step might be to commend portability by various means of communication—from the pulpit, through newsletters, and if possible, by the testimony of laypersons who have experienced its value personally. The planter may want to underscore the importance of portability because the church is still in formation. In the same way that Israel utilized a portable tabernacle during the forty wilderness years and well after, so the new congregation can be a portable church.

Good stewardship. The planter can help church members understand portability as good stewardship. Many people benefit from pastoral reminders to invest money in church staff members and in efforts to reach the unchurched, rather than in building or buying a facility. Refocusing members on priorities for reaching the community through stewardship of resources will help members center on such priorities for many years to come. By the time the church does build, members will have matured to the point where they view the building as a tool for ministry.

Call out workers. Many people cannot teach or lead in worship, but they can set up chairs or the audio system—and will enjoy doing so. Involving them in set-up efforts is important not only to make everything ready for worship, but also to cultivate their participation and their faithfulness in service. Although the pastors or core group leaders *could* perform the task, involving others who have no other church job enables them to feel that they are making a valuable contribution. Leaders should praise these people publicly and privately for their faithfulness in this important ministry. Such persons are "body parts" in Christ who, though seemingly of lesser value, actually become more valuable through their service to the kingdom.

Seven-day facilities. Although it is almost certain to be more expensive, another way to avoid rental fatigue is to lease a seven-day facility. This around-the-clock rental arrangement provides building access every day for office space and weekday ministries. It also solves the portability problem because no one else uses the building or needs to have the church's furnishings removed each Sunday. Even if this arrangement is initially impossible (or unnecessary) for the new church, the congregation might consider the feasibility of such a facility within the first few months. Several factors—rental fatigue, developing church ministry needs, and financial ability, among other factors, signal the church's readiness for a seven-day facility.

Nomad Churches

Although the thought surprises our building-centered values, some congregations actually find a "nomadic" existence—*permanently* moving to new meeting sites as needs change—a way of life. This approach to church planting has become increasingly popular, particularly in expensive urban settings. The reasons for such developments are understandable.

No available acreage. Land in some urban settings is prohibitively expensive. In other areas, churches find that purchasing land on which to build is legally impossible because very old—occasionally even dilapidated—buildings have received civil protection as historic landmarks. This most frequently occurs in the northeastern United States, where many communities guard their colonial heritage. Some open land in urban areas is off-limits to development for houses and churches as a matter of wildlife protection. In still other places, religious, political, or social pressures may prevent a new congregation from purchasing land or from putting up a building.

Available but insufficient. Even if land is available, it may not be large enough to meet needs. Generally, since churches need one acre for every 150 persons, a projected congregation of fifteen hundred will need ten acres of land. Manhattan Island, in the heart of New York City, contains no available tracts that size. Northern Virginia offers virtually no land for purchase today. Even if available, land costs may soar to a price of millions of dollars for one acre.

The Singapore solution. The island nation of Singapore, which lies just off the tip of the Malay Peninsula, faces overcrowding and shortage of space, just as in some North American urban areas. As a result, churches have met for many years in hotels, office buildings, and similar structures.

"It is almost impossible to find any meeting place to rent in the city on Sundays as the Christians have already taken up everything available."[6]

New paradigms for new times. If evangelicals are to be successful in reaching North American urban centers in church planting, we must abandon the thinking that ten acres of land and a brick building are essential in order to be successful. A true New Testament church can meet on the sixteenth floor of a high-rise building just as surely as any First Presbyterian Church can meet on the county seat town square. With the birth of the twenty-first century and the changes it has ushered in, we must redefine good stewardship in the context of land purchase and buildings. We need new paradigms for new times.

Shared Facilities

Sharing facilities is another alternative to the exorbitant costs of building permanent church structures. Congregations across the United States and Canada have discovered the economic advantages of this approach in which two congregations—or even multiple groups—share the same meeting space. This practice sometimes includes churches of different denominations and, certainly, of different ethnic backgrounds.

A Permanent Building

At some point, the congregation may desire a building to call its own. Although not every call for a permanent site signals the time to buy or build, there are times to consider the need.

Cultural needs. For example, if a church cannot secure even marginally adequate facilities at a reasonable price, few realistic options remain except to buy or build. Another common situation is the community's perception of the church's permanence.

Buffalo, New York, is a heavily Roman Catholic area. As a whole, Roman Catholics (as well as others) seem to be "building-centered." Despite the fact that our prospects were *nonpracticing* Catholics in many cases, they would hardly give our new church a second glance until we "had a church"— until we owned our own building. On a number of occasions, I heard prospects or contacts say, "When you get a church, I'll come to see you." In response to this cultural need, we eventually purchased a 150-year-old church building and remodeled it to suit our needs and the needs of the focus group. Cultural preferences sometimes dictate the need for a new church to occupy its own facility.

Just one chance to get it right. The church should never let the shoe determine how big the foot will become. If it decides to build or buy, a congregation must be certain that the space it chooses does not limit the growth of the church. Churches that are determined to build must look as far as possible into the future to determine whether their planned building will be sufficient for next week as well as for today and even tomorrow. Churches *can* overcome underplanned facilities but not without headaches and great costs. They have only one chance to get it right—the first time they build.

With a rented facility, the church simply moves when it has outgrown its space. Over several years, Seminole Community Church met at a funeral home, a gym, a movie theater, and an elementary school before building a more permanent facility.[7] They moved to a different site as they needed.

Location for Building

If a congregation decides that it must build, location is a highly important consideration. Many have observed that location does not *always* matter—particularly to strong, established churches. For example, Thomas Road Baptist Church in Lynchburg, Virginia—one of the largest churches in the United States—lies at the end of a road that is difficult to find. Because the church already had established its identity in the community and was growing rapidly, its location did not keep it from becoming a megachurch.

Location, location, location. When a *new* church decides to build, its choice of location is crucial because it is different from an established church. The new congregation does not have an established reputation in the community. Visitors will not easily find the church facility unless it sits in plain view and is easily accessible. A building located on a convenient, accessible site can enhance the fledgling congregation in developing its community identity.

Many acres; how much use? The congregation must consider how much of the land will actually be usable. Lakepointe Community Church purchased twenty acres of land for construction. Approximately one-third of that land is wetland and is not available for construction. Fortunately, the congregation knew well before the purchase that the land would not be useful for their construction purposes, and they planned for that reality. But not all churches are so fortunate or thorough. Skilled consulting engineers can help the church avert costly, discouraging problems.

Zoning Laws

Along with plans for purchasing land, the congregation should develop its awareness of local zoning issues. Failing to do so can prove costly to the new church. The "Religious Land Use and Institutionalized Persons Act of 2000" addressed the creeping problem of local zoning laws by giving more power to local churches. Under the new law, the government must have a "compelling governmental interest" to exclude a church from a zoning category.

Laws to restrict churches. Churches should clearly understand that government entities sometimes use zoning laws to restrict the activities and development of churches. The Web site of well-known Christian activist/attorney Jay Sekulow explains that churches are "increasingly facing discrimination from local zoning authorities."

Search and obey. If a new congregation plans to build, it must find real estate that meets three criteria: first, it must provide adequately for the present and future needs of the church, as described above. Second, it must be financially affordable. Third, its intended use must conform to zoning laws.

The consistent U.S. Supreme Court pattern over recent years has been to rule on the side of governments, not on the side of churches in matters regarding zoning. These decisions send a chilling message to congregations that hope to build facilities in the near future, particularly congregations that are not recognized and respected by local government officials. The recently passed national Religious Land Use Act may make things better, but as of this writing, it has not been tested in court. (See www.new-churches.com/legal for updates.)

A place to begin. In order to avoid costly and frustrating battles over zoning issues, the congregation should begin its building plans in the zoning office of the local government. Informed representatives of the church should first determine the present zoning of the proposed site. Next, they should determine whether local government entities already have or are preparing to change zoning regulations in ways that would impact the church's plans. Although new legislation in the United States holds out renewed hope for churches, congregations must be careful in their dealings with local government agencies and agents.

Building Campaigns

If a congregation plans to build, it *must* have a plan not only for building but also for financing its purchases. As a rule of thumb, most consultants feel that a church can raise three times its annual budget income for a building campaign. LifeWay Christian Stores administers one such plan through their Together We Build program for fund-raising.[8] This program has proved its worth over a number of years and has been used by all kinds and sizes of churches.

But not with a fund-raiser. I do not recommend that a new congregation engage a professional fund-raiser. Many of these agents, while superb in their skills, require costly fees that can discourage the financially challenged church, which usually pays 5 to 15 percent of the fund-raising proceeds to the agent.

Other alternatives. An alternative program, "A Time to Build"[9] was designed by and successfully used by Saddleback Valley Community Church for their building campaign.

Another option is to request the services of your denominational consultant who can be skilled in effective, nonmanipulative fund-raising techniques. His or her skills should help raise the money. In addition, the consultant should leave the congregation matured in their stewardship and feeling respect for the agency that dispatched the agent to the congregation.

Church Loans

A new church has several options for securing a building loan.

Conventional loans. Conventional lending institutions such as banks, savings and loan institutions, and credit unions may provide the resources a church needs. The church may find borrowing locally of some advantage in building a solid reputation in the community.

Local denominational entities. Some denominations loan money for church building purchase or enhancement. Even if *all* needed funds are not available through these groups, they may provide sufficient seed money to enable the church to pay for architectural plans and other start-up costs.

Foundations. Many states and localities have small agencies or wealthy laypersons with resources for grants and loans. You should ask local churches or denominational leaders what opportunities are available. For example, the Oldham Little Church Foundation[10] provides grants for church building repairs and upgrades. Although their grants are not large, their target is small churches. Many small, new churches may find this brick-and-mortar agency helpful.

Only one-third of income for debt service. Regardless of the lender or means by which a new church purchases property, it should commit no more than one-third of its weekly receipts for debt service. Many church planters will confirm that churches which do not heed this warning place a strain on the spirit of the congregation and choke its life and ministry.

Conclusion

A meeting place is indispensable to the life of a church, but facilities should never control the direction of the church, whether by their cost, their size, their need for maintenance, or some other factor.

Whether you rent or buy, pay cash or secure a loan, build new or remodel another congregation's structure, the building in which you meet is God's gift for *ministry,* not a monument to be protected. Plan its use well.

Resources for Further Reading

Bowman, Ray, and Eddy Hall. *When Not to Build.* Grand Rapids: Baker Book House, 2000.

Callahan, Kennon L. *Building for Effective Mission: A Complete Guide for Congregations on Bricks and Mortar Issues.* San Francisco: Jossey-Bass, 1997.

Warren, Rick. *"Bigger Buildings?"* at http://www.purposedriven.com/articles/practice/display.asp?id=41

CHAPTER TWENTY-TWO

Getting the Attention of the Media

Charles Chaney, author of *Church Planting at the End of the Twentieth Century*, would often begin conferences by saying, "Every time a church is planted, it is a miracle." He is right. Sadly, in many cases, just a few people hear about this miracle. This chapter will help you enlist the secular media in order to tell the story of the new church.

As a church planter, you need to create what is called "top-of-mind awareness" with your focus group. Top-of-mind awareness is reached when people in the community think of your church plant as a place where they can find spiritual fulfillment (when they decide they are ready). Getting the attention of the media and getting them to tell your story will get the word out and help create awareness.

Secular advertisers look for top-of-mind awareness every day. When asked to think of hamburgers, many people think of McDonalds. When cola is mentioned, many think of Coke. But when spirituality is mentioned, most people do not think of a church; they think of the spirituality section at Barnes & Noble or a Wayne Dyer spirituality program on PBS. The planter who gets advertising and media recognition can help raise the top-of-mind awareness among the church's focus group. Then the people in the community will know where to turn when they have a spiritual need. Creative advertising and free media can help with this.

Media Recognition

Media recognition begins with understanding that you must have newsworthy events—events which are newsworthy to the media, not to you. Some pastors may believe that when seven people are saved and a revival speaker is preaching at his church, ABC News should send a correspondent to cover the story. Realistically, media types seldom see this as newsworthy. It is a great story for the kingdom, but the secular media are not interested. The newspapers that print the story will probably put it in the religion section. The church planter who wants to get media coverage must do something "newsworthy." News that gets reported usually focuses on the unusual or the sensational.

Instead of church planters becoming sensationalists to attract the news, I recommend that they be "wise as serpents and gentle as doves." What are some things that catch the media's attention that will get people to hear about your church and respond? You can do a number of things. Sojourn Church in Louisville opened an art gallery, and the local newspapers covered the event and their new church. Journey Church on the Upper West Side of Manhattan planned a dog party as an evangelistic outreach, and the media covered it. When I was at Millcreek Community Church, we built a new building with volunteer labor—and all four local stations covered the story.

www.new-churches.com/media has sample press releases and articles.

You can get the press to come to your facility every week if you do goofy things or if you do things that raise opposition. This type of media coverage will cheapen and distort the gospel.

Today there is increased pressure on news outlets to have some positive news. This is great news for church planters. You can help them and in the process help yourself. Begin by contacting the person at the local station who covers the public interest section.

The Press Release

Write a press release for each media source in the area. Make sure the release is geared toward the appropriate medium. If you plan to do a press release for a newspaper, do not talk about whatever you are doing as you would for a television clip. If you plan to do a radio spot, do not just say what something looks like; be visually descriptive. Add some audio imagery. Write something that catches people's interest.

We are not being persecuted when the media ignore our events. Many times Christians are just viewed as boring. Do not write a press release like this: "The Lord is clearly working at Grace Christian Church. Sixty-four people have been saved in the last week." That will not turn the ear of the unchurched. We must catch the interest of people across the city in a way that would cause them to say, "Wow, I am glad they told me about the revival at such-and-such church. Something exciting must be happening there." We should ask ourselves why the unchurched public should be interested in this event. Then write a press release to answer that question.

Many radio station employees are very busy; it's a good idea to provide for them a press release with taped quotes. Sometimes I will send in a press release and will have one of my staff members take a recording so the station's time can be saved. But the first time you do a press release, do not show up with the tape and the written material. Instead, offer to put a recording together that the station can listen to. After listening to this recording, they can make their decision on whether to air the material.

For television, a press release with visual imagery is required. For example, when we did construction work at our church, we showed tractors driving around; we had pictures of people doing construction. We specifically included shots of teenagers doing work. Give the media visual imagery that is interesting to them. Give the press release visual imagery.

With newspapers, you are dealing with verbal imagery. Many newspapers are eager to print local stories. Give the local newspaper the press release and include a picture. Avoid the religion section. The only people who read the religion section are Christians, and your plan is to reach non-Christians.

When we were planting Millcreek Community Church, we found out that the day we were opening, the oldest church in Erie County was closing. This was a newsworthy story. We met with the pastor of this Presbyterian church and said, "We could really honor God in the midst of these events. Would you consider helping us put a story together?"

The plan was simple. I said, "Let's transfer some of the assets of your church to our church." We did not request anything that was of great value. We asked that they give us a Bible holder and some offering plates. We collaborated on a press release and got some of our members involved in the event. The headline read, "Oldest Church Helps Newest Church Get Started." (You can see the article at www.newchurches.com). It turned out to be the lead story on the front page of the local newspaper. This event helped us raise top-of-mind awareness.

The Right Contacts

Be sure to get the news director's name and fax number at the local radio station, television station, and newspaper office. Use these names and numbers to be certain that the right person receives your story. In addition, send the press release a week before the event. Keep in mind that newsrooms are very busy places. Sometimes things that were meant to be published get lost, delayed, or never published at all. With this in mind, contact the news director two days before the event and say, "Hey, did you receive so-and-so?" I have made calls such as this in both a large city (Buffalo) and a mid-sized city (Erie), and I have never found anyone to be irritated by my follow-up call.

If you are told that they are too busy to publish your story, always respond positively and assure the media that you will plan to contact them the next time you have a newsworthy event. A cooperative and positive attitude will help you get good news coverage.

Interviews

Being prepared for an interview is an important but simple process. Generally, you should prepare and memorize a two-sentence summary about what the church is doing. This summary is called a "sound bite." Politicians are masters at this. This is an example of a sound bite that I memorized and used: "We're excited to be starting a new church for those who don't attend church. This will be a place where people unfamiliar with stained glass and pews will feel comfortable."

When I would say this, I would consciously eliminate the pause between the sentences. If you insert a pause, the editors might cut the sound bite when they produce the final product. Watch the news programs tonight. Almost everyone in a story has only one sentence to say. Although the reporter may spend an hour with the interviewee, only one sentence will be heard on the television or be quoted in the newspaper.

The sound bite is your theme. Get your theme across while sounding professional. Speak naturally but without pause. If a camera is present, do not look at the camera while you are speaking; look at the reporter. Do not try to copy what you see on television.

Dress appropriately for the context. If you are doing a sports clinic story, do not show up in a suit and tie. If you are doing construction of the church, wear a tool belt. Always be among the people. If you are going to be on camera, try to have an appropriate backdrop. If you are starting a church that is meeting in a theater, do the story in front of the theater. If you are conducting a construction project, do the story in front of where the construction is going on. Reporters and photographers are often open to background suggestions.

Miscellaneous Issues

When the interviewer arrives, provide him or her with a copy of the press release so he will be familiar with what you are doing. Sometimes you will be interviewed by an intern who has not yet received the press release that you sent to the studio or office.

Try to build a relationship with the newspaper editor. Sometimes the editor will be very helpful in getting your information out of the religion section. I spoke with one editor who believed that many of the religious stories should be out of the religion ghetto. He wanted his stories on the front page of the paper, and we were glad to work with him to make that happen.

Utilize free sources like public service announcements, local cable stations, and the community calendar of Christian radio. Some committed believers work for media sources. Contact area churches about possible press contacts. Try to find where these people work, and ask them for assistance.

Conclusion

Someone is going to be on the news; it might as well be you. When people hear good news about your church—what it is doing, who it is serving, how it is growing—they are more likely to remember your church when they are at a point of spiritual need. You have helped create top-of-mind awareness—a seed that the Holy Spirit can bring to fruition at the right time.

Resources for Further Reading

Shawchuck, Norman. *Marketing for Congregations: Choosing to Serve People More Effectively.* Nashville: Abingdon Press, 1992.

Barna, George. *A Step-by-Step Guide to Church Marketing: Breaking Ground for the Harvest.* Ventura, Calif.: Regal Books, 1992.

CHAPTER TWENTY-THREE

The Launch—Birth of a New Church

Some planters put so much effort into the conception-prenatal period of planting that they fail to remember the importance of the actual birth *day*. This chapter outlines the final days immediately before birth and the day of the launch. We will also consider a few matters related to the first days of new church life after launch day.

Pre-Birth Announcements: Advertising the Launch

There are several different ways to tell the community that a new church is about to be launched. Some people have compared the prelaunch period to a pregnancy. The vision for the new church is the conception. The pre-launch growth of the new church is the prenatal period. The birth is the launch day.

Advertising is a proven means for reaching large numbers of people in a limited amount of time. Effective advertising can generate a large attendance, but it can also break a budget. Church planters may choose from a number of options when advertising the birth of the new church. Following are some of the best-known advertising options.

Direct Mail

Aubrey Malphurs notes the two most effective ways to gather a crowd are direct mail and telemarketing.[1] While telemarketing is used much less frequently today, direct mail is very common and the most cost-effective. In a recent focus group of seven church planters from across Canada and the United States,[2] I asked for their thoughts on direct mail. Three of the planters ranked direct mail as their most effective outreach tool, two thought it was moderately effective, and two thought it was ineffective in their context. Direct mail is working—but not everywhere.

I was surprised at where direct mail was working. Many churches are using direct mail and having success. This surprised me because many discard the idea—yet many others are still using it as a tool to reach postmoderns. The key question is, Will it work among my focus group? Consider some direct-mail strategies that church planters are using.

Single mass mailing. An invitation letter is the most widely used one-time mailing. This type of letter is most effective when the letter identifies the needs of the focus group and addresses those particular needs. The letter should express enthusiasm and excitement for the future of the new church, the readers, and those who become involved in the new congregation.[3] The letter must anticipate and overcome the reader's concerns about church and spiritual matters. It should help the reader put aside fears that surface at the mention of "church." It should be understandable and completely free of theological and church terms as well as grammatical errors. As recipients finish reading the letter, they should feel energized and ready to attend the new church.

Examples of different types of church planting mailers can be found at www.new-churches.com/example. Church planters wanting to share their own example mailers may do so there.

Double mailing. Some churches have found it more effective to do two mailings—one ten days before the first service and one five days before. The impact of the mailer is multiplied, and the message is reinforced with two mailers.

Multiple mailings. When it comes to advertising, more is usually better. Some churches have sent five or more mailers to the same area to reinforce the message of the new church, but more mailers cost more money. Those wishing to start with a big first service generally find that the single mailing does not produce the best results.

Telemarketing

Even today, the second most widely used method for initiating contacts is telemarketing. This methodology must not be thought of as merely making phone calls. Rather, it is part of a combined phone-and-mail strategy.

Norm Whan explained, "Over 30,000 churches have used 'The Phone's for You!' kit to plant or grow their churches since 1985. The program works better today than ever before."[4]

Another option is an automated call system like Tellstart. The ministry, a part of Southside Community Church, explains:

TellStart is a program whereby we telephone up to 50,000 homes per day on your behalf, seeking interested people for your church. . . . Essentially, we take about five seconds and ask if the person answering the phone would be interested in a new (or re-focusing) church in the area. . . .

If they press #1 they are given an additional one-minute message containing details about your church. At the close of this section they are invited to leave their name and address for follow-up and more detailed information. Those who have left their names after the tone are prospects for your church.[5]

However, my impression is that telemarketing is becoming less effective over time. Caller ID and unlisted numbers may mean that this strategy will eventually become less and less helpful. Furthermore, more people are reacting negatively to unsolicited phone calls. However, that time is not *yet* here. Telemarketing *still* works. It can help jump-start the process to making relationships with the unchurched.

If telemarketing was unproductive and fruitless, business marketers would stop using the methodology. Those called may not respond every time, but they are much more likely to respond if they perceive a personal need for the "product," in this case, a church, offered by the telemarketer. This method can reach a husband and wife who recently discussed returning to active church life. It can stir to life the individual whose interest in spiritual matters has grown because of watching a Billy Graham television event. Marketers cannot reach everyone every time, but they *do* reach someone every day.

Millcreek Community Church's 55,000 dial-ups before the launch service helped develop a list of 2,151 persons who agreed to receive more information. From that list, more than two hundred people in addition to our core group attended the first service. At the time, we were the largest Southern Baptist launch service in history in the northeastern United States.

Telemarketing served as a superb resource—a major reason Millcreek Community Church became a church-starting success.

The most obvious objection is to the telemarketing itself. But one church planter described the results as follows:

> When people comment on (telemarketing), they frequently say that it will not work in my area because people are adverse to telemarketing. . . . I held the same opinion. I hate telemarketers—though Jesus tells us to love our enemies. However, after a lot of prayer, I felt God calling us to use the phones for your strategy. We made over 13,000 phone calls and ended up with 330 people at our launch.
>
> I found that while people were negative toward telemarketing, they were excited to have a phone call from a new church. We only had one truly negative response out of 13,000 dial-ups. Because all of our phone numbers were newly assigned, they either did not identify the caller on people's caller ID's or people were just curious. Frequently, we had people get our number off their caller ID and call us back to see what we wanted. Go figure![6]

The Phone's for You. The best-known procedure for telemarketing was designed by Norm Whan. He created The Phone's for You! Whan designed his excellent resource on a marketing formula assuming a 10 percent positive response. A caller making 20,000 phone calls would identify about 2,000 persons willing to receive more information about a new church. Over 1,200 churches used the program in 2002.[7]

After calling, mail. After collecting the needed information, the church sends a series of five mailers to the 2,000 respondents. Whan discovered that typically 10 percent of the original pool of positive respondents respond positively to mailers and attend the first service of the church.[8] Since these figures vary somewhat from place to place, Whan developed a test instrument of 1,000 calls in order to help telemarketers project the predictable response in any given market.

Telemarketers' target. Church planters who use telemarketing are looking for people who are not involved in church. Their sample question in some way asks whether the person is "actively involved in church." In some areas of North America that are influenced heavily by cults or sects, the sample questions could be modified to: "Are you actively involved in a church *that teaches the Bible?*" The caller's question should be contextualized to the area.

Next step. The telemarketer's second question, if the first generates interest, is, "May we send you information about a new church that will be starting in the area this fall?" The vast majority of people will decline. Of those who say yes, about 10 percent will remain sufficiently open and actually attend the church's first service.

Telemarketing is not for everyone. In some communities, it may even cause the church's reputation to suffer. But it has worked in many locations and continues to be used widely.

Preview Services

The preview service is a new method. It usually consists of a series of monthly meetings just before the first official service of the new church. It allows many people to be exposed to the new church while gradually increasing the size of the attendance that will show up at the first official service. Be cautious not to do such a large mailing for the first preview service that there are two hundred in attendance at a preview service and then only one hundred present at the first official service. This shift in size becomes anticlimactic, and the momentum will be lost.

Do not have more than three preview services before the launch. People soon begin to get impatient and want to start regular services. The preview services also give the group an opportunity to try out the worship leadership. Tell the people who are present, "We are glad you are here for this service. This is the first time we've been together, so everything might not be perfect." The worship team is allowed some slack to make some mistakes that are generally not permitted after the launch service. Many churches have found this a successful method of core building through existing relationships.

E-mail

E-mail is a controversial method. Just as people receive junk mail at home, junk E-mail can be sent to the inbox on a computer. This type of unsolicited E-mail is called "spam" and is the equivalent of Internet direct mail. Every day pornography and "get-rich-quick" schemes are sent out to random E-mail accounts. But the world is already using the Internet—and the Internet is ripe for the gospel of Jesus Christ to be proclaimed via E-mail methods.

No matter what approach is used, complaints should be expected. When we used the telemarketing approach, we were amazed at the number of people who were using *69 and calling us back wanting to know who we were and why we called. If you use a postage-paid return address card, there will be responses that do not always glorify the Lord. Some people will believe you are interfering because to them their faith is a private matter.

Some church planters have decided to avoid all methods of mass outreach. They reason that a postmodern world is now relational and that all forms of outreach will be received negatively. This has not been my observation. The only postmoderns I have seen offended by mass outreach are Christians who have determined it worldly or lacking authenticity. Spiritually seeking postmoderns are generally not offended by outreach.

Statistical evidence supports that new churches utilizing a big-launch method are larger than those that do not. Although the difference is not as significant as I expected, those who use a "large first meeting" to start their church do evidence a larger attendance in the second through fourth years:

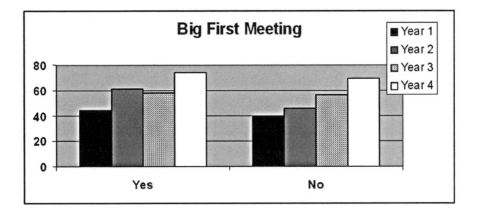

Some Approaches to Avoid

I usually do not encourage church planters to use the newspaper. It covers too broad an area for a local church in most cases. Newspaper ads are also expensive. Local and ethnic papers of small towns may be exceptions to this rule. If you do use the newspaper, make sure the ad is eye-catching.

I also usually discourage the use of radio. Radio touches an audience that is too broad. When the audience is too broad, you do not reach your target. If you decide to use radio, make sure you do so through a station that uses the musical style to which your church is accustomed or the style your church will use when it launches. For example, do not advertise on a classical station unless there will be classical music in the worship services.

Billboards are another media source generally to be avoided. They are too expensive for the amount of return they yield. People who have used this method tend to put up an eye-catching billboard with a countdown to the first service. When Big Sky Church[9] used a billboard, they placed a big invitation with a note advertising their launch Sunday.

A major problem with billboards is that they are so common they often go unnoticed. The only billboards people really look at are those that catch the eye. So if you use billboards, make sure they are eye-catching.

Television time is also extremely expensive. Cable access is one possible exception. Advertising on one of those thirty-minute cable access programs where someone sits in a chair with a Bible and preaches are not effective in church planting. Some cable access channels do sell local time on CNN, MSNBC, and FOX news. Local ads on national networks may work.

Gathering the Large Group

The point of using any of these methods is to gather a large group. You need to gather a group so you can move from one stage to another. No matter the number of people you begin with, when you go public with the worship service, make it an important event. Have the core people invite all their friends. Tell the core group that is assisting in the church plant, "We are starting a new church. Let's bring all our friends. Let's focus together and see what God can do in this new church." The launch might attract thirty people or three hundred. Either way, make sure you use your methodology wisely.

The Launch Event

Most new churches today start with a "large launch." The core group works to attract a large number of people for the first public worship service. Getting unchurched people to come is one task; helping them feel comfortable about being there is another matter.

Seven out of ten people in attendance at the launch service are typically unbelievers without church experience. Two out of ten may be churched, but they do not know anyone at this church. It is a challenge to create an atmosphere that will break down anxiety and stimulate the desire of the attendees to hear of and experience God's presence.

I encourage church planters not to launch with a crowd more than ten times the size of their core group. A core of twenty should not plan for a first service of over two hundred. I call this the crowd-to-core ratio. If a core of ten launches with more than three hundred people, the core is frequently overwhelmed because there are not enough workers for music, child care, assimilation, etc. New churches should plan their launch service to match an adequate core group.

Conclusion

Planting a church eventually involves a public worship experience. Church planters have learned that a public launch is often most effective. But such a launch requires efficient planning and quality execution. The kingdom of God is to be built up in a strategic and biblical manner.

The church's worship must not alienate unbelievers but lead them to Christ. We will explore this topic in the following chapter.

Resources for Further Reading

Chaney, Charles L. *Church Planting at the End of the Twentieth Century.* Wheaton: Tyndale House, 1991.

Logan, Robert. *Church Planter's Tool Kit.* St. Charles, Ill.: ChurchSmart Resources, 1991.

Rainer, Thom S. *Surprising Insights from the Unchurched.* Grand Rapids: Zondervan, 2001.

CHAPTER TWENTY-FOUR

Worship in the New Church

*T*he purpose of church planting is to begin a church that gathers to praise God in corporate worship. We are planting a *church*. By definition, churches are "people of worship," but writing about worship is like talking about driving. Everybody does it and thinks they do it best.

Much has been written about worship in recent years. Worship authorities debate the "right" musical styles for worship. Seeker sensitivity has spawned controversy. Many committed believers question what forms are appropriate in the worship setting.

Some believers believe worship has been given to Christians only. They reason that the church should gather for worship and Bible teaching. The people will be built up spiritually and go out and evangelize. This notion is incomplete. The church and its worship are not intended solely for believers. We are called to please God. This includes the edification of believers, but the true purpose of the church is as broad as the purposes of God. It is the *missio Dei*—the mission of God. It includes all that God includes—because we are an extension of his work in the world. The *missio Dei* includes worship but evangelism, ministry, encouragement, and pastoral care as well.

Some church attendees are being drawn to Christ and are "called" but have not yet committed to Christ. The Bible refers to the church as the *ekklesia*—those "called out ones" who have made a commitment to follow Christ. When the called are brought together, the planter must present God's message in such a way that it challenges believers and also encourages unbelievers toward commitment.

Hundreds of years after the birth of the church, Augustine still lamented the impossibility of separating the wheat (faithful) from the tares (unbelieving). His implication is plain: in this church age, the unchurched and Christians will always coexist in the local congregation. If this were not true, why would Paul have to write the Corinthians about what unbelievers think when they enter the worship service? (see 1 Cor. 14).

The purpose of the worship service is not just to arouse attendees' passions to hear preaching. The true objective is to enable believers to encounter God in worship and the Word. The purpose of worship is also to allow unbelievers to observe the divine-human encounter and to yearn for their own personal relationship with God.

Congregations such as Willow Creek Community Church believe that their seeker service prepares seekers for the presentation of the gospel message. This argument rests upon their strategy for reaching the unchurched population through large group meetings. Going to Willow Creek on Sunday morning is the equivalent of going to an evangelistic crusade. It is not intended for the worship and edification of believers. The worship and edification of believers occurs at the midweek "new community" service.

Much of the criticism directed at the seeker-driven church is a result of the misunderstanding of their strategy. In seeker-driven churches, Sunday morning is not supposed to look like church. It is designed to be an ongoing evangelistic service. A student who visited Willow Creek with me commented that the service looked like a Young Life meeting—a low-key evangelistic service with an opportunity for those who attend to go deeper at another time. The strategy has worked for Willow Creek, but it is not one I embrace for theological reasons.

Instead of focusing on a seeker-driven worship service, it is better to ask why the church exists—and then to ask questions about the content of the worship service. Churches should exalt God, edify believers, and evangelize the world.[1] Worship services, first and foremost, should exalt God. This statement underscores the imperative of God-centered worship. Believers should also be built up in the faith. Finally, authentic worship can evangelize unbelievers.

Believers who assert that the church is intended only for Christians assume continued preaching to believers will mature them to the point where they will evangelize the unchurched. I have yet to see this happen. Churches that are not *intentionally* evangelistic do not *become* evangelistic through quality Bible teaching *alone.*

When the church exists for feeding believers *only,* those believers become spiritual sponges that absorb more and more knowledge. If those sponges do nothing but soak in a pool of their own learning, they eventually sour. An unchurched person can hardly feel welcome in such a setting.

God-Centered Worship

The challenge is to create an atmosphere for worship that is appropriate for both believers and unbelievers. The worship service should be God-centered or even God-*driven.* Unchurched persons benefit from seeing believers enter the presence of God. Sally Morgenthaler's book, *Worship Evangelism,* is an excellent resource for this type of worship experience.[2] Churches should recognize that the unchurched need to experience the presence of Jesus—not because they *are* Christians, but because they are *around* Christians. They need to see Christians worship God.

Seeker-Sensitive Worship

The primary means for creating a welcoming atmosphere for unbelievers is designing worship that is sensitive to the needs of unbelievers. This sensitivity can build bridges to the unchurched by beginning where they are.

Seeker-sensitive, not seeker-driven. Churches must center themselves on the worship of God and the proclamation of his Word while also being in tune with the needs of seekers. The need to reach seekers must not take the place of Christ-centered, Bible-based, Spirit-led values. In order to reach unbelievers, effective churches must become seeker-*sensitive.* The place to begin expressing this caring openness is the church's public worship service.

Evangelism through worship. One of the most effective evangelistic methods a church can use is exposing the unchurched to the authentic worship of God. Unbelievers learn worship as they witness the worship of believers. Seeker-sensitive worship gatherings create an experience of both "God-centrality" and openness toward the needs of seekers. Seeker-sensitive worship is a gathering that offers God honor—through worship and the preaching of the Scriptures—while providing a relevant atmosphere in which unbelievers are challenged to come to saving faith in Christ.

Seeker-*sensitive* and seeker-*driven* worship gatherings are not the same. Seeker-sensitive worship asks, How can we make the unbeliever understand and feel as comfortable as possible in this context? We must remember that the unbeliever *cannot* be made completely comfortable because the cross is not seeker-sensitive, but the message of the cross still contains Good News. Seeker sensitivity asks how to conduct worship and to communicate convictions in ways that welcome outsiders, yet simultaneously honor God, his Word, his directives, and Christian practices.

Every church is seeker-sensitive to some degree. If we are worshiping in the local language, wearing local clothing, and singing music written in the last one thousand years, we are using a worship style that is sensitive to those who attend. (The pre-Vatican II Roman Catholic Church was a good example of a truly non-seeker-sensitive church. They worshiped in Latin regardless of the location.)

The real question is to what *degree* we will be seeker-sensitive. Will the church explain what the song means? Will the church tell when everyone will stand? Will the church demonstrate how to take the Lord's Supper? Will the church avoid the use of confusing language? Every church has seeker-sensitive worship—but how sensitive is it?

An Atmosphere of Acceptance

Part of a church's task of sensitivity toward unbelievers is simply making them feel wanted and welcomed. Many pastors preach "How to Be Friendly" messages to their congregations. Creating an atmosphere of acceptance is not as easy as one might think, because unbelievers and the unchurched do not act or live like Christians.

Acceptance is not approval. Accepting people without approving of their lifestyles can be very challenging. While loving people, we must be careful not to appear to approve or condone their un-Christian behavior. Leading such people to life-changing discipleship is not likely to occur unless they hear the claims of Christ during a worship event. The church must allow unchurched persons who are living in sinful lifestyles to enter and hear. These persons will not disrupt the well-being of the congregation or taint the saints.

Here we stand. The church's stand on holiness should emerge at the point of church membership. Allowing sin to go unchecked among *members* is fundamentally different from welcoming the unchurched to a worship service.

The church must make clear that anyone may come and find acceptance, no matter their lifestyle. But coming to Christ and becoming his disciple requires a life change. Christ expects change, and the church should expect change. Part of the congregation's commitment to new members must be to ensure that members' lives mature in Christ. Congregational integrity demands such accountability. The church should love unbelievers as Jesus loved them, but it should also call members to life-changing discipleship, just as Jesus did.

Meeting Spiritual Needs in Worship

Needs of believers and unbelievers are often similar. Christians suffer from the same rate of divorce as non-Christians. Christians face the same rate of emotional breakdown as unbelievers. Christians and non-Christians alike need help with parenting, finances, and priorities. God's Word applies to all in need. God's Word relates to all kinds of life issues. The church must proclaim God's Word to unbelievers in such a way that they are encouraged to take new directions in life. Making the scriptural and musical messages understandable aids this transformation process.

Make the music clear. We must never underestimate the power of music to transform lives. For many people, music can touch the heart in a way that preaching cannot. Since music has an intense power in the formation of the human spirit and in the transmission of truth, we must ensure that the worship songs are theologically sound and worship-appropriate.

Music should relieve anxiety and create interest for unbelievers who have not attended church for years. When people enter, they have no idea what is about to take place. Spiritually empowered music can relieve their anxieties and stir their hearts to hear God's voice.

During our second service at Millcreek Community Church, we sang a song titled "The Lord Reigns." It is a great song, but the chorus can confuse the unchurched. The lyrics read, "A fire goes before him and burns up all his enemies. The hills melt like wax at the presence of the Lord."[3] We needed to explain those words to those in attendance in order to make the lyrics understandable to the unchurched.

From oral to visual. Our culture changed from oral to visual orientation with the advent of television half a century ago. Younger people are even more visual than their parents are. In order to secure and hold their attention, churches should consider using audiovisual equipment.

Electronic aids. Electronic communication through overheads, PowerPoint presentations, and video clips also enriches worship. At the very least, the church should print the morning's Scripture texts and provide a fill-in-the-blank outline to help listeners stay engaged as the preacher presents the information using an overhead projector.

Consider preaching a series. Besides the use of electronic and written resources, another way to help listeners stay engaged is to develop a thematic series for preaching. These plans will help unbelievers and young believers alike build a body of knowledge that will serve as a foundation for their faith development for the rest of their lives. Preaching is God's chosen method for communicating the Word of God. Effective preachers will use multiple approaches to give their preaching the greatest possible impact. (See chapter 25 for an in-depth treatment of preaching in the new church.)

Consider language and behaviors. The typical evangelical church often demonstrates confusing activities: everyone suddenly stands and shakes other persons' hands on cue, everyone contributes an offering, and people walk down the aisle after the sermon. The unchurched guest, given no explanation, may find these actions strange and uncomfortable.

Aubrey Malphurs says it well: "Rather than attracting new people *to* Christ, many worship services are distracting them *from* Christ."[4] Church planters should remain sensitive to the concerns of the unchurched. If we consider visitors as guests, then we should treat them as guests. We must be careful to explain everything that could cause confusion in their minds.

Music

If church planting is missionary work, then the church planter and the planting team should think like missionaries in planning worship music. Leaders should choose the music based on the context. Music should be missiological ("like a missionary") and serviceable in the context.

Early Hawaiian missionaries failed miserably in this regard.[5] When they arrived on the islands, they had the islanders dress in Western clothing, and they taught them European music and hymns. These insensitive activities limited missionary effectiveness for that time and, perhaps, for all time among the indigenous people of Hawaii.

Although members of liturgical churches in colonial North America enjoyed stately English hymns, persons of lower station neither liked nor understood them. One creative missionary along the frontier adapted a tavern tune to tell the gospel story in response to that reality. The church then learned the good news from the lyrics of "Amazing Grace, How Sweet the Sound."[6] Contextual music is always better, but we must remember that songs that were clear one hundred years ago may not be understandable to many people today.

The sensitivities expected of international missionaries should compel North American church planters who also work in pluralistic cultures. Planters and team members should select worship music that is culturally appropriate for their specific context.

One way to determine the music is to know your focus group. What is their favorite musical style? This can be determined by listening to popular radio stations or looking at a local music shop in a culturally creative neighborhood.

Once we have determined their preferred musical style, wisdom calls us to adapt our own tunes and style to the preferred style of our focus group. Just like the frontier evangelist who adapted the tune of "Amazing Grace," we must also write or adapt Christian lyrics suitable to that particular style. As the frontier evangelist might have said, "There is no such thing as Christian music, only Christian *lyrics*." Adapt the unchanging gospel to a changing musical style.

Statistical evidence supports the fact that worship style does impact church size. When comparing six styles and looking at attendance over four years, contemporary and seeker churches tend to be larger than the other worship styles:

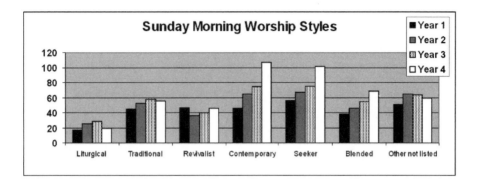

The Enduring Struggles

The church planter must decide whether to think like a missionary, or to be compelled by the values of supporters and what they want the planter to do. An effective church planter needs to demonstrate a great concern for gospel expressions that relate to unchurched people. Effective missionaries do not ask the focus group what the content of their preaching and music should be; they ask what vehicles—preaching style and music style of the focus group—will change the most lives in the most effective way.

If the style of music or preaching overwhelms the message, the missionary-church planter is making a serious mistake. Worship requires words—words of truth. The vehicle—music, style of proclamation, and so forth—must edify Christians and encourage the unchurched to consider Christ.

Conclusion

Worship should touch the heart and the mind. It should be cognitive, touching the brain like the kenotic hymn of Philippians 2; it should be affective, stirring the emotions like the Psalms. We need both experiences in new churches today.

Not every service has to include both elements. These elements should receive attention in order to touch and change the lives of your focus group. Every worship time, regardless of stylistic content, should emerge from the leadership of God and rest solely on his Word. True worship must be both *God-centered* and *seeker-sensitive*.

Resources for Further Reading

Blount, Ken. *What Jesus Taught About Praise & Worship*. Tulsa, Okla.: Harrison House, 2000.

Morgenthaler, Sally. *Worship Evangelism: Inviting Unbelievers into the Presence of God*. Grand Rapids: Zondervan Publishing House, 1995.

Shelley, Marshall, general ed. *Changing Lives Through Preaching & Worship*. Nashville: Moorings, 1995.

Sorge, Bob. *Exploring Worship: A Practical Guide to Praise & Worship*. Canandaigua, N.Y.: Oasis House, 1987.

CHAPTER TWENTY-FIVE

Preaching in the New Church

*P*reaching should both edify believers and encourage nonbelievers. We must grow in our preaching skills if we cannot do both. While Jesus preached a straightforward gospel, he demonstrated that preaching is not just opening the Bible, reading words, and providing a commentary.

Preaching should be simple but not simplistic. The Scriptures are given not only for information but also for *transformation*. The preacher may impress listeners with arcane theological truths that offer no life and hope, or the preacher may help transform lives with the truths of Christ's life-changing presence. The latter result is God's intention for Christian preaching.

Relational Truth Preaching

Hershael York[1] advocates moving listeners from *felt* needs to *real* needs during the preaching event. In planning a sermon series on the lordship of Christ to be presented to a weekly business luncheon, York estimated that 40 percent of those attending would be either unbelievers or uncommitted believers. He promoted his sermon series as a study on time management, but he actually designed the series to address the underlying issue of the lordship of Christ, who can reorder personal priorities, including the best use of time.

Unchurched people often cannot recognize their *real* personal needs, so the preacher must explain those needs and allow the biblical text to *meet* those real needs. York calls this process "moving from felt needs to real needs."

In a seeker-sensitive message, the preacher begins with relational truths and moves toward the presentation of theological truths. The church planter may wish to address, for example, Bible teachings about stress and worry. Rather than approaching the text with preconceived ideas, the church planter should research Scriptures related to these topics and allow the text to set the tone and content of the message. After completing this research, the planter would design a message or a series of messages that present God's truth on those topics.

The seeker-sensitive service usually does not focus with intensity on theological truths without application. When the Bible presents theological truth, it almost always weds that revelation to relational application. The high kenotic hymn in Philippians 2:6 says this about Christ: "Who, being in very God, did not consider equality with God something to be grasped." This is theological material, but it is important to remember how the hymn begins: "Have this attitude in yourselves which is also in Christ Jesus." Any presentation of the theological truths (about the pre-existence of Christ, etc.), needs to include practical application (about how our attitude is to be changed by Christ's example).

Listeners need a time for hearing technical theological truths because they serve as foundations for life changes. The seeker-sensitive service is not the best time to do this. The seeker-sensitive service aims not at theological lessons alone but at biblical truth leading to life application—a change of attitude, feeling, or commitment.

Expositional Preaching

All biblical preaching should be expositional preaching. *Expository* means a presentation of the meaning or intent. All true preaching explains the meaning and intent of the Bible. This does not necessarily mean that preaching has to be a verse-by-verse study of the Bible. It does mean that it has to convey accurately the meaning and intent of the Bible.

The unmistakable admonition of 2 Timothy 4:2–4 is, "Preach the Word." These verses do not commend personal opinions, nor do they validate fads. Paul's directive to Timothy was, "Preach the Word."

Scripture-based preaching is not always popular. Unchurched people and believers yet to define their biblical values clearly often take offense at the preaching of the cross. Such thinking may create friction between the pastor and unchurched people. The church planter, nevertheless, has been called to "preach the Word; be prepared in season and out of season; correct, rebuke and encourage—with great patience and careful instruction" (2 Tim. 4:2). The church planter must allow the text to set the agenda and to address the issues.

It has been interesting to be a part of, and now an observer of, the church growth movement of the 1980s and 1990s. Some people taught cultural truths with scriptural footnoting. They would describe some universal truth (you should be good to your spouse, for example), and then explain that the Bible agrees. In the last few years, such preaching seems to be less common. Increasingly new churches that are reaching postmoderns are saying, "This is what the Bible says, and this is how to apply it. We are trying our best to apply it in our lives, and you can too." I think that is good news.

On the other hand, there seems to be a significant minority who say that all preaching needs to be verse-by-verse. For some people, expositional preaching has become synonymous with verse-by-verse preaching. This causes some to argue that verse-by-verse exposition is the only valid form of preaching. Were this the case, the early church heard no preaching at all for at least 350 years, until the time of John Chrysostom, who popularized this form.

For the purposes of this book, I will define expository preaching as "proclamation that exposes people to the truths of God's Word." Albert Mohler asserts, "For a sermon to be genuinely biblical, the text must set the agenda as the foundation of the message, and not as a spiritual authority cited for spiritual footnoting. Scripture should be central."[2] Expositional preaching does not make statements and look to the Bible for support; it begins by examining the Scriptures.

Although much criticism of seeker-sensitive preaching has arisen from misunderstandings, some new churches *have* abandoned biblically based, expositional preaching. The Bible is *not* their sermon text; it barely *impacts* their sermon text.

I have seen too many churches advocate subtly that winning people to Christ necessitates laying aside the Bible. One pastor in a Bible Belt state explained his strategy as having people attend a "little pep talk" each Sunday morning in order to offer them encouragement and then send them home. That church has shortened its service time to a maximum of forty-five minutes. The end results will be disastrous if the pastor-planter does not preach the Word. The pastor-planter *must* preach the Word.

Four Kinds of Expositional Preaching

There are many different kinds of expositional preaching. The four most common are: verse-by-verse, thematic, narrative, and topical.

Verse-by-Verse Preaching

Verse-by-verse preaching is the systematic reading and explanation of a biblical text. In involves a unified book of Scripture and its piece-by-piece analysis. Mars Hill Church[3] in Seattle is a well-known church that is effectively reaching postmoderns. The church Web site explains, "The beginning, the end, and everything in between. The Bible defines Mars Hill."[4] The site lists recent messages from Pastor Mark Driscoll and other teaching pastors including text and MP3 files of each message. Recent messages include studies of Song of Solomon, Romans, Jonah, and other Scripture texts.

Thematic Expository (or Doctrinal) Preaching

Thematic preaching is an excellent form for preaching Bible doctrine. The speaker can focus on everyday topics by expounding a specific biblical text. The pastor can focus on Bible sayings on any relevant subject by a careful study and exposition of relevant biblical passages.

Thematic expository preaching generally appears in a sermon series over several weeks and introduces many Scriptures focused on the same theme. Thematic messages may include as many as ten or twelve Scripture passages in each sermon. Since the Bible tends to provide teachings on themes dispersed through different books, this form of preaching is a good way to preach the "whole counsel of God." This method also introduces new believers or unschooled unbelievers to general themes and patterns that appear throughout the Bible.

Narrative Expository Preaching

Narrative preaching presents the biblical text in the form of story and follows that story to completion. A narrative sermon functions as a lengthy illustration that uses a biblical text as its beginning and end.

When using this form, the speaker shares a story from the gospel such as that found in the account of Jesus and the Samaritan woman (John 4). In telling the story, the preacher asks the listener to join in the narrative. As a result, the listener sees the fullness of Jesus' words and teachings. This type of expository preaching can be highly effective in postmodern North American culture, which has rejected most of our traditional approaches.

Some time ago, I discovered the value of narrative preaching during a church-starting crusade in West Africa. Although I believed I had preached a great message on the first night of a crusade, I found that the nationals had not connected with my verse-by-verse exposition of Luke 14.

On the second night, I adapted my style to use narrative exposition of the Nicodemus story from John 3. Those in attendance responded to the unfolding story with enthusiastic applause at key points. Their excitement grew. When I told of Nicodemus's presence at the foot of Jesus' cross, the crowd exploded with joy. Many responded to the gospel invitation that night. Over one hundred attended the first service of the new church.

Narrative preaching will grow more popular in the coming years. This is good news as long as the narratives remain consistent with biblical texts. Jesus demonstrated the value of narrative preaching by his use of parables.

Topical Expository Preaching

Of the four forms of exposition, I recommend this form the least. Its weakness grows out of the limits of time and the speaker's inability to include enough biblical text about the topic in one sermon. Although I discourage this form, it is helpful at times.

Topical exposition generally revolves around one passage, centering on one theme. It is topical because it is usually a single message on a single subject. It is expository because it uses the biblical text as its source.

Most preachers use this form on special occasions such as Mother's Day, Father's Day, and Easter, but topical preaching does not provide adequate time to address the whole counsel of God as other methods do. Topical preaching limits opportunities for presenting proper understandings of the context as opposed to verse-by-verse preaching. In addition, the topical approach does not offer the opportunity to use the graphic and powerful images of narrative preaching. The church planter will probably use topical exposition, but it should be used sparingly.

Application

Any good message starts with the primary question: what is the purpose of the sermon?[5] If people find the purpose interesting, they will listen. Pastors often do not answer the questions that people ask. The pastor may be preaching on the benefits of the Old Testament law while a woman in the pew is wondering if her marriage will last. The pastor may be explaining the importance of the chiasm in Philippians while a husband is considering an adulterous relationship.

The pastor needs to answer the questions that people are asking and answer them in a way that influences people's lives. The sermon should be biblically sound first—and then mnemonically effective, visually stimulating, and encouraging.

Mnemonically Effective

It has been my experience that the most effective sermons are those that are simple and easy to remember. Paul provides some examples. Pithy sayings can be very effective. Each of the following Scripture passages can be readily quoted:

"Bad company corrupts good character" (1 Cor. 15:33).

"For the letter kills, but the Spirit gives life" (2 Cor. 3:6).

"If a man will not work, he shall not eat" (2 Thess. 3:10).

"Don't you know that a little yeast works through the whole batch of dough?" (1 Cor. 5:6).

Visually Stimulating

Paul used illustrations from many sources, including athletics and the military.[6] These were appropriate because they were from the world in which he lived. Illustrations are essential. Good messages have memorable illustrations.[7]

Encouraging

Paul had no difficulty in appealing to the emotions of his hearers.[8] Chris Seay, now pastor of Ekklesia[9] in Houston, explained how he shared his struggles with honesty and transparency. He wanted to show others that they could make it if he could: "Basically my preaching style is to get up in front of them and say: 'This is where God "beat me up in the Word" this week and this is an area where I have sinned.'"[10]

Instead of trying to amaze congregations with the use of primary sources and exegetical methods, a wiser course is to share personal shortcomings and struggles through the text together.[11] This is where genuineness comes into play.

Paul was not considered a great orator. Much has been written about this topic, and it seemed to be a great weakness of the apostle Paul.[12] Delivery hardly seemed to be of great importance to the spread of the gospel. It was stated of him, "His letters are weighty and forceful, but in person he is unimpressive and his speaking amounts to nothing" (2 Cor. 10:10). But Paul's heart was always open. He derived his speaking authority from his genuineness and broken nature.

Shaped by the Listener

I remember sitting in a well-known church after a national tragedy. The pastor did not mention or address what was on everyone's mind—why did such things happen? Instead, he continued through his text as he had planned months before. He failed to take into account the needs of the listener.

The Scriptures model a different paradigm. For example, Paul varied his message depending on the needs and spiritual conditions of the listeners. The chart below illustrates his changing style:

TEXT	PLACE	AUDIENCE	APPROACH
Acts 13:15–41	Antioch of Pisidia	Interested Jews	Much history and Hebrew Scripture
Acts 14:15–17	Lystra	Idolaters	Nature is a bridge to the gospel
Acts 17:22–31	Athens	Educated philosophers	Quotes a Stoic poet and acknowledges their religious quest
Acts 22:3–21	Jerusalem	Mob of Jews	Gives a personal testimony

Conclusion

When a new church is launched, the messages will not tend to be as deep as they might be in the future. In the beginning stage of a new church, the sermons should be more like what Larry Moyer defines as an evangelistic sermon—a message with a sharper focus, an awareness of the biblical illiteracy of the audience, less work with the text, simple organizational structure, revealing of life, filled with illustrations, and humorous.[13] Good preaching in a new church will eventually evolve into a more thoroughly biblical, yet practical, preaching. Some have called this "life-situation preaching."[14]

We must not only stay immersed in the Word, but we also must study the culture in order to understand the people to whom we preach.[15] The most effective form of preaching to postmodern culture seems to be indicative induction.[16] This form of preaching lays out propositional truth, allowing the hearer to decide in a nonthreatening manner. We do not have to talk them into anything or convince them that the Bible makes sense; instead, we can share the Bible as authoritative and allow them to decide whether to accept it.

Calvin Miller explained that the purpose of the sermon is not education; it is encounter with God.[17] It is my hope to be able to lead people into that encounter while remaining faithful to the Word of God.

My desire is to be able to repeat the words of John Calvin: "I have not corrupted one single passage of Scripture, nor twisted it as far as I know. . . . I have always studied to be simple."[18] Preaching in a postmodern age, as in any age, needs to be biblical preaching. Styles of delivery should change, but we still must "preach the Word." It is good news that emerging postmodern congregations are rediscovering the value of biblical preaching.

There was a school of thought that emerged in the 1990s—in order to reach the lost you had to water down the biblical content. Ralph Moore explains:

> We at Hope Chapel sometimes take a little heat for our
> bibliocentric approach. One time a delegation from another
> congregation visited my church. As soon as I asked people to
> open their Bibles to the text for the evening, these people

began rolling their eyes and punching each other in the ribs. Later I discovered they were young pastors in training. They had been taught that it is not sensitive to the unchurched to use the Bible in church.[19]

If it is not clear by now, let me try to make it so. The only message you have is Christ and the Bible. Downplaying the prominence of that message for any reason is a dangerous compromise. You can reach out to the unchurched and still be honest about your message—and the Book that contains that message.

Resources for Further Reading

Anderson, Kenton C. *Preaching with Conviction: Connecting with Postmodern Listeners.* Grand Rapids: Kregel Publications, 2001.

McDowell, Josh. *The Disconnected Generation.* Nashville: Word Publishing, 2000. (This is a good resource to help understand the postmodern mind-set and can also be used for messages.)

Willard, Dallas. *The Divine Conspiracy: Rediscovering Our Hidden Life in God.* San Francisco: Harper & Row, 1998.

Sermon materials on the www.pastors.com Web site.

www.preachingplus.com

www.sermoncentral.com

CHAPTER TWENTY-SIX

Assimilation in the New Church

Church growth expert Win Arn lists eight characteristics of an "incorporated member." These characteristics not only describe a person successfully assimilated by a new church but also help the congregation develop methods for assimilation.

1. New members should be able to list at least seven new friends they have made in the church.
2. New members should be able to identify their spiritual gifts.
3. New members should be involved in at least one (preferably several) roles/tasks/ministries in the church, appropriate to their spiritual gifts.
4. New members should be actively involved in a small fellowship (face-to-face) group.
5. New members should demonstrate a regular financial commitment to the church.
6. New members should personally understand and identify with church goals.
7. New members should attend worship services regularly.
8. New members should identify unchurched friends and relatives and take specific steps to help them toward responsible church membership.[1]

Discipleship

At some point, the church planter must move beyond immediate follow-up to create an ongoing disciple-development program. Disciple development occurs through opportunities in which individuals consistently grow toward spiritual maturity.

Discipleship does not occur by accident. Jesus told his followers, "If you hold to my teaching, you are really my disciples. Then you will know the truth, and the truth will set you free" (John 8:31–32). Church planters are called to create *disciples,* not just *believers.* By definition, a disciple is a follower of Christ. A disciple is a learner.

A disciple is also a believer who practices biblical habits that enable him or her to live the Christian life effectively. A mature believer displays many behaviors or habits. These habits include prayer, sharing faith, Bible study, and fasting. The disciple must intentionally *practice* these habits in order to develop effectively as a disciple.

Many churchgoers and leaders assume that younger believers develop these habits because they hear about the need to practice them. Although this assumption is probably not true in an established congregation, it certainly does not apply in a new church. Habits leading to Christian maturity must be *practiced* in order for a disciple to become developed.

The effectiveness of the approach used in a new church for disciple making is much more important than the particular approach used. The important question is whether the church's approach produces maturing disciples. As long as the discipleship strategy is biblically based and God-focused and produces maturing believers, it is a serviceable disciple-making approach.

Part of the church planter's task is to create an atmosphere—a congregational culture—in which discipleship and disciple-making surface as core values.

Sequential Discipleship Plans

Probably the most common approach for new church discipleship is a L.I.F.E. class curriculum.[2] L.I.F.E. classes usually meet in a four-hour block or for one hour per week over a period of four weeks. Courses focus on specific aspects of the Christian life and the local church's ministry. Participants are encouraged to sign a covenant to practice the matters they have studied prior to the conclusion of each course.

101 and Beyond. The L.I.F.E. process of study begins with course 101. Class 101 focuses on the topics of salvation, the Lord's Supper, and baptism. Affiliated churches will also explain their denominational connection.

The class ends with a discussion of congregational vision, direction, future, and central values.

Disciplines of 201. The second class, course 201, focuses on several basic disciplines: Bible study, prayer, small-group *koinonia,* and tithing. At the close of 201, participants respond to a covenant opportunity to read the Bible regularly, to pray daily, to gather weekly with a small group of other believers, and to begin tithing.

301: Disciples Taking Shape. L.I.F.E. course 301 emphasizes each participant's calling to confirm his or her spiritual giftedness and to identify a ministry interest (calling) within the congregation. Most churches using L.I.F.E. classes use the Saddleback Church's gifts-assessment tool, S.H.A.P.E., discussed in chapter 6, an acronym that stands for:

- Spiritual gifts,
- Heart passion,
- Abilities,
- Personality type, and
- Experiences in life.

Since *every* believer has qualities identifiable in the S.H.A.P.E. profile, this profile enables new churches to determine the best place of ministry for each participant.

401 My Mission. The final 401 L.I.F.E. class focuses on evangelism and missions. Participants explore God's expectations—the implications of living their personal faith in the larger world outside the church. In keeping with this study and the discovery of their personal S.H.A.P.E. during course 301, members articulate their personal mission statements.

Examples of the L.I.F.E. classes from several churches can be found at www.new-churches.com/examples.

These L.I.F.E. classes center on four fundamentals: personal faith and church values; basic disciplines of the Christian life and small-group involvement; self-discovery of spiritual giftedness and ministry calling; and the development of a personal mission statement. Most churches modify them for their particular situation.

The next stage of training. Beyond these fundamental areas, every individual needs more individualized training. For example, parents might benefit from the study of *Parenting by Grace*.[3] Believers who are still grop-ing for God's direction for their involvement in his will may benefit from the discipleship course *Experiencing God*.

In one of my church plants, we continued to use the college course numbering system for this variety of discipleship studies and training opportunities. Since the 201 course emphasized Christian spiritual disci-plines, *Experiencing God,* which provided greater focus on these disciplines, was offered as another 200s course. Since we related 301 to dis-covering one's ministry, courses such as "How to Teach the Bible" fit into that same family and received a 300s course number.

The new church should first equip all members with the fundamentals in the four L.I.F.E. classes. Thereafter, the church will need to offer a bal-ance of other training opportunities based on members' perceived and actual needs. Progressive, creative planning throughout the disciple-making process will keep members motivated and excited and will reinforce the cli-mate for church discipleship and disciple making.

Discipleship by Environment

Some churches in a postmodern age are moving away from linear discipleship models. Instead, they are emphasizing opportunities for disciple-ship that are offered simultaneously or in a random order.

Northpoint Church[4] invites attendees to participate in three "environ-ments." They explain them as follows:

> foy•er (foĭ er, foi ya´) *n.* an entry.—It's the place in your
> home that serves as the welcome area for guests and new
> friends. It's the first step, and it's often your only chance to
> make your guests feel comfortable enough to return. That's
> exactly how we've designed our entry environments at North
> Point Community Church. Our Sunday morning worship
> services are "foyer" environments. We want our guests to
> come back, so we do everything with them in mind. Each
> area of our church also has its own foyer: middle school has
> Xtreme, high school has Rush Hour, families have KidStuf,
> and singles have 7:22. These environments are where most
> people will experience NPCC for the first time, and they

serve as the perfect place to introduce newcomers to the life of North Point Community Church. So, come on in . . .

liv•ing room (liv´ing room) *n.* a room in a home, with sofas, chairs, etc., for social activities, entertaining guests, etc. Once your guests arrive and are welcomed into your home, you invite them into the living room. Everyone finds a comfortable place to sit, and the interaction begins. (Now you're getting the picture.) This is where you connect with people like yourself. Single adults have Area Fellowships. These are monthly or bimonthly social events held in various locations around Atlanta. Smaller and more interactive than the foyer environment, this is a real-life, genuine opportunity to begin friendships . . . just like you would in your home. Married adults have MarriedLife Live—quarterly events designed to encourage your hearts, draw you closer together and offer you essentials for a healthy marriage . . . all in a casual, fun environment. Now that you're in the living room, what's next. . . .

kitch•en (kich´en) *n.* a room or place for the preparation and cooking of food.—OK, so Webster's doesn't help us much here, but think about it: What's the most popular room in your house? Where do you end up when guests or family come over? That's right. The kitchen. And that's the kind of environment we're shooting for in our small groups: Community Groups, Starting Point and Crown. These groups consist of six to eight individuals or five to six couples who meet regularly for Bible study and prayer and commit to accountability, friendship and support. This is a safe place to open your heart and share your feelings. It's a safe place to ask tough questions. This is where lasting friendships are made. It's about commitment and strength and security. And we want to help you get there.

Pastor Andy Stanley explained to me, "Life is not sequential. . . . People need to be in all three environments."[5] The church provides places of connection to people on their timetable.

Nonsequential Discipleship

New Horizons Fellowship[6] in Apex, North Carolina, defines its purposes and its assimilation strategy with an atom:

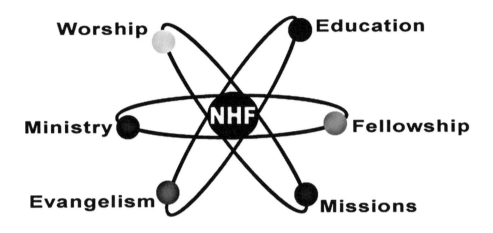

Instead of encouraging members to go through a sequential process, Pastor Ray Wickham tells church attendees they can start anywhere in the process. A church attendee might begin with a mission project helping to build a Habitat for Humanity house. Alternatively, they might start fellowshipping in a small group. On the other hand, they might begin at a discipleship class. Any point can be an entry point. The church does encourage all attendees to work all the way "around" the atom.

> [At New Horizons] we encourage believers to make sure
> that they have balance in their spiritual lives. Balance
> involves making sure that you're "doing" the six purposes of
> the Christian life. . . . We believe that if you just emphasize
> one or two of these, it's like eating just chocolate or meat and
> not all the elements of the food pyramid! It's essential to have
> balance for spiritual health and growth.[7]

Create a Culture of Discipleship

Whatever approach the church chooses for disciple development, the pastor and other leaders must cultivate a congregational culture. The pastor should decide before beginning the new work what disciple-development plan the congregation will follow. Without an intentional developmental approach, the church is likely to become "a mile wide and an inch deep."

Great expectations. Entrepreneurial planters, especially gifted teachers, may be able to design discipleship materials for a new church. "Franchisees" (as we used the term earlier) probably will be wise to adapt someone else's materials for their new church's needs.

Whichever approach for materials the church follows, the planter should set clear standards for all members in their personal discipleship. These great expectations should appear in church literature. The planter-pastor should announce these expectations in meeting settings, in teaching, and in proclamation. This intentionality will help create a "congregational disciple-making culture" that will endure throughout the life of the church.

A culture *and* a ministry. Discipling as a personal ministry is different from discipleship as a design for the congregation's life. Although the two are intertwined, the church planter, while encouraging the entire congregation to become mature disciples, can personally disciple only a handful of leaders. Disciple making is *both* a culture for the congregation *and* a personal ministry for the church planter.

What is the difference? *Discipling* is a process of spiritual mentoring performed by the pastor for only a few individuals. *Discipleship* is a process in which all church members grow in faith, assisted by congregational programming. The church must provide discipleship curriculum as part of a discipleship culture designed to train all members. The planter-pastor mentors (disciples) only a few of those members personally. These functions are intertwined; both are important.

Who to disciple? Developing a leadership training methodology is important. Even more crucial than methodology is the question of who should become the planter's disciples.

The planter should mentor a few handpicked individuals—three to five disciples—at any one time. Persons whom the pastor mentors need not function in high levels of leadership, but they should be people of great potential. The church planter should invest disciple-making time almost exclusively with leaders or potential leaders for the long-range well-being of the congregation.

Biblical principles. The Holy Spirit must grant discernment to the planter in the selection of persons to mentor. Human beings are highly susceptible to temptation; God does not choose leaders based on outward appearances but on the purity of heart (1 Sam. 16:7). Our discernment must be tempered by prayer in order to be sound. Although we readily affirm this instruction, we practice it too seldom. The Son of God spent all night in prayer before choosing his closest companions in ministry (Luke 6:12–13). Each of those twelve failed at some point. But because of his training—and the power of the Spirit—his disciples ultimately grew to replicate much that Jesus had done—as he had promised they would.

Expecting the Best from Believers

Great expectations disciple making is one component of a larger pattern found in healthy congregations. Such congregations expect great sacrifices and commitments from their members. Some church starters believe that if they require too much of people, members will not commit.

Some people *will* leave. Some marginal or insincere people will withdraw because they have no interest in deep and costly commitment. Some sincere and committed people may also leave because they are not convinced of the strategy. For example, one family in our church stopped attending our discipleship training events. They explained that they had been believers for twenty years and that the husband in that family had served as an elder at their former church. I told them that I understood their feelings and their position on the matter, but I also reminded them that the church had agreed to high standards for church members.

By their continued absence from these training opportunities, they demonstrated that they did not agree with my reasoning or with the congregation's policy. I finally confronted them with the choice of attending and conforming to the church's expectation or finding another church home. They soon found another church home.

Like attracts like. Some prospects, and even members, may become offended by such high expectations. Planters should remember that like attracts like. The greater the number of people interested in deep levels of commitment, the higher the spiritual intensity of the church will become. In addition, even highly committed persons ultimately will be swallowed by the mediocrity of the many.

Demand evokes commitment. When a church planter articulates high expectations and describes the vision of the congregation, members will respond positively. High expectations summon surprising commitments. High-expectation churches evoke serious commitments because human beings want to commit themselves to something bigger than themselves. High-expectation churches attract and affirm members who commit themselves to high standards of performance and discipleship.

Statistical research also demonstrates that the presence of high membership standards seemed to have a positive correlation in several samples. Each time a membership requirement was included, an increase in mean attendance was noticeable. Churches that expect more from their members are larger than those that do not.

Not in words, but in principle. Some people may question why a church imposes high standards for membership and discipleship, especially if the Bible records no specific mandate for those demands.

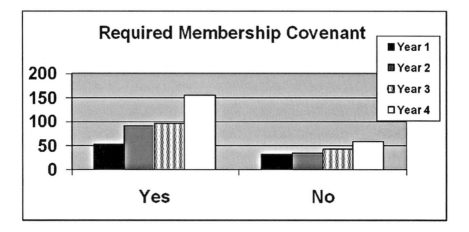

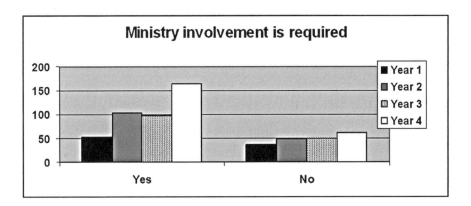

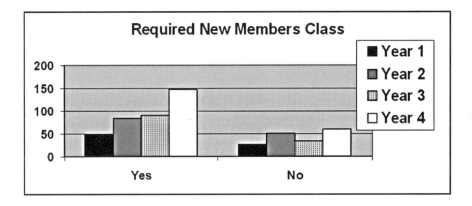

The first answer is that while the specific *words* may not appear in Scripture, the underlying *principles* do appear. Second, and perhaps more practical, the church's practice reflects the congregation's values in practicing its commitments. There is nothing wrong with a positive mind-set.

Help sincere but uncomfortable believers find a comfortable place. Disagreement by members or prospects about such policies does not mean that they are unspiritual because of their views. Nor does it mean that the congregation is too zealous when it sets requirements. Some people simply need a different type of church home. Helping these people see their need for a different church home is an important part of the planter's task of shepherding the entire flock.

Spiritual Infants

God entrusts churches with incredible gifts, unbelieving persons who come to relationship with Jesus Christ. As "foster parents," stewards, of those spiritual infants, congregations must take the task of discipling new believers seriously. Following God's path for our lives must not be taken lightly.

Sunday worship, no matter how effective and spiritual, cannot provide sufficient spiritual nourishment for a new believer. The church needs to provide more support and instruction than one hour on Sunday mornings. Whatever the curriculum and delivery system, the church must provide instruction in Christian fundamentals. Beyond this basic instruction, the congregation should plan, provide for, and monitor the effectiveness of discipleship instruction through which the entire congregation finds resources to continue growing in their faith.

Although many persons teach and enable disciple making in the congregation, the central role remains with the planter-pastor. The church planter is the person who must select and mentor the church's first generation of leaders. The church planter must choose the initial framework and system for disciple making. The pastor must also take the initiative in modeling and communicating the importance of ongoing discipleship. If the planter performs these functions properly, the new congregation should mature, develop young believers, and honor God through the lives of many persons that will impact the new congregation over the course of its lifetime.

Assimilating Guests into the Fellowship

Assimilation is the process of enabling and encouraging prospects and visitors to become members and active participants in the church. Many guests attend for a week or two and then stop coming. Some will attend only sporadically. The object of assimilation is to encourage attendees to become fruit-bearing disciples.

New believers; unique challenges. Although churches frequently do not recognize these needs, new believers present unique challenges. New churches must discern the needs of new believers in order to assimilate them. The church must identify goals for a follow-up program and design a system that enables the church to retain new believers.

Beyond church as a service. The congregation must move beyond the perception that "church" is a worship service that leads to more worship services. When the church allows itself to be perceived as a series of meetings, it deteriorates into nothing more than a gathering of people with unmet needs. A church needs a system to help people find stability that leads to long-term spiritual growth.

New Habits of Stability

The need for stability is fundamental to all human beings, but most especially to new believers.[8] Most people come to Christ before the age of eighteen. If they come to Christ later, they often do so in the midst of a personal crisis. Since the years of youth are filled with upheaval, we may assume that crisis plays a major role in most decisions to accept Christ.

Crises usually do not disappear when a person becomes a Christian. Although the crisis of discovering one's need for a Savior can be resolved by a commitment to Christ, most unbelievers become Christians through other kinds of crisis: a recent divorce, the death of a family member, the loss of a job, or some other catastrophic event that opens them to the saving work of the Holy Spirit.

The task of the church is to introduce Christ into people's lives when their stability is crumbling. Believers can help non-Christians understand that Christ alone is the way to experience lasting stability. Stability can take several different forms: biblical, relational, and functional.

Biblical Stability

Unchurched people cling to the idea that one can become a Christian without forsaking nonbiblical ideas. New believers may still read horoscopes or continue in unholy activities in which they participated before accepting Christ. The church cannot wait for the new believer to discover that such practices contradict biblical and doctrinal beliefs. We need to instruct new believers from the beginning. We should model behaviors which aid them in grounding their lives doctrinally and biblically in Christ.

Establishing stability. The church that establishes new believers in the faith must provide help for young believers in a variety of areas: assurance of God's forgiveness, certainty of their salvation experience, and confidence that God hears their prayers. New believers need support as they develop a maturing understanding of God, Jesus Christ, and the church.

Stability born of God's Word. New believers develop doctrinal stability in their lives when the church teaches and preaches God's Word as powerful, authoritative, and true. This area of stability is the easiest of the three to develop as long as new believers continue to attend church gatherings and pay attention to what they hear.

The sincere milk of the Word. The congregation should make every effort to teach young believers to rely on God's Word for insight (1 Pet. 2:2). If the church teaches new believers to study and search the Scriptures from the beginning of their relationship with Christ, they will discover the necessity of the Word becoming their daily bread and spiritual sustenance. In learning this truth, they learn to find and digest their own spiritual food. As they study the Scriptures, new believers develop a habit that can transform their lives over the course of their lifetime.

Relational Stability

William Hendricks, in his book *Exit Interviews,* argues that new Christians are likely to leave the church within the first six months of faith if they do not develop seven significant relationships with the congregation in that time.[9]

These relationships pose an important challenge because the new church's ministry of assimilation must develop an atmosphere that encourages the relational stability that novice believers need. This atmosphere will develop as members model healthy relationships and as the church emphasizes relational accountability through small groups or Sunday school.

New believers need close Christian friends, especially disciple makers who can accept them as they are while challenging them to mature. Many Christians make little effort to cultivate new friends because they feel comfortable with the friends they already have. New congregations must learn to accept the immaturity of new believers and make befriending them a priority. This attitude is the spirit of the hero of Acts, Barnabas. Without Barnabas, two young, aspiring leaders—Saul (later Paul) and John Mark (later the Gospel writer)—might not have become powerful, effective leaders in God's kingdom. If believers do not involve new converts in their circle of faith, they will likely never become mature believers.

The writer of Hebrews exhorted his readers to assemble with other believers for the purposes of fellowship and encouragement (Heb. 10:25). Leading new believers to regular participation in fellowship activities will not be simple. Such intimacy requires trust and an assurance of being accepted by others. This level of fellowship demands personal intimacy with God raised to a group level. Such intensity of fellowship can be intimidating to maturing believers and even more intimidating to younger Christians.

The church should encourage new members toward a small-group experience. Sometimes low-key events such as a meet-the-pastor luncheon or a *Survival Kit for Young Christians* study can encourage new people to get more involved in small-group fellowship opportunities.

Small-group ministry can nurture relational stability. Churches cannot assimilate people in crowds of a hundred or a thousand. Assimilation occurs individually and in small groups. These small groups should be a bonding place for new relationships. Small groups should not be used for an in-depth Bible study. Interaction between members should serve as the focus of small groups.

Functional Stability

New believers also long for functional stability. If they still wrestle with drug abuse, sexual immorality, and other concerns, they will be unable to focus on issues of spiritual maturity and discipleship until they settle these matters. New churches usually have few mechanisms for dealing with such high-demand issues.

We cannot assume that becoming a Christian will change new Christians' lives automatically. The church needs a way to expose new believers to systematic Bible teaching while also helping them overcome the moral or psychological baggage they bring from their pre-Christian life.

Functional stability is the most difficult area to develop. A recovery ministry (something like a twelve-step program) is one example of such a program for promoting functional stability in new believers.[10] Such ministry requires the skills of trained leaders.

If the young congregation needs such a ministry but cannot find internal resources to staff and direct it, one option may be to ask the help of another church that already sponsors a recovery group. This sister congregation may be willing to provide counseling resources while the new church's people link with their support groups.

Some people need resources for learning how to handle a personal crisis. Many may not need the church or the pastor to handle the crisis with them. Such resources may take the form of support from outside the church family or may include fee-based or sliding-scale fee counseling.

Certain habits in the Christian believer nurture personal growth and speed up growth. The church cannot expect new believers to demonstrate good spiritual habits immediately. The church must help them take ministeps of commitment that will eventually develop into habits displayed by mature believers.

Most churchgoers assume that sincere Christians attend church weekly. Such behavior is a big commitment for people who have not attended church in months or years—or ever. The new church must accept the fact that regular church attendance may be a difficult habit for a new believer to master.

The secret is to encourage baby Christians to make baby-step commitments that the church celebrates. Expecting too much of new believers can be a great discouragement to people who are new to the faith. The church should encourage them to make short-term commitments and allow them to see the benefit of developing new habits.

New believers must perceive the importance of the Scriptures as soon as possible. The church must take the initiative to identify and address specific issues that new believers bring to their new experience of faith. A well-designed one-on-one or small-group discipling program to foster meaningful assimilation of new believers can help with this need.

Many churches lose young believers because they never address the functional issues that plague almost everyone who is new to the faith. Some congregations find ways to help immature believers only in areas of biblical knowledge. Many churches succeed at the relational or doctrinal areas, but most churches miss the mark in helping new believers in areas of functional stability. Pastors and church planters do not have to counsel everyone personally, but congregations must take the responsibility for providing help in addressing issues of functional stability. God uses disciple makers to sharpen and shape new disciples in Christ.

Resources for Further Reading

MasterLife, available through LifeWay Christian Stores, 1-800-458-2772.

Arn, Win, and Charles Arn, *The Master's Plan for Making Disciples: Every Christian an Effective Witness Through an Enabling Church.* Grand Rapids: Baker Books, 1998

Barna, George. *Growing True Disciples.* Colorado Springs, Colo.: Water Brook Press, 2001.

CHAPTER TWENTY-SEVEN

Growth in the New Church

Sometimes church planters invest so heavily in launch-day preparation that they flounder in the days following the birth of the new church. This often hampers the planter and the new church plant. This chapter is designed to prepare the starter for this letdown and to strengthen the planter to nurture the newborn church toward maturity.

Growth of the new church begins the first day after the launch. Growth requires growing a relationship list, developing an immediate follow-up process, designing an assimilation plan and a small group development strategy, and working toward legal recognition of the congregation.

Building a Relationship List

If the new church intends to follow up with persons who visit church events, the church must, in some thorough fashion, record and organize the names of attendees to the first—and every—service. Not all churches decide to collect the names of guests. Some reason that it is better to allow people to attend without asking their name.

I think a better way to proceed is to encourage people to share their names and other pertinent information to the degree that they are comfortable. For example:

Welcome to New Hope. We are glad you are here today. To the degree that you're comfortable, sing, pray, and participate with us. At the end of the service, each person in the church family fills out a card where they communicate with us prayer requests or other needs. If you are a guest and you would like more information about the church, you can fill it

out as well. No one will visit you unannounced. But if you
write down your address, we will mail you information. If
you include your phone number, I will call you. So please
complete the card to the degree that you are comfortable.

This provides a low-key way for guests to indicate their interest. Asking
only the guests to complete information cards singles them out. When
guests have attended several times, they are not likely to continue completing the cards unless everyone does.

It is best to ask *all persons* to complete response cards *each* time they
attend. This process, especially as the church grows, can become unwieldy,
but the benefits of having updated information outweigh the difficulties. An
accurate database grows only from intentional and consistent encouragement of the congregation to complete these cards.

The Day After

The day after the congregation's first service is likely to be a day of rejoicing. Many churches meet their first-service attendance goal. Most consider
their first service a success. But after several months of core development,
advertising, and hard work, the big day passes quickly. Most church planters
struggle with what steps to take in the days that follow the first service.

No one can fault the planter for being preoccupied with the launch day.
The importance of that day cannot be overstated, but it must not be allowed
to prevent planning and preparing for follow-up and the second service.

Follow-up should begin immediately after the first service. The congregation could follow a definite schedule to follow up those wanting more
information. Here is an example:

Sunday: Launch Day
- The follow-up team prepares a letter from the church outreach
  leader to guests. The outreach leader signs and transports the
  letters to the main post office.[1]
- The follow-up team makes brief phone calls to express welcome
  and gratitude to the guests who attended the service.

Monday
- Most follow-up letters arrive.
- The follow-up team completes their "thank you" phone calls.

Tuesday
- The follow-up team submits the list of attendees to the pastor.
- The pastor prepares and sends his personal follow-up letter.

Wednesday
- Most of the pastor's letters arrive at the homes of attendees.
- The pastor and follow-up team prepare and mail postcard invitations to all of the prospects on the mailing list.

Thursday
- Most postcards arrive.

Friday and Saturday
- The pastor personally calls every family to invite them to return for the second service. The pastor may arrange a personal visit if the guests are responsive.

This system enables the new congregation to make five contacts with church guests who have given their names and information within the first week following launch Sunday. Three contacts arrive by mail. One comes through a personal call from the pastor and one from a church member.

Maintaining Direction and Growth

Maintaining direction and growth following the launch service is crucial. The planter is not the only one who invested heavily in the launch service, so keeping core group members and others motivated can be difficult.

Losing the core group after launch. Core group members often leave the new start after launch day. In fact, the bigger and more successful the launch, the more likely it is that core group members may withdraw. The group, which once had intimate, frequent contact with the planter, no longer experiences that intimacy. Suddenly, the planter has become preoccupied with assimilating dozens or even hundreds of people who had not been present before launch day.

Prepare them for the problem. The first step in addressing this problem is to warn the core group of the typical difficulties of transition following the launch service. The best way to keep the core group is to keep them focused on the vision.

Burnout and plateaued growth. The church planter functions as a shepherd before the launch. The planter knows every member by name and stands ready to help and support the entire core group. This is simple when twenty people are involved. But when the church explodes to ten times that number, this shepherding becomes both impossible and unhealthy for the pastor. First, it pulls the planter toward burnout. Second, the impossibility of the planter's presence everywhere with everyone means that the church will quit growing unless the style of leadership changes.

Layers of leaders. Lyle Schaller refers to this as a shift from "shepherd mode" to "rancher mode."[2] Schaller's metaphor explains that a shepherd is responsible to oversee and care for a flock of sheep. A rancher is different. A rancher *oversees* and *equips* shepherds for their caretaking role. Wise ranchers spend the majority of their effort training shepherds. The church planter actually shepherds leaders who, in turn, shepherd the remainder of the body.

Limitless potential for growth. When the rancher mode operates successfully, the potential numerical growth of a congregation has no limit. In this pyramid of influence and care, the pastor continues to shepherd the shepherds. As the congregation grows, each of those shepherds maximizes his or her care group. In this way, the congregation forms a new layer of shepherd-leaders who begin to care for multiple families under their umbrella of responsibility. The church can create more layers of new leaders as the church grows in size.

Loss of control. The core group will face not only a loss of intimacy but also a loss of control. Prior to the launch, the core group has supplied so much energy and input that they probably have come to "own" the church. But after the launch, a much larger congregation holds stock in the new church. These new members will not know about the prelaunch efforts of the core group, and they probably don't care about the costs to get the church started. These new people will present different ideas on how the church should be organized. The core group must learn to embrace these new members and new ideas.

Lost hope for realized vision. The final thing for which core group members must prepare is the possibility of failing to actualize their visions for the church's future. Core group members usually appear to adopt the planter's vision, but often they adopt only *part* of that vision. Many core group members develop their personal visions, thinking as a bride- or groom-to-be, "I will change things after we marry." After the church launches, some core group members realize that the new direction is not the course for which they had hoped.

One common expression of this conflict occurs in reaching people. Many core groups really intend to reach unchurched persons, but when they realize the cost of succeeding—the changes that come with the addition of new people and their ideas—many balk. Suddenly they awaken to the "death of their vision." Their grief and anger become so compelling that they leave the congregation rather than stay and reinvest in the new church.

The departure of core group members does not mean that they were dishonest about their commitments. More likely, they did not realize what it would take to reach new believers. Such discoveries can become so uncomfortable that many cannot continue. As the church reaches unbelievers, lost people who act in ungodly ways mingle with believers. "Church-cultured" members often become offended and frightened by persons who have yet to adopt Christian lifestyles.

Vision Hijacking

Following the launch, when tensions begin to rise between the original core group and newcomers, a phenomenon called "vision hijacking" may occur. Vision hijacking is an attempt by church members, often highly invested core group members, to redirect the church away from the planter's vision, *especially* when the original vision no longer seems workable. This usually happens at a low point in the life of the church.

Our original vision. About eighteen months after the birth of Millcreek, we witnessed the stagnation of our original vision. We felt called to become a cell-based church expressed through celebrative worship, home-based care groups, and discipleship courses. We had taught and reinforced this concept in new members' classes and had shared it with everyone who visited our church.

The moment of crisis. At the low point, about eighteen months following our launch day, a few of our families decided the congregation should pursue a vision that was different from mine as the church planter. Their attempt at redirection (vision hijacking) was not intended to destroy the church but to save and reenergize the congregation because we found ourselves at a low point. They just had a "better way" than our church's stated vision. (In case you are wondering, they stayed and were able to refocus on the original vision when I recast it to them.)

Thwarting attempts at vision hijacking. Churches and planters cannot avoid attempts at vision hijacking. The fact that new churches need strong core members in order to succeed also introduces the possibility that these members may try to redirect the church in a time of frustration. Every church planter I have known has experienced an attempted vision hijacking within the first three years of the church start. Although planters cannot avoid attempts at vision hijacking, certain steps can minimize their success.

The first step to avoid successful hijacking is to educate new members about the church's vision and direction. The pastor probably should be the teacher of these early classes because no other leader understands or can articulate the vision as well.

Second, the planter must recast the vision *each month* without exception. Listeners and followers have incredibly short memories. The leader must repeatedly and consistently recast the church's vision and values in order to cement members to the vision.

A third step in averting the success of an attempted hijack is to prepare the core group for painful transitions that usually follow the church's launch. To be forewarned is to be forearmed.

Fourth, the pastor should involve every person in the church's mission and ministry. People who *row* the boat cannot easily *rock* the boat. New congregations always have at least one oar for every person; every member should pull an oar. As everyone gets involved and people begin to "own" the church and "own" a particular ministry within the church, the church will grow—in health as well as in numbers.

Keeping Vision Before the People

By keeping the vision before the people, the planter reminds them of the direction for the new church. The planter must continually remind the entire congregation of the vision. People forget. Church members often lose track of the "main thing." The vision of the planter must be shared with the church—and not just once. Andy Stanley observes, "All God ordained visions are shared visions. Nobody goes it alone. But God generally raises up a point person to paint a compelling verbal picture. A picture that captures the hearts and imaginations of those whom God is calling to embrace the task at hand."[3]

The planter should meet with key leaders at least monthly. Among the many details that must be addressed in that meeting, one central feature should be the recasting of vision. The planter must also make a weekly effort to place the vision before the entire group in order to keep everyone headed in the same direction. Although the planter may see such repetition as risky or boring, the people will benefit from a regular reminder of who they are and where they are going.

Vision is more than just a set of propositions, value statements, or truths; it requires a mental image. It should touch people's hearts and motivate members to get involved in the purpose of the congregation. Vision should cry out, "This is something you long to be a part of, a purpose to which you want to make a major contribution." People must "in-vision" the core values of the congregation before they can become part of that vision.

Credibility and Vision

The power of the vision also requires a credible vision-caster. If the church planter's attitudes, behaviors, and values suggest that he is not credible, the congregational vision suffers.

On the other hand, vision gains credibility with each success and with the anticipated likelihood of success. Each time the planter successfully casts a vision for the congregation or the core group, this experience prompts the followers of the congregation to believe more fully in the long-term vision.

In the same way that the planter's "credibility tank" fills with each success, failed efforts diminish credibility. Members and group leaders become energized and excited when anticipated successes lead to realized dreams. But underachievements or catastrophes strain the vision-caster's credibility.

The Peak-to-Peek Principle

A successful mountaintop experience enables participants to adopt a greater vision and to work toward its achievement. The issue of credibility dovetails with the "peak-to-peek principle," which specifies that the time to cast a vision for the next endeavor is atop the peak of the current success.

At Millcreek Community Church, our staff envisioned an Easter service attendance of over 700, even though our normal attendance at that time was only 250. Instead of casting the vision for 700 people, we rented the facilities of a local high school that would hold over 700, and we cast the vision for more than 500 people. We knew that the church was not yet ready to believe it could reach more than 500 people, so we were careful to cast a credible vision. On Easter morning, 750 people attended. On that day, we cast the vision for our next endeavor.

Halfway through the service, I again greeted our guests and members: "It is so great to see you today! Let me tell you what God will do through Millcreek Community Church this fall—we will start two daughter churches which will become the largest churches ever started by Southern Baptists north of the Mason-Dixon line." We started these churches six months after that Easter service.

The valley, which inevitably follows every peak experience, can be overcome by focusing the church on the next peak. The size of the present peak is not the major concern; visioning from that peak is crucial. Giving the people a "peek" of what is next is the key.

The church start with five persons prepares for the climb to ten. That success will set the stage for an immediate turn of the congregation's energies and attention to doubling again, or to some other worthy goal. Peak size in and of itself is not the concern; timing and consistency from the middle of the previous success are the things to pursue.

Become a Vision-Caster

Established churches sometimes demonstrate no apparent need for vision-casting. This observation does not mean that such churches have no need for vision but that traditions and established patterns can project the *appearance* of vitality—for a period of time.

In a new church, vision-casting is imperative. Asking people to make sacrifices—to attend a yet-to-be-established church, to wait until the new church is ready to launch, or to deny their kids an established children's ministry—is more sacrifice than many families can accept. Creating a vision for such families is indispensable in securing their confidence and involvement.

One of the ways a church planter can help people envision the future is to demonstrate where a similar vision is already functioning successfully. Even if this investigation means traveling some distance or viewing a high-quality videotape, both the planter's credibility and the core group's visioning capacity may benefit. Either of these options can enable core leaders to see what is still just an idea for them—just words. Afterwards, they will develop the ability to *see* the future and to commit themselves to that future.

Conclusion

Maintaining direction and growth is essential. Many new churches start and then fizzle out months later. They are unable to maintain momentum. They are distracted and often lose focus. Good planning and vision-casting from the start help to avoid these obstacles.

Resources for Further Reading

Maxwell, John C. *Failing Forward*. Nashville: Thomas Nelson Publishers, 2000.

McIntosh, Gary L. *One Size Doesn't Fit All: Bringing Out the Best in Any Size Church*. Grand Rapids: Fleming H. Revell, 1999.

Minirth, Frank, and others. *What They Didn't Teach You in Seminary*. Nashville: Thomas Nelson Publishers, 1993.

Stanley, Andy. *Visioneering*. Sisters, Oreg.: Multnomah, 1999.

CHAPTER TWENTY-EIGHT

Children in the New Church

One of the biggest challenges that a new church faces is children's ministry.[1] If the children do not like the new church, the parents may not return. We must think beyond providing baby-sitting services for preschoolers while their parents go to church. Ministry to preschool children and their parents is *real* ministry. Sikes and Niles observe:

It's multifaceted. It's multidimensional. It's a multi-targeted ministry. Your church [child care] provides a mission field for those who are called to serve, a first impression for many new families, respite and training for parents, and most importantly, a child's first contact with the family of God outside his or her own home. It's a place where babies [and small children] can learn that the God who created them is Lord of all there is to know. And it's a place where we become even more awed by the wonder of God through [children].[2]

New churches often neglect children's ministry because they focus on a myriad of other things. In some cases, this works for a time. Nelson Searcy explains that his church does not have a children's ministry because there are so few children on the Upper West Side of Manhattan.[3] But in most cases, children's ministry is an essential part of the strategy of a new church.

Most new churches will not have a full children's ministry from the first service. People will understand that the church is just getting started. But the church planter must let the church know that a ministry for children is needed, and it is coming soon. The planter must keep this vision of what it will become before the people, especially the parents. Once things have settled for the rest of the church and more people have been raised up to be leaders, more time and energy can be invested in children's ministries.

The children's ministry does not have to be functioning like a well-established church weekday program, but there are some important principles and key factors that must be applied from the very beginning.

Most new churches start with only a nursery or preschool. In North American culture today, most parents are comfortable with their children being elsewhere when they are trying to learn. The nursery and preschool should be designed with the security of the parents and the preschoolers in mind. "Security means providing a worry-free environment where the child knows he is welcome, safe, and free from harm. . . . Guidance is direction given to help the child make choices . . . [and] a sense of accomplishment results from having been given opportunities to succeed."[4]

Security is provided to parents by letting them know their children are well cared for in a safe environment. Many churches today use pager systems. Parents will sign in their children and receive a numbered vibrating pager. They receive their children back only when they return that pager. This provides a good security check to put parents at ease. They know they can be contacted in the service if a problem occurs, and they know that no one can pick up their child unless the person has a specific pager.

Recruiting and training children's workers is very difficult when a church is new. A preschool worker should be a "Christian growing in his relationship with Christ; a member of the church in which he(/she) serves; a person who is willing prayerfully to prepare and train; a person who loves preschoolers; a person who is punctual, flexible, and dependable; a person with a gentle, cooperative spirit; a person who demonstrates maturity, tact, and enthusiasm; and a committed Christian who will teach, visit, and reach out to preschoolers and their families."[5] If such a person does not yet exist in the new church, it may be necessary to get help from a nearby church.

Background Checks

All workers in a church nursery should fill out an application. This application should ask some key questions. It should also include permission to do a criminal background check. Every person working with children needs to undergo a criminal background check—no exceptions.

Without background checks, churches open themselves to serious liability. But that is not the most important reason. Without background checks, churches expose children to danger. A church should be a safe place, free from harm or scandal. It is sometimes difficult to do background checks with so much else going on. But this is essential.

Sample applications can be found at www.new-churches.com/examples.

Identifying Workers

All workers in church nurseries should have some sort of identification. This helps parents know who is working with their child. It also helps with security. Some churches have workers wear smocks or aprons with a monogram of the church name. The workers should also have name tags. Some churches print up photo ID badges for all workers.

Ministry to Parents

The first question that most parents will ask their child is, "Did you have fun?" So it is important that children's activities be enjoyable and enthusiastic. When children have fun, they will want to return and bring their parents.

The second question most parents will ask is, "What did you learn?" I have a four-year-old daughter, and she never remembers. But she will often give me a sheet of paper with the lesson and say, "This!" So as you teach preschoolers, be sure to give them something to take home to show their parents. This will show that they learned something, and the parents might even read it.

Vineyard Christian Fellowship[6] in Columbus, Ohio, considers ministry to children a good way to reach families. They send a large fluorescent postcard to the children of all guests. (It is large—it folds out to 17 x 24!) All it says is, "Thanks for coming to Vineyard." Ultimately, it is not the children who are reached by such a gesture. It is the parents.

Conclusion

Clean nurseries, staffed with quality people who serve in a safe environment, are much more welcoming than "a place to keep kids" (a small, unpainted room with old donated cribs). New churches should pay close attention to what quality child care looks like in the churches in their area and emulate what they see.

Here are some closing rules from a friend that should help every children's ministry:

Thou Shall Nots for Children's Ministry

1. Thou shall not leave children with children; children's workers should be over the age of eighteen.
2. Thou shall not have anyone work who has not undergone some form of criminal check.
3. Thou shall not use unsafe or hand-me-down cribs, toys, sheets, and blankets.
4. Thou shall not give any child any food that has not been approved by the parents. Allergies are deadly.
5. Thou shall not have an unclean room. All toys, cribs, and other things that little hands touch need to be washed with bleach.
6. Thou shall not have a child in the room without having the parents fill out a form with the child's name, allergies, and physical problems listed.
7. Thou shall not recruit people who are not called to children's ministry.
8. Thou shall not use people who are not trained in children's ministry and in child development.
9. Thou shall not see children's ministry as a necessary evil in order to attract their parents.
10. Thou shall not use the very short time given to just baby-sit. This is the time to teach children in the way they should go. Don't use VeggieTales videos to substitute for children's ministry.[7]

Resources for Further Reading

Capehart, Jody, with Lori Haynes Niles. *Touching Hearts, Changing Lives: Becoming a Treasured Teacher.* Loveland, Colo.: Group, 1999.

Sanders, Thomas, and Mary Ann Bradberry. *Teaching Preschoolers: First Steps Toward Faith.* Nashville: LifeWay Press, 2000, 17–18.

Children's Ministry Magazine.

Part 6

Making It Official

CHAPTER TWENTY-NINE

Congregational Formation

*A*fter planting a new church, the time for official congregational formation eventually comes. This process moves the congregation from functioning as just a concept or even a worshiping group of people to becoming a legally and administratively recognizable unit.

Milestones in the New Church's Life

A newborn human separates from its mother at birth but remains in intimate dependency upon her. Likewise, new churches generally separate from the mother church but retain a degree of dependence for a period of time. If both congregations are healthy, their relationship soon becomes an expression of interdependence within a reasonable period of time. The new church must complete several tasks and pass several milestones successfully in order to enable maturation and healthy interdependence between congregations.

Statement of Faith. The first major milestone for a new church is the adoption of a confessional guide. Denominational churches generally adopt the organization's statement of faith. Others may draw on the statements of churches they admire. Either way, the statement should address core issues and make clear the church's position on theological issues.

Samples of statements of faith, constitutions, incorporation papers, and sample chartering services can be found at www.new-churches.com/examples.

Constitution. The church document known as a constitution describes the new church. The congregation votes to adopt the document as a written expression of the beliefs and principles around which it will organize its ministry. A constitution usually includes the congregation's articles of faith. Our church also included a section on church discipline to explain our values and systems. We required everyone who joined our church to read the constitution.

A new church should not constitute at its launch service. Although great things happen on that day, the church has not matured in several crucial areas that need to be addressed before it is ready to pass the milestone of constitution. The congregation should have developed consistent giving and growth patterns and should have established a solid leadership core before taking this step. Andy Stanley often advises the church planters that he mentors, "Put off constituting as long as you can. . . . If you have a clear idea, make sure the people around you share it before you constitute."[1]

Before a church constitutes, it *needs a reason* to do so. The reason is usually that the church is able to support itself. Larry Lewis believes the new congregation should have at least one hundred faithful resident members before constituting as an official congregation.[2] Although I would not assign an attendance limit, it is essential that constituting is an event that establishes a separate and distinct identity for the church.

The constitution should be simple. Long constitutions that articulate every possible problem indicate mistrust rather than congregational health. Collecting samples from other church plants helps move the process along.

Bylaws. Bylaws give more specific information about church operations than the constitution. Bylaws (and an operations manual) should be simpler to change than the articles of the constitution. If the congregation articulate them prudently in the beginning, the church's core values (found in the constitution) should rarely change.

Bylaws and operations procedures should be simple to change because they explain the *methodologies* the church is using to incarnate and live out its core values. Changes in the constitution should be made only through the vote of the entire body. Alterations in bylaws and operations manuals should be possible through decisions of the administrative team or the elders.

Incorporation. Incorporation is the step that signals official legal recognition by governmental entities. It is a true milestone. In almost every state and in Canada, the congregation should be incorporated. This procedure protects the ministers and the officers of the church in the event that someone brings a lawsuit. The ministers and officers can be held personally liable for any problems if a church is not incorporated. Incorporation also signals that the congregation now stands on its own as a legal entity separate from the mother church.

In most nonhierarchical churches, once the church is incorporated, it is its own "entity" and needs to call a pastor. The new church should call the pastor and record that call in the official minutes of the church business for the pastor's role to be official. In most cases, the church issues its call through a vote of the entire congregation.

No person can be a member of the new church until the congregation constitutes. At the time of constitution, charter membership is the first opportunity for a person to become a church member. The congregation should plan this opportunity as a major congregational and community event.

Many churches require charter members to attend the new members' class, to sign a membership covenant and an original charter document, and to attend the chartering service.

Conclusion

Church planters often show no interest in such details as constitution and bylaws, but they are vitally important. Not only do these documents encourage and protect the vision of the church, but they also safeguard the congregation from conflict.

Although the planter needs to be involved to some degree, careful consideration should be given to delegating the details of this work to people in the congregation. If you are fortunate enough to have a lawyer or someone who works with legal issues, this person could take the lead. In addition, if you are affiliated with a denomination, a representative will have helpful checklists and advice. I realize more and more the need for a good attorney in this process. It is possible to find a good Christian attorney who will work pro bono.

Resources for Further Reading

Lewis, Larry. *The Church Planter's Handbook.* Nashville: Broadman Press, 1992.

"Church Constitution Guide" available at www.newchurches.com.

CHAPTER THIRTY

Churches Planting Churches

Church planting should not end with the establishment of one church. The process can repeat itself when a new church matures to the point of becoming a sponsoring church.

Some of the readers of this book will become church planters. Those planters will work hard at planting and growing the church. Many will say, "It is taking all I have to make this church plant work. We cannot help start another church." But the new church is the best source for expanding upon a zeal for church planting. Churches of all sizes and ages can be a part of a church plant.

As a professor of church planting, I am disappointed when gifted church planters have not, after three years, "mothered" a second church. I am not disappointed in the *church*; I am disappointed in the *planter*. Church planters need to be the best advocates and sponsors of next-generation churches.

Casting the Vision

The planter is the person who develops and instills the vision to start new churches. Bob Logan tells us that a new church that does not plant a church within its first three years of life probably never will. From the first day of a new church plant, the planter should also strategize for reproducing that church, and for advancing the kingdom of God by producing daughter churches.

The planter initiates a daughter church by casting a church planting vision. This vision must come from the *pulpit,* from the words and heart of the *pastor.* This vision must come from the pastor because God has uniquely anointed him to present God's vision to the congregation.

Furthermore, the vision must come from the *pulpit,* because presenting the vision through preaching signals to the church that, of all the many important matters the pastor could have preached, the church planting vision has taken precedence. This vision for a new church is not to be mentioned casually like idle hallway conversation. The vision must be cast to the entire body.

Once the pastor has presented the vision, the people must *catch* that vision and then cast it among themselves. For the vision to survive, the church must catch it; for it to thrive, they must adopt and promote it as their own.

Another step toward planting a church is the church's appointment of a planting leadership team that is empowered to establish new congregations. When the pastor promotes the church from the pulpit and when the leaders of the congregation close ranks behind the pastor in the divine vision, the remainder of the church will join them in the important ministry of church planting.

The Great Commission presents concentric circles through which to share the gospel (Acts 1:8): Jerusalem, Judea, Samaria, and the world. The center should be called the church's Jerusalem, the equivalent of a hometown or immediate area surrounding the congregation. The first circle from the center is Judea, which might be identified as one's association, county, or state. The Samaria circle perhaps describes a distinct ethnic or language group that lies a geographical distance or cultural distance from Jerusalem. The third and final concentric circle represents the world—every place where the name of Christ remains unproclaimed. All of these four echelons for evangelism also identify forums in which a church might strategize to start a daughter congregation.

Reasons to Sponsor a Daughter Church

Becker and Williams have outlined several reasons why existing churches should plant daughter churches.[1]

1. **To evangelize the unchurched.** Evangelistic effectiveness is one of several practical reasons to start new churches. The evangelist's longing to reach people soars to its zenith in church starting. Although every church, no matter its age, must strategize to evangelize, established churches make

greater progress in kingdom evangelism by initiating new daughter churches. This commitment is necessary because evangelism occurs more rapidly in new churches than in longer-established congregations.

2. **To develop new leaders.** One crucial imperative of new churches is leadership development. When new congregations demonstrate this capacity, leaders often arise at a more rapid pace than in older churches. The appearance of new leaders may actually outpace the new church's needs. As new leaders find fulfillment in their Spirit-anointed ministries, they often become dissatisfied with just occasional opportunities to serve.

If a new church develops several worship teams who alternate in leading, one team might receive the church's blessing in becoming leaders for a daughter church start. Each team—both those who leave and those who stay—would have the opportunity to lead worship more than occasionally during the month.

This type of situation allows leaders to continue to develop their abilities. Many pastors and planters testify that as their churches have commissioned leaders and sent them out, God has replaced those leaders and allowed even more people to get involved in the leadership core of the church.

3. **To grow the kingdom.** A maturing *kingdom* awareness is more important than a local church mentality. Church leaders need to look beyond their local churches. Leaders who are unwilling to make organizational sacrifices for the benefit of the kingdom are stunted in growth and are immature in understanding God's larger purpose. When congregations initiate daughter churches, God accomplishes his purpose more effectively than when churches conserve resources in order to optimize local organizational strength and vitality.

4. **To transmit a lasting legacy.** Another reason for sponsoring new churches may be termed "the family legacy." Enduring families manifest a family heritage, a noble tradition passed from one generation to the next. This awareness of their family heritage creates excitement and energy for each new generation.

The same claim may be made for churches. Daughter churches can look with feelings of contentment upon their parentage in the faith. Their legacy lends strength to these churches, enabling them to feel more thoroughly rooted and grounded in history.

Sponsoring churches also become excited as they see God's people multiply and God's kingdom grow because they are passing along their heritage to a new generation of churches. The excitement swells as these new-generation churches initiate their own daughter congregations. Sponsoring churches experience a kind of divine honor reserved for those who enable the success of their children, for they know that they played an important role in that success.

5. **To grow the denomination.** Although denominational growth often can model a kind of imperialism, there is clearly a difference between denominations that foster kingdom church plants—and grow because of those efforts—and denominations that initiate churches for sectarian reasons and for institutional survival.

6. **To meet ethnic and language group needs.** At the dawn of the twenty-first century, urban centers of the United States and Canada have attracted ethnically diverse people groups. Today, as never before, North American believers can carry out international missions without leaving their own neighborhoods. Churches—whether new or long-established—face the opportunity to plant language and cross-cultural churches in North America, just as we plant congregations around the world among the same ethnic and language groups.

7. **To glorify God.** Although many people in a community may never attend your new church start, your presence represents the presence and the power of God to a community. God proclaims who he is as his people establish new churches. New churches are great testimony to a great God![2]

Becoming a Sponsoring Church

Leading a congregation to sponsor daughter churches presents its own set of challenges. In the 1970s, Jack Redford authored a practical study that addressed many of the challenges of church sponsorship. Redford gave nine sequential steps for planting a daughter church.[3]

1. **Select a missions committee.** A church planting effort without a skilled, effective leadership-advisory team is like a ship without a rudder. The committee should be made up of missions-hearted persons who have the new church's best interest at heart. The committee may even be a church planting team charged with the specific task of leading the new church start.

2. **Select the area.** This step may seem obvious, but a number of factors will influence the choice: size of the population, affinity of the planting team to the focus group, sociological congruity between the focus group and the sponsoring church, and other characteristics.

The presence of other churches can make a difference as well. If the sponsoring church takes the initiative in picking a location, the new work benefits greatly. The sponsoring church lends credibility to the start. If site location includes the sponsor's purchase of property, the advantages to the new congregation are considerable.

3. **Prepare the sponsoring congregation.** Preparation involves explaining to the proposed sponsoring church the events that must occur in order to plant a new church successfully. This explanation should include a thorough list and an anticipated time line for coming events. Such explanations should include not only *what* will be done but also *why* it should be done. Laying out all of these factors in the beginning enables the sponsoring church to feel it has the adequate information to make an intelligent, responsible decision. If emergencies arise later, sponsoring church members can more easily accept such contingencies as a normal part of church planting.

4. **Cultivate the field.** The first reason for cultivating is to locate potential members and, especially, core group members. A second is to determine the community's needs that the new church may address. Third, cultivation stirs interest for the church that will emerge publicly in just a few months.

5. **Start home Bible studies.** Although this terminology describes Jack Redford's era and methods, the reader should understand this stage as the core group development phase described earlier in this book. After field cultivation comes the time for small group design. The planter or team should locate interested persons and then follow up immediately by involving them in a small group. Taking too much time between contact and involvement may squander good opportunities because some prospects may lose interest if not followed up quickly and appropriately.

6. **Establish the mission chapel.** With the successful initiation of one or more small groups, the sponsoring church should move toward establishing public worship. In Redford's day, this did not involve a public "launch." Either way, this step means coalescing the small groups meeting at different locations into a larger group. This larger group is intended ultimately to be

a church gathered publicly. It will gather publicly for worship as well as be scattered throughout the community.

7. **Plan finances.** The new mission should have a simple organization at this stage. The fellowship has not yet become a church. It probably collects no funds or, at best, limited financial gifts. Simplicity of organization will direct energies to stimulate vision development among core group members. Simplicity will also maximize small group development. An overly sophisticated organization may impose unnecessary burdens on the new work. The sponsoring congregation probably should continue managing the mission's finances during this period.

8. **Secure facilities.** This involves finding a place in which the new church will meet. This step demands a particular wisdom. Ill-advised decisions can send wrong messages to the community if the sociological values reflected in the facility are out of step with the tastes of the community. An extravagant meeting place can saddle the mission with unmanageable financial burdens. Too little space may hamper the development of the new congregation.

9. **Constitute the church.** The final step in the process from missions committee to a new church is the actual constitution of the new body. The sponsoring church will have transferred control and direction of the new church's finances to the fledgling congregation. The new church also should now take responsibility for all of its own administration and leadership.

Steps for Planting a Daughter Church

1. Select a missions committee.
2. Select a target area.
3. Select a sponsoring church.
4. Cultivate the target area.
5. Start home Bible studies.
6. Begin a mission chapel.
7. Plan the finances.
8. Secure the facilities.
9. Constitute the church.

Time-Honored Principles

The terminology in the discussion above is a little dated, but the principles remain sound. Sojourn is following this model right now. They are a church reaching culturally creative types in a gentrified community of Louisville. They believe God is calling them to plant a new church in the south side of Louisville. The south side is what Pastor Daniel Montgomery calls a "redneck" part of town—a big stretch from the tattooed and pierced members of Sojourn. They are in the process of forming a church planting team that will follow these steps and plant an indigenous church in south Louisville.

North America is filled with pastors and churches that are not willing to sponsor daughter churches and to make the sacrifices necessary to support a new church start. It will require thousands of churches willing to sponsor church plants to reverse the self-destruction of North American culture.

Dino Senesi explained his church's practice to me as follows:

> When I was pastor of a parent church we had a celebration of all congregations once a year. Most all of our churches were ethnic, which worked really well. They shared in the service and we fellowshipped over ethnic food afterwards. This was strategically placed before budget time in the mother church. Our people loved it and caught on. We had as many as six churches and missions and their pastors for the celebration. They sang, preached and testified. By far it was the most blessed and strategic thing that we ever did to encourage church planting through our congregation.[4]

When churches sponsor churches, they have the privilege of seeing lives changed because of their efforts.

Sponsorship and the Church Planter

Our discussion in this chapter has centered on the sponsoring church's responsibility. Ultimately, one person is primarily responsible for leadership in the new start. That person is the church planter. The sponsoring church must play a leading role in finding the church planter-pastor. In doing this, the sponsoring church must address several concerns.

Theological matters. The candidate's agreement with the theological convictions of the sponsoring church is important. The sponsoring church must decide what level of theological disagreement—if any—is acceptable. Churches vary widely on this matter. Some insist that the planter agree with the supporting church in every area of theology. Other congregations bend on some minor areas of theological understanding in view of the candidate's connection with the demographic focus group. The sponsoring church should define its expectations *before* beginning the search process.

Ministry experience. Another issue that the sponsoring church should consider is its expectations of the candidate in regards to ministry experience. Must the candidate be a seasoned church planter? Has the candidate successfully ministered alongside other persons on a multiple-member church staff? Does this person demonstrate strong interpersonal skills and the ability to cooperate with others? Has this person shown responsible handling of authority? Can this person lead by modeling?

Behavioral assessment. The sponsoring church may use a behavioral assessment[5] to aid in finding a planter. Such tools enable the sponsoring church to determine whether a candidate is just a strong leader—or a strong leader gifted for church planting. The assessment can help locate individuals who have church planting skills while also revealing those persons who, though strong in many areas, lack the essential giftedness for the planting task.

Supervisory accountability. Other concerns worthy of consideration in calling a church planter are the issues of accountability, supervision, and mentoring. No matters are more important in the sponsor-church planter relationship. Supervisory accountabilities must be spelled out. Supervision, expectations about attending sponsoring church staff meetings, and detailed performance expectations must be agreed upon by the church and the candidate before his call to the new church field. The planter must understand the need for selecting a mentor or coach to assist in providing the emotional support that every new church planter needs.

Conclusion

The role of a sponsoring church is vital to the church planting and church-reproduction process. Church planters should remember their divine calling not just to plant one church but also to continue planting churches long after their first church has been launched and developed. Pastors of established churches should use this information to create a tradition—a legacy of missions and church planting for their churches.

Resources for Further Reading

Allen, Roland. *Missionary Methods: St. Paul's or Ours?* Grand Rapids: Eerdmans, 1962, reprinted 2001.

Becker, Paul, and Mark Williams. *The Dynamic Daughter Church Planting Handbook*. Dynamic Church Planting International, 1999.

Coursey, Claylan. *How Churches Can Start Churches*. Nairobi, Kenya: Baptist Publications House, 1984.

Faircloth, Samuel D. *Church Planting for Reproduction*. Grand Rapids: Baker Book House, 1991.

Logan, Robert E., and Steve Ogne. *Churches Planting Churches*. St Charles, IL: ChurchSmart Resources, 1995.

CHAPTER THIRTY-ONE

Breaking the Mold: Church Planting Movements

*P*rayer, Jesus' purposes, and the Spirit's presence are at the heart of church planting. These three factors provide the focus of this brief conclusion. This book started with biblical, theological, and spiritual foundations. This is where it ends.

Foundations for Church Planting

Spiritual preparation is sometimes neglected when training church planters. This emphasis is crucial because church planting attracts energetic and entrepreneurial persons who are generally more activity-driven than contemplative and prayerful! Furthermore, training for church starting usually emphasizes practical areas and often neglects the spiritual. In the Master's business of planting his churches, there is no better place to begin than in gaining direction and purpose from him through prayer.

The Gospels record Jesus' use of the term *church* only two times. In the first he explained, in response to Peter's affirmation of faith, "I will build my church, and the gates of Hades will not overcome it" (Matt. 16:18). By these words, Jesus indicated that he is the source of church growth. He did not advocate the centrality of *methodology*—but the centrality of *deity*: He promised that he would build his church.

In the second use of the term, Jesus focused on his protection and purification of the church. In Matthew 18:17, he explained how believers should react when their brothers and sisters refuse their admonitions: "If he refuses to listen to them, tell it to the church; and if he refuses to listen even to the church, treat him as you would a pagan or a tax collector."

Jesus will build; Jesus will purify his church. By definition, *church* refers to "ones who are called out." Clearly, these tasks of building and purifying begin with and emanate from Jesus but are acted out through those he has called out. The spiritual foundations of church planting suggest that Jesus is the source of church growth and holiness. In order to know how to build and how to purify *his* church, we must remain in touch with the Lord of the church.

Church planting does not focus on advertising, organization, music, and worship. Planting does, of course, *include* all of these concerns, but it is *not* these things. Planting churches centers on touching, winning, and congregationalizing the lost. The wise church planter must remember to focus on what matters: the Lord and his purposes for the church.

A Personal Reflection

Some observers attributed the successful launch of Millcreek Community Church to effective advertising. Perhaps there is a degree of truth in that assessment. Advertising was important, but it was not the key. It was a useful methodology, but it was *not* the center of the church's successful launch.

On the night before our grand opening at Millcreek, I lost my voice. I felt deep frustration—even anger—at having spent a year in preparation, only to become an "absentee father" at the moment the congregation was to be birthed. Our core group's prayers for my healing in order to preach on launch Sunday yielded no immediate results. Even my prayers on the morning of the launch, focusing all the faith I could muster, seemed of no avail.

Other problems also arose on that morning. Attendees trickled in to the service. As I stood in front of the stage, I experienced a crisis of faith. I prayed to God and said to myself at the same time, "God, I came here because I believed you wanted me to. I have invested my life in these people because I believe you called me. I am now here to serve you by evangelizing this crowd and I believe it to be your will. Please God, in your grace let me have the privilege of sharing with these people your Word. You knew of my voice. You knew of the people who would attend. God, I am sorry for trusting in myself. I want you to be glorified here today."

As I ended the prayer, I stepped on the stage. In that instant, my voice returned. By the beginning of the service, my concern was not about the number of those who attended, but in God's activity in their midst that day. A total of 234 people visited the first service of Millcreek Community Church.

Immediately following the service, a television reporter covering our grand opening asked me, "Pastor, how do you account for such a great response to a new church where so many churches are declining?"

I suddenly found that my voice had again disappeared. I encouraged the reporter to talk to our designated spokesperson, and I walked to the side of the tent. With tears welling in my eyes, I prayed, "God, thank you. Thank you for showing me—though I could send out thousands of mailers, make more than fifty thousand phone calls, develop a core group, plan a service, and even create a facility—that, 'Unless the LORD builds the house, its builders labor in vain' (Ps. 127:1)." God showed me on that day that training is important, that planning is essential, but, *most* importantly, that God's Spirit is the only truly indispensable factor in church planting.

I would be grieved if a church planter or church planting student were to read this book as just a tool kit of techniques for church starting. I hope it includes a great number of tools and techniques. But my greater intention is to move the reader to seek the Lord—the true Church Planter. I hope that, by reading these pages, the student will experience a taste of church start- ing—how awesome and humanly impossible it is. I want the reader to understand the centrality and indispensability of the One who founded and established the church—Jesus Christ, without whose presence the starter starts and the planter plants in vain.

When God is at work, a church is planted. It is always a miracle. When we allow ourselves to be used of God to plant churches that plant churches that plant churches, a church planting movement can emerge.

Church Planting Movements

Church planting movements have caught the attention of missionaries in the international field. In a few places, churches are exploding among people groups. Entire people groups are coming to Christ, and churches are being planted.

David Garrison has written an influential little book titled *Church Planting Movements*. It is available in its entirety at http://www.imb.org/CPM. The book describes and analyzes several church planting movements. The following lengthy edited quote describes the universal characteristics of such a movement:

1. Prayer. It is the vitality of prayer in the missionary's personal life that leads to its imitation in the life of the new church and its leaders. By revealing from the beginning the source of his power in prayer, the missionary effectively gives away the greatest resource he brings to the assignment.

2. Abundant gospel sowing. We have yet to see a Church Planting Movement emerge where evangelism is rare or absent. Every Church Planting Movement is accompanied by abundant sowing of the gospel.

3. Intentional church planting. In every Church Planting Movement, someone implemented a strategy of deliberate church planting before the movement got under way. There are several instances in which all the contextual elements were in place, but the missionaries lacked either the skill or the vision to lead a Church Planting Movement. However, once this ingredient was added to the mix, the results were remarkable.

4. Scriptural authority. Even among nonliterate people groups, the Bible has been the guiding source for doctrine, church polity and life itself. . . . In every instance, Scripture provided the rudder for the church's life, and its authority was unquestioned.

5. Local leadership. Missionaries involved in church planting movements often speak of the self-discipline required to mentor church planters rather than do the job of church planting themselves. . . . Walking alongside local church planters is the first step in cultivating and establishing local leadership.

6. Lay leadership. Church planting movements are driven by lay leaders. These lay leaders are typically bivocational and come from the general profile of the people group being reached. . . . Dependence upon seminary-trained—or in non-literate societies, even educated—pastoral leaders means that the work will always face a leadership deficit.

7. Cell or house churches. Church buildings do appear in Church Planting Movements. However, the vast majority of the churches continue to be small, reproducible cell churches.

8. Churches planting churches. In most church planting movements, the first churches were planted by missionaries or by missionary-trained church planters. At some point, however, as the movements entered a multiplicative phase of reproduction, the churches themselves began planting new churches.

9. Rapid reproduction. Most church planters involved in these movements contend that rapid reproduction is vital to the movement itself. They report that when reproduction rates slow down, the church planting movement falters. Rapid reproduction communicates the urgency and importance of coming to faith in Christ.

10. Healthy churches. Church growth experts have written extensively in recent years about the marks of a church. Most agree that healthy churches should carry out the following five purposes: (1) worship, (2) evangelistic and missionary outreach, (3) education and discipleship, (4) ministry, and (5) fellowship. In each of the church planting movements we studied, these five core functions were evident.[1]

Church planting movements have occurred before in North America. Baptists and Methodists on the western frontier planted thousands of churches in two decades. Calvary Chapel and Vineyard churches multiplied greatly in the 1970s and 1980s; and some consider this a church planting movement.

Scholarly articles about these two movements can be found at www.new-churches.com/ research.

But there is no such movement today, and none is on the horizon in North America. Churches are being planted, but as of yet there is no movement. Some are trying to encourage systems that promote church planting movements. The most common system seeking to promote a church planting movement is described in Kevin Mannoia's *Church Planting: The Next Generation.*

The twenty-first century church planting system is the planting strategy of the Free Methodist Church. This book is a description of their strategy with a strong emphasis on application in denominational leadership structures. Although it specifically deals with the Free Methodist denominational structure (and often reads like an internal denominational document), its application is much broader.

The text provides more than just the example of the work of one denomination. The system described is an expansion and explanation of the system created by Bob Logan. (Logan wrote the forward and Mannoia calls him "the leading resource on church planting in America.") Due to the pervasive influence of Bob Logan, most denominationally based North American church planting has developed a similar structure.[2]

For a full review of this and other major church planting books, see www.new-churches.com/books.

The Church Planting System

Mannoia divides the system into the following categories: Parent Church Network, Profile Assessment System, New Church Incubator, Recruitment Network, Pastor Factory, Church Planter's Summit, Maturing Church Cluster, Strategic Planning Network, Harvest 1000, and the Meta-Church Network.

The Parent Church Network is the development of a church planting vision in a group of local or regional congregations. Mannoia includes this first because it requires no large commitment of staff or resources—just a commitment to explore the possibilities of planting. The Parent Church Network generally develops into a cluster of three to five churches interested in planting and multiplication.

The Profile Assessment System is designed to objectively measure "skills, performance, and personality profile in prospective planters." Mannoia believes that the assessment system is the most important aspect for short-term impact and that proper assessment leads to a 90 percent success rate for planters.

The New Church Incubator is a resource rooted in fellowship. Planters are provided an empowering environment to assist them in the development of new churches. The incubator generally meets once a month and is generally run by a trained facilitator. Between these monthly meetings, a coach meets with each planter. This provides the emotional support needed for the planter and family.

The Pastor Factory is a resource to train laypeople to become founding pastors. This process generally is intended for the cell-based church. But any congregation with a leadership structure can use this system. This is generally divided into two categories: a leadership training system and a Pastor Factory network. They are divided by a sense of ministry call and the behavioral assessment mentioned earlier. Those who are called and assessed move from the leadership system to the factory network.

The Church Planter's Summit is a regular event, perhaps two or three days in length, to initiate new planter candidates. Candidates are generally invited to the event after they have completed the behavioral assessment and received a recommendation.

The Maturing Church Cluster is intended to provide new churches with needed support after the first year. The shift from year-old church to maturing church is significant, and the needs are significantly different. As the role of planter changes, the people must be included in the process in a different way.

The Strategic Planning Network is a network of pastors and lay leaders who want to avoid the pitfalls of institutionalization while focusing on the planting of new congregations. The intent is not to focus on new church planting exclusively, but on the development of stronger established churches as well.

The Harvest 1000 is focused on the financial resources necessary for the creation of a church planting movement. The goal is to raise funds specifically designated to new church plants. This task is one of the most difficult, since there is no visible need—only a vision.

The Meta-Church Network is a cluster of churches committed to implementing the ideas of the metachurch. The term, coined by Carl George, refers to a church that changes people through small-group ministries.

Mannoia's book ends with resources for implementation. The flow-chart provides a visual picture that denominational leaders can understand and implement. The implementation time line for developing a comprehensive church planting program is both realistic and challenging.

Many groups and denominations have adopted these systems, and they have helped raise church planting capacity. More churches are being started, and more of them are being successful.

Conclusion

Perhaps as we combine the power of the Spirit and Spirit-led systems, church planting movements *can* emerge in North America. My prayer, now that you have read this book, is that God will bless you as you begin this journey of planting his church. May God guide and empower you. In the words of Christian history's greatest church planter, "Now to him who is able to do immeasurably more than all we ask or imagine, according to his power that is at work within us, to him be glory in the church and in Christ Jesus throughout all generations, for ever and ever! Amen" (Eph. 3:20–21).

May God lead you to plant churches. There can be no greater task than evangelizing and conregationalizing North America. As we join God in this task, we become missional—on mission with God to see his kingdom expanded. We become participants in the *missio dei*. Who knows what God will do through us!

Resources for Further Reading

Akins, Thomas Wade. *Pioneer Evangelism*. Rio de Janeiro: Convenção Batista Brasileira, 1995.

Garrison, David. *Church Planting Movements*. Richmond, Va.: International Mission Board, 1999.

Mannoia, Kevin. *Church Planting: The Next Generation*. Indianapolis, Ind.: Light and Life Communication, 1994.

Nevius, John L. *Planting and Development of Missionary Churches*. Nutley, N.J.: Presbyterian & Reformed, 1958.

Patterson, George. *Church Multiplication Guide*. Pasadena, Calif.: William Carey Library, 1993.

Robb, John D. *Focus! The Power of People Group Thinking*. Pasadena: MARC Publishing, 1989.

Endnotes

Foreword

1. Ewa Czarnecka and Aleksander Fiut, *Conversations with Czeslaw Milosz*, trans. Richard Lourie (San Diego: Harcourt Brace Jovanovich, 1987), 136.

2. As quoted in Jack Kemp, "A Cultural Renaissance," delivered at Hillsdale's Shavano Institute for National Leadership Seminar, "Culture Wars: The Battle over Family Values," in Raleigh, N.C. See *The Christian Library: A Cultural Renaissance*, http://www.christianityinternational.com/culturalren.html. Accessed 2 June 2002.

3. For another treatment of the relationship between face and place, see Erving Goffman, *Interaction Ritual: Essays on Face-to-Face Behavior* (Chicago: Aldine, 1967), especially 5–8, 41–45.

4. John Haines, "Roots," in his *Living Off the Country: Essays on Poetry and Place* (Ann Arbor: University of Michigan Press, 1981), 85.

Chapter 1

1. Aubrey Malphurs, *Planting Growing Churches for the 21st Century* (Grand Rapids: Baker Book House, 1992), 22.

2. Bill Easum, http://www.easum.com/church.htm

3. Cited in Malphurs, *Planting Growing Churches*, 44.

4. C. Peter Wagner, *Church Planting for a Greater Harvest* (Ventura, Calif.: Regal Books, 1990), 11.

5. Tom Clegg and Tim Bird, *Lost in America: How You and Your Church Can Impact the World Next Door* (Loveland, Colo.: Group Publishers, 2001), 30; with additional information from an unpublished paper by Tom Clegg. Clegg is vice president for church multiplication, Church Resource Ministries, P.O. Box 202217, Des Moines, IA 50310. See www.crmnet.org.

6. "Excerpts from *The Easum Report*, accessed 6 March, 2001; available from http://easum.com/church.htm.

7. Of course, seminary education is extremely important in helping

provide doctrinal stability, ministry skills, and spiritual depth. The point, however, is that years of academic training are not necessary to start a church. In fact, waiting for a seminary-trained pastor in many cases delays God-called people from starting a church.

8. Roland Allen, *Missionary Methods: Saint Paul's or Ours?* (Grand Rapids: Eerdmans, 1962), 106.

9. Bivocational is having two vocations: a pastor and a secular job.

10. See Roger Fink and Rodney Stark, *The Churching of America, 1776–1990: Winners and Losers in Our Religious Economy* (New Brunswick, N.J.: Rutgers University Press, 1994).

11. Unfortunately, doctrinal error easily emerges in movements that do not provide adequate basic theological training. Wise denominations provide a middle option: offering training by extension for interested lay leaders and bivocational pastors.

12. These areas constitute what many experts call "multihousing" communities. By even conservative estimates, approximately 40 percent of the United States (with more in Canada) live in such housing, but merely 5 percent of those multihousing dwellers (an estimated 5,000,000 of the 100,000,000 persons!) have *any significant* connection with *any kind of church*. This population segment constitutes the largest unreached people group in North America. Sixty percent of the unchurched in North America live in multihousing communities.

13. Cited in Malphurs, *Planting Growing Churches*, 44.

14. Stuart Murray, *Church Planting: Laying Foundations* (Scottdale, Pa.: Herald Press, 2001), 21.

15. Ibid., 25.

16. George Hunter, "The Rationale for a Culturally Relevant Worship Service," *Journal of The American Society for Church Growth, Worship and Growth* 7 (1996): 131.

17. Win Arn, cited in Malphurs, *Planting Growing Churches*, 32.

18. Win Arn, *The Pastor's Manual for Effective Ministry* (Monrovia, Calif.: Church Growth, 1988), 16.

Chapter 2

1. Craig Van Gelder, ed., *Confident Witness—Changing World* (Grand Rapids: Eerdmans, 1999), 1.

2. Wilbert R. Shenk, *Write the Vision* (Harrisburg, Pa.: Trinity Press International, 1995), 43.

3. Craig Van Gelder, *The Essence of the Church* (Grand Rapids: Baker Books, 2000), 98.

4. The Southern Baptist Convention plants the most churches of any evangelical denomination—about 1,700 per year. The North American

Mission Board of the Southern Baptist Convention plans to help start 60,000 churches by 2020. The reason for this is the desire to have 100,000, churches in North America. That means that 50,000 churches are needed in order to reach that goal. Therefore, the plan is to plant 50,000 new churches in order to reach the goal of 100,000, leaving 10,000 for attrition.

5. Richard J. Mouw, "The Missionary Location of the North American Churches," in *Confident Witness—Changing World*, ed. Craig Van Gelder (Grand Rapids, Mich.: Eerdmans, 1999), 4.

6. Christendom, for the sake of this book, represents the realm/time where Christianity was the assumed religion of the West.

7. Douglas John Hall, "Metamorphosis: From Christendom to Diaspora," in *Confident Witness—Changing World*, ed. Craig Van Gelder (Grand Rapids, Mich.: Eerdmans, 1999), 69.

8. Wayne C. Stumme, "Interaction of Global and Local: A New Look at Mission Responsibility and Planning for Churches in the U.S.A. and Canada," in *Mission at the Dawn of the 21st Century*, ed. Paul Varo Martinson (Minneapolis, Minn.: Kirk House Publishers, 1999), 185.

9. James V. Brownson, *Speaking the Truth in Love* (Harrisburg, Pa.: Trinity Press International, 1998), 4–5.

10. An important point also needs to be addressed. As the North American church has become less missional, it has also become less mission-minded. Engel's Lilly Endowment study observed that "North American Christian commitment to world evangelization (mission) is in sharp retrenchment." See James F. Engel, "North American Global Mission: A Clouded Future," in *Mission at the Dawn of the 21st Century*, ed. Paul Varo Matinson (Minneapolis, Minn.: Kirk House Publishers, 1999), 190.

11. Mouw, "The Missionary Location of the North American Churches," 15.

12. Douglas John Hall, *The End of Christendom and the Future of Christianity* (Harrisburg, Pa.: Trinity Press International, 1997), 66.

13. Mouw, "The Missionary Location of the North American Churches," 5.

14. Charles Van Engen, *Mission on the Way* (Grand Rapids: Baker Books, 1996), 71.

15. Lesslie Newbigin, *A Word in Season* (Grand Rapids: Eerdmans, 1994), 67.

16. Van Engen, *Mission on the Way*, 164.

17. This scale was developed by Robert Don Hughes and is used here by permission.

18. Shenk, *Write the Vision*, 47.

19. Wilbert R. Shenk, "The Culture of Modernity as a Missionary Challenge," in *The Church Between Gospel & Culture,* ed. George R. Hunsberger and Craig Van Gelder (Grand Rapids: Eerdmans, 1996), 69.

20. George R. Hunsberger, "Sizing Up the Shape of the Church," in Hunsberger and Gelder, eds., *The Church Between Gospel & Culture,* 1996), 338.

21. Hall, *The End of Christendom and the Future of Christianity,* 55.

22. Shenk, *Write the Vision,* 47.

23. George R. Hunsberger, "The Newbigin Gauntlet," in *The Church Between Gospel & Culture,* ed. George R. Hunsberger and Craig Van Gelder (Grand Rapids: Eerdmans, 1996), 5.

24. Aubrey Malphurs, *Planting Growing Churches for the 21st Century* (Grand Rapids: Baker Book House, 1992), 27.

25. Craig Van Gelder, "Defining the Center—Finding the Boundaries," in *The Church Between Gospel & Culture,* ed. George R. Hunsberger and Craig Van Gelder (Grand Rapids: Eerdmans, 1996), 45.

26. Paul McKaughan, Dellana O'Brien, and William O'Brien, *Choosing a Future for U.S. Missions* (Monrovia, Calif.: MARC, 1998), 22.

27. Hunsberger, "The Newbigin Gauntlet," 5.

28. Charles Trueheart, "Welcome to the Next Church," *The Atlantic Monthly* [on-line], accessed 22 August 2002, http://www.theatlantic.com/issues/96aug/nxtchrch/nxtchrch.htm.

29. Ibid.

30. Calvin Guy, "Theological Foundations," in Donald A. McGavran ed., *Church Growth and Christian Mission* (William Carey Library, 1976 reprint), 44.

31. Stuart Murray, *Church Planting: Laying Foundations* (Scottdale, Pa.: Herald Press, 2001), 33.

32. Some have proposed that Paul's actions here are descriptive and not a good strategy. Since the Athenians "sneered," they reason that it proved to be an ill-advised strategy. This is a minority position. By connecting with the Athenian culture, he was able to connect with a resistant people.

33. Mouw, "The Missionary Location of the North American Churches," 8.

34. William J. Larkin, "Mission in Acts," in *Mission in the New Testament,* ed. William J. Larkin Jr., and Joel F. Williams (Maryknoll, N.Y.: Orbis Books, 1998), 180.

35. Martin Kähler as quoted in McKaughan, O'Brien, and O'Brien, *Choosing a Future for U.S. Missions,* 21.

36. James A. Scherer, "Key Issues to Be Considered in Global Mission Today: Crucial questions about mission theology, context, and expectations," in *Mission at the Dawn of the 21st Century,* ed. Paul Varo Martinson (Minneapolis, Minn.: Kirk House Publishers, 1999), 12.

37. Wilburt Shenk, "The Culture of Modernity as a Missionary Challenge," in *The Church Between Gospel and Culture*, ed. George R. Hunsberger and Craig Van Gelder (Grand Rapids: Eerdmans, 1996), 69–78.

38. Shenk, *Write the Vision*, 86.

39. Scherer, "Key Issues to Be Considered in Global Mission Today: Crucial questions about mission theology, context, and expectations," 12.

40. Shenk, *Write the Vision*, 90.

41. Martin Erdmann, "Mission in John's Gospel and Letters," in *Mission in the New Testament*, ed. William J. Larkin Jr. and Joel F. Williams (Maryknoll, N.Y.: Orbis Books, 1998), 212.

42. Andreas J. Köstenberger and Peter T. O'Brien, *Salvation to the Ends of the Earth* (Downers Grove, Ill.: InterVarsity Press, 2001), 269.

43. International Missionary Council as quoted in James A. Scherer, "Mission Theology," in *Toward the 21st Century in Christian Mission*, ed. James M. Phillips and Robert T. Coote (Grand Rapids: Eerdmans, 1993), 194–95.

44. Köstenberger and O'Brien, *Salvation to the Ends of the Earth*, 269.

45. Wilbert R. Shenk, "Mission Strategies," in *Toward the 21st Century in Christian Mission*, ed. James M. Phillips and Robert T. Coote (Grand Rapids: Eerdmans, 1993), 221–23.

46. Larkin, "Mission in Acts," 175.

47. Shenk, "The Culture of Modernity as a Missionary Challenge," 71.

48. This was not an illegitimate mission, but it was an incomplete mission view.

49. Van Gelder, *The Essence of the Church*, 55.

50. Peter Beyerhaus, "Indigenous Churches," in *Concise Dictionary of Christian World Mission*, ed. Stephen Neil, Gerald H. Anderson, and John Goodwin (Nashville, Tenn.: Abingdon Press, 1971), 278.

51. Donald R. Jacobs, "Contextualization in Mission," in *Toward the 21st Century in Christian Mission*, ed. James M. Phillips and Robert T. Coote (Grand Rapids: Eerdmans, 1993), 236.

52. Hunsberger, "The Newbigin Gauntlet," 24.

53. Roland Allen, *Missionary Methods: Saint Paul's or Ours?* (Grand Rapids: Eerdmans, 1962), 98–99.

54. Van Gelder, ed., *Confident Witness—Changing World*, 66.

55. Mouw, "The Missionary Location of the North American Churches," 14.

56. International Missionary Council, "The Growing Church: The Madras Series," Papers Based on the Meeting of the International Missionary Council, at Tambaram, Madras, India, December 12–29, 1938. Vol. 2 (New York, International Missionary Council), 276, cited in

Mark Terry, Ebbie Smith, and Justice Anderson, eds., *Missiology* (Nashville: Broadman & Holman, 1998), 311.

57. Jacobs, "Contextualization in Mission," 240.

58. Some put the break with Judaism as early as the 1960s (G.B. Caird, *The Apostolic Age* [London: Gerald Duckworth & Company, Ltd., 1955], 141), but this is only partially true. Clearly there is a break, but Christians remained in the synagogue until they were forcibly expelled. Expulsion does not happen to a people uninvolved in synagogue life.

59. Adolf Harnack, *The Expansion of Christianity in the First Three Centuries* (Eugene, Oreg.: Wipf & Stock Publishers, 1997), 72.

60. Justin, *Dialogue with Trypho,* Chapter XLVII: "Justin Communicates with Christians Who Observe the Law. Not a Few Catholics Do Otherwise" [on-line], accessed 22 August 1999, http://www.ccel.org/fathers2/ANF-01/anf01-48.htm#P4424_915856.

61. Justin, *Dialogue with Trypho,* Chapter XVII: "The Jews Sent Persons Through the Whole Earth to Spread Calumnies on Christians" [on-line], accessed 22 August 1999, http://www.ccel.org/fathers2/ANF-01/anf01-48.htm#P4043_787325.

62. Irenaeus, *Against Heresies,* Chapter XXVI: "Doctrines of Cerinthus, the Ebionites, and Nicolaitanes" [on-line], accessed 22 August 1999, http://www.ccel.org/fathers2/ANF-01/anf01-58.htm#P6642_1589520.

63. Shenk, "The Culture of Modernity as a Missionary Challenge," 72.

64. C. Peter Wagner, *Church Planting for a Greater Harvest* (Ventura, Calif.: Regal Books, 1990), 11.

65. Shenk, *Write the Vision,* 48.

66. Shenk, "The Culture of Modernity as a Missionary Challenge," 74.

67. John R. "Pete" Hendrick, "Congregations with Missions vs. Missionary Congregations," in *The Church Between Gospel & Culture,* ed. George R. Hunsberger and Craig Van Gelder (Grand Rapids: Eerdmans, 1996), 304.

68. David J. Bosch, *Transforming Mission* (Maryknoll, N.Y.: Orbis Books, 1998), 21.

69. J. Andrew Kirk, *The Mission of Theology and Theology as Mission* (Valley Forge, Pa.: Trinity Press International, 1997), 39.

70. Dean S. Gilliland, "Contextual Theology as Incarnational Mission," in *The Word Among Us,* ed. Dean S. Gilliland (Dallas: Word Publishing, 1989), 10–11.

71. Van Gelder, *Confident Witness—Changing World,* 14–15.

72. Bosch, *Transforming Mission,* 495.

73. Tom A. Steffen and David J. Hesselgrave, *Reconnecting God's Story to Ministry: Cross Cultural Storytelling at Home and Abroad* (Center for Organization & Ministry, 1997).

74. Bosch, *Transforming Mission*, 494.

75. Malphurs, *Planting Growing Churches*, 46

76. Dean S. Gilliland, ed., *The Word Among Us* (Dallas: Word Publishing, 1989), vii.

Chapter 3

1. Talmadge R. Amberson, "The Foundations for Church Planting," in *The Birth of Churches*, ed. Talmadge R. Amberson (Nashville: Broadman Press, 1979), 45.

2. Elmer Towns, *Getting a Church Started: A Student Manual for Theological Foundation and Practical Techniques of Planting a Church* (Lynchburg, VA.: Church Growth Institute, 1985), 8. This book is now available free at www.elmertowns.com. Towns includes Mark 16:15 in his list. However, the oldest and best Greek texts of Mark have not included this verse, suggesting that it is a later addition to the original text. Thus, I have included only four.

4. Outline created by John Worcester, http://www.churchplanting.net/resources/index.htm.

5. John Mark Terry, unpublished document.

6. http://www.redeemer2.com/rucpc/rucpc/index.cfm.

7. This meaning is exactly the reason for the eunuch's joy (Acts 8:39). He who loved the Jewish nation and the Jewish law could not, because of his emasculation, become part of the community and was denied baptism by the Jews. The gospel of Christ included even him and meant he could be baptized without first undergoing (an impossible) circumcision. See Frank Stagg, *The Book of Acts* (Nashville: Broadman Press, 1954), 106–109.

8. *ChurchNext: Quantum Changes in How We Do Ministry* (Downers Grove, Ill.: InterVarsity Press, 2000), 11.

9. Ibid., 33.

10. The Philippian emissary, Epaphroditus, serves as a perfect example of a major city church which sent its own to serve, and probably to become an evangelist, in this case, alongside Paul (see Phil. 2:25–30; 4:18).

Chapter 4

1. Biblical and historical examples here, and in the rest of this chapter, were researched and partly written for me by my former teaching assistant, J. D. Payne. Today he serves as a church planting professor. He also has written an excellent Ph.D. dissertation examining current church planting practice in North America. He can be reached at jpayne@sbts.edu.

2. John B. Polhill, *Acts,* in the New American Commentary, vol. 26 (Nashville: Broadman Press, 1992), 319.

3. Justo L. Gonzalez, *The Story of Christianity: The Reformation to the Present Day,* vol. 2 (New York: HarperCollins Publishers, 1985), 246.

4. John Mark Terry, *Evangelism: A Concise History* (Nashville: Broadman & Holman Publishers, 1994), 128–29.

5. Robert E. Logan and Steven L. Ogne, *Churches Planting Churches: A Comprehensive Guide for Multiplying New Congregations* (Carol Stream, Ill.: ChurchSmart Resources, 1995), VHS tape, "Churches Planting Churches."

6. V. Simpson Turner Sr., "A History of African-American Evangelistic Activity," in Lee N. June, ed., *Evangelism and Discipleship in African-American Churches* (Grand Rapids: Zondervan Publishing House, 1999), 21.

7. See http://homechurch.org/registry/index.html for a directory of house churches.

8. John Dee, "China Report 1999: A Visit with the Underground Church Now 85 Million Strong." See http://www.hccentral.com/magazine/china2.html.

9. Charles Brock, *Indigenous Church Planting: A Practical Journey* (Neosho, Mo.: Church Growth International, 1994), 262.

10. Brock, *Indigenous Church Planting,* 86.

11. Steve is the founder of the U.S. Center for Church Planting (www.churchplantingcenter.com).

12. Terry, *Evangelism,* 130.

13. C. Peter Wagner, *Church Planting for a Greater Harvest: A Comprehensive Guide* (Ventura, Calif.: Regal Books, 1990), 71–72.

14. Some may argue that Titus could also be an example of this paradigm, but this is not the case. An examination of the ministry of Titus reveals a similarity to that of the ministry of Paul. Titus 1:5 says, "For this reason I left you in Crete, that you might set in order what remains, and appoint elders in every city as I directed you" (NASB). Titus was not confined to one location but rather was to minister across the island in the various cities. Timothy, on the other hand, was to concentrate on the church in Ephesus.

15. Michael Nicholls, "Missions, Yesterday and Today: Charles Haddon Spurgeon (1834–92), Church Planter," in *Five Till Midnight: Church Planting for A.D. 2000 and Beyond,* Tony Cupit, ed. (Atlanta: Home Mission Board, 1994), 94.

16. Ibid., 94

17. Ibid., 96.

18. http://www.stonecreekonline.org.

19. http://english.fgtv.com.

20. Wagner, *Church Planting,* 61–62.

21. http://pccchurch.com.

22. http://www.roccnet.com.

23. http://www.millcreek.org.

24. Terry, *Evangelism,* 48.

25. See Loyd Childs, "Teams Multiply Churches in Malaysia/Singapore," *Urban Mission* 2 (1985): 33–39; Ben A. Sawatsky, "A Church Planting Strategy for World Class Cities," *Urban Mission* 3 (1985): 7–19; Roger S. Greenway, "The 'Team' Approach to Urban Church Planting," *Urban Mission* 4 (1987): 3–5.

26. James E. Westgate, "Church Planting Strategies for World-Class Cities," in Harvie M. Conn ed., *Planting and Growing Urban Churches: From Dream to Reality* (Grand Rapids: Baker Books, 1997), 205.

27. Westgate, "Church Planting Strategies," 204.

28. Ibid., 205.

29. http://kensingtoncc.org.

30. http://www.newhope.org.

31. From the author's Ph.D. dissertation, "The Impact of the Church Planting Process and Other Selected Factors on the Attendance of Southern Baptist Church Plants."

Chapter 5

1. David W. Schenk and Ervin R. Stutzman, *Creating Communities of the Kingdom* (Scottsdale, Pa.: 1988), 43.

2. David J. Bosch, *Transforming Missions: Paradigm Shifts in Theology of Mission* (Maryknoll, N.Y.: Orbis Books, 2001), p. 132 citing W. H. Ollrog, *Paulus und seine Mitarbeiter* (Eukirchen-Vluyn: Neukirchener Verlag, 1979).

3. Stott, *The Message of Acts,* 300.

4. Longenecker, *The Expositor's Bible Commentary,* 284.

5. Craig Wurst, student paper, "Who Can Plant Churches?"

6. Daniel Sanchez, Curt Watke, Ebbie Smith, *Starting Reproducing Congregations* (Cumming, Ga.: Church Starting Network, 2001), 33–34.

7. From "The Impact of the Church Planting Process and Other Selected Factors on the Attendance of Southern Baptist Church," Ph.D. dissertation of the author.

8. Kevin Maples, student paper, "Who Can Plant a Church?"

9. Joe S. Ratliff, *Church Planting in the African-American Community* (Nashville: Broadman Press, 1993), 51.

10. These categories describe thirteen qualities from chapter 2 of Charles Ridley's *How to Select Church Planters* (Pasadena, Calif.: Fuller Evangelistic Association, 1988), 7–11.

11. http://www.christian-faith.com/evangelism/churchplantingman-ual.html.

Chapter 6

1. Aubrey Malphurs, in his 1992 book *Planting Growing Churches for the 21st Century* (Grand Rapids: Baker Book House), advocates full-time staff members. Although this model best fits the biblical teaching on governance, I believe elders may be either paid staff members or unpaid volunteers.

2. See Rick Warren, *The Purpose-Driven Church* (Grand Rapids: Zondervan, 1995) for some helpful guidelines on organizing a church for growth.

3. Larry L. Lewis, *Church Planter's Handbook* (Nashville: Broadman & Holman Publishers, 1992), 84.

Chapter 7

1. Larry L. Lewis, *Church Planter's Handbook* (Nashville: Broadman & Holman Publishers, 1992). I have altered his time allocations to some extent; Lewis treats the varied responsibilities of church planters comprehensively. This resource, though slightly dated, remains a serviceable resource, especially for planters in rural areas.

2. See www.sermoncentral.com for a listing of sermon resource sites.

3. Both of these graphs come from my Ph.D. dissertation.

Chapter 8

1. We will consider *vocational* (full-time) church planting teams at a later point.

2. Aubrey Malphurs, *Planting Growing Churches for the 21st Century* (Grand Rapids: Baker Book House, 1992), Malphurs, *Planting Growing Churches* (Grand Rapids: Baker Books, 2000), 289, citing Schaller, "Southern Baptists," 8.

3. See Bob Logan, *Church Planter Toolkit,* tape 7, "Getting Your Ministries Ready for Birth." Available from ChurchSmart resources (www.churchsmart.com).

4. www.riverside.org

5. Steve Sjogren and Rob Lewin, *Community of Kingness* (Ventura, Calif.: Regal by Gospel Light, 2003), 207. See also Steve Sjogren, "Growing Pastor [Past the] Temptation to Quit," online at http://www.plantthefuture.org/pdf/Growing_Past_the_Temptation_to_Quit _by_Steve_Sjogren.pdf.

Chapter 9

1. The importance of this assertion cannot be stated too strongly. Not understanding the culture of one's focus group is sure to result in failure or diminished effectiveness.

2. Exegesis, pronounced "ex-uh-GEE-sus," this term, from Greek, means "to show the way," or "to guide." Thus, to "exegete" the culture is to study the setting in such a way that one receives guidance for understanding the meanings of cultural patterns, systems, and behaviors.

3. Adapted from Thom Rainer, *The Bridger Generation* (Nashville: Broadman & Holman, 1997).

4. One helpful resource for such studies is Paul G. Hiebert, *Anthropological Insights for Missionaries* (Grand Rapids: Baker Book House, 1985).

5. One overview of these groups and issues in ministry with them is *Three Generations* by Gary McIntosh (Grand Rapids: Revell, 1995). Although McIntosh focuses only on Builders, Boomers, and Busters, Thom Rainer's *The Bridger Generation* (Nashville: Broadman & Holman, 1997) provides one understanding of the newest demographic grouping. Elmer Towns has also provided helpful contrasts between the Builders and Boomers in his conference on "How to Reach the Baby Boomer." Much of the following material is influenced by Towns's resource.

6. http://www.bgct.org/content/30/generic.cfm?ContentUUID= AA342D31-4F8B-4EBC-A4644E29C9749CEA&state=detail.

7. Unpublished document from John Worchester, church planting consultant, Fort Worth, TX. Visit his Web site, www.churchplanting.net.

8. http://webuildpeople.ag.org/wbp/leader_development/ 9201_baby_boomer.cfm.

Chapter 10

1. Jimmy Long, *Generating Hope: A Strategy for Reaching the Postmodern Generation* (Downers Grove, Ill.: Intervarsity Press, 1997), 13.

2. Tim Celek and Dieter Zander, *Inside the Soul of a New Generation* (Grand Rapids: Zondervan Publishing Co., 1996), 20.

3. http://www.theooze.com/articles/read.cfm?ID=98&CATID=4.

4. Leonard I. Sweet, *Soul Tsunami: Sink or Swim in New Millennium Culture* (Grand Rapids: Zondervan Publishing House, 1999), 25.

5. Long, *Generating Hope,* 41.

6. Bill Stoneman, "Beyond Rocking the Ages: An Interview with J. Walker Smith," *American Demographics,* May 1998.

7. From a post by Gerald Pineda at http://www.fourthturning.com/ cgi-local/netforum/politicsandeconomics/a.cgi/14—14.28.1.

8. Celek and Zander go so far as to defend the comparison of the Buster era to that of the Great Depression. Ibid., 70.

9. Ibid., 20.

10. Sweet, *Soul Tsunami*, 389.

11. Darrel L. Guder, *Missional Church* (Grand Rapids: Eerdmans, 1998), 47.

12. Stanley E. Grenz, *A Primer on Postmodernism* (Grand Rapids: Eerdmans, 1996), 174.

13. Richard J. Mouw, "The Missionary Location of the North American Churches," in *Confident Witness—Changing World,* ed. Craig Van Gelder (Grand Rapids: Eerdmans, 1999), 4.

14. Craig Van Gelder, *The Essence of the Church* (Grand Rapids: Baker Books, 2000), 98.

15. Wilbert R. Shenk, *Write the Vision* (Harrisburg, Pa.: Trinity Press International, 1995), 43.

16. Walter Truett Anderson, *Reality Isn't What It Used to Be* (San Francisco: Harper and Row, 1990).

17. Millard J. Erickson, *Postmodernizing the Faith: Evangelical Responses to the Challenge of Postmodernism* (Grand Rapids: Baker, 1998), 17.

18. Oden in David S. Dockery, ed., *The Challenge of Postmodernism: An Evangelical Engagement* (Grand Rapids: Baker, 1995), 45.

19. Nietzsche is best known for his inflammatory "death of God" language. Nietzsche's point was not that God died. His point was that Christianity had lost its influence in culture without anything to replace it.

20. Grenz, *The Challenge,* 92.

21. Grenz, *Primer,* 5.

22. Long, *Generating Hope,* 61.

23. Conyers, *Eclipse of Heaven,* p. 175, cited in Long, *Generating Hope,* 125.

24. Grenz, *Primer,* 45.

25. Grenz, *Revisioning,* 65–66.

26. Eddie Gibbs, *ChurchNext: Quantum Changes in How We Do Ministry* (Downers Grove, Ill.: InterVarsity Press, 2000), 22.

27. Wells, 286.

28. Wells, 101.

29. Long calls 1968 the decade in microcosm (*Generating Hope,* 66).

30. Erickson, *Postmodernizing the Faith,* 19.

31. Grenz, *Primer,* 131.

32. Robert E. Webber, *Ancient-Future Faith: Rethinking Evangelicalism for a Postmodern World* (Grand Rapids: Baker, 1999), 21; italics Webber's.

33. Ibid., 23.

34. Guder, *Missional Church,* 40.

35. Grenz, *Primer,* 40.

36. Ibid., 93.

37. Ibid., 12.

38. Jean-François Lyotard, *The Postmodern Condition: A Report on Knowledge,* trans. Geoff Bennington and Brian Massumi, "Theory and History of Literature," vol. 10 (Minneapolis: University of Minnesota Press, 1984), xxiv.

39. Guder, *Missional Church,* 39.

40. Grenz, *Primer,* 8.

41. Long, *Missional Church,* 71.

42. Grenz, *Primer,* 44.

43. http://www.mit.edu/~dmaze/leg_morality.html; accessed February 1, 2002.

44. Grenz, *Primer,* 15.

45. Erickson, *Postmodernizing the Faith,* 20.

46. Grenz, *Primer,* 13.

47. Ibid., 166.

48. Lesslie Newbigin, *A Word in Season* (Grand Rapids: Eerdmans, 1994), 67.

Chapter 11

1. Leonard I. Sweet, *Soul Tsunami: Sink or Swim in New Millennium Culture* (Grand Rapids: Zondervan Publishing House, 1999), 23.

2. http://www.theooze.com/articles/read.cfm?ID=70&CATID=4

3. Robert E. Webber, *Ancient-Future Faith: Rethinking Evangelicalism for a Postmodern World* (Grand Rapids: Baker, 1999), 13.

4. Sweet, *Tsunami,* 18.

5. Eddie Gibbs, *ChurchNext: Quantum Changes in How We Do Ministry* (Downers Grove, Ill.: InterVarsity Press, 2000), 33.

6. Nash, 50.

7. Nash, 55.

8. Sweet, *Tsunami,* 45.

9. Darrel L. Guder, *Missional Church* (Grand Rapids: Eerdmans, 1998), 1.

10. Eddie Gibbs, *ChurchNext* (Downers Grove, Ill.: InterVarsity Press, 2000), 10.

11. Ibid., 43.

12. Ibid., 11.

13. Ibid., 33.

Chapter 12

1. Nash, 77.

2. Mark Swan contributed to the research and writing of this section as part of a study group, "Church Planting in a Postmodern Age."

3. Coupland, 359 from Long.

4. Nash, 49.

5. Mouw, "The Missionary Location of the North American Churches," 8.

6. http://www.gospelcom.net/tmattingly/2000/ col/col.05.17 .2000.html.

7. Eddie Gibbs, *ChurchNext: Quantum Changes in How We Do Ministry* (Downers Grove, Ill.: InterVarsity Press, 2000), 174.

8. Morganthaler, 44.

9. Gibbs, *ChurchNext*, 174.

10. Dan R. Stiver, "Much Ado About Athens and Jerusalem: The Implications of Postmodernism for Faith," *Review and Expositor,* 91 (11/94): 98.

11. Ralph Greenwell contributed to the research and writing of this section as part of a study group, "Church Planting in a Postmodern Age."

12. Sweet, *Soul Tsunami,* 215.

13. Gibbs, *ChurchNext,* 69.

14. Survey response from Freeway Church in Baton Rouge.

15. Celek and Zander, *Inside the Soul of the New Generation,* 99.

16. Ibid.

17. Debbie Dornfeld contributed to the research and writing of this section as part of a study group, "Church Planting in a Postmodern Age."

18. Sweet, *Soul Tsunami,* 342.

19. Leonard Sweet, *Postmodern Pilgrims: First Century Passion for the 21st Century World* (Nashville: Broadman & Holman Publishers, 2000), 61.

20. Survey response from Downtown Community Fellowship, Athens, Georgia.

21. Ken Baugh and Rich Hurst, *Getting Real* (Colorado Springs, Colo.: Navpress, 2000), 65.

22. Ibid., 82–83.

23. Celek and Zander, *Inside the Soul of the New Generation,* 140.

24. www.newhorizonsfellowship.com.

25. Mark Swan contributed to the research and writing of this section as part of a study group, "Church Planting in a Postmodern Age."

26. Celek and Zander, *Inside the Soul of the New Generation,* 138.

27. Sweet, *Soul Tsunami,* 209.

28. Darrel L. Guder, *Missional Church* (Grand Rapids: Eerdmans, 1998), 29.

29. Long, *Generating Hope,* 147.

30. Sweet, *Soul Tsunami,* 210.

31. From Faithworks, http://www.theooze.com/articles/read.cfm?ID=113&CATID=2.

32. Ford, 199.

33. Morganthaler, 84.

34. Sweet, *Soul Tsunami,* 199.

35. Ibid., 307.

36. Jonah Paffhausen in http://www.theooze.com/articles/read.cfm?ID=133&CATID=4.

37. Beaudoin, 161.

38. Morganthaler, chapter 5.

39. http://www.imagodeicommunity.com/.

40. http://www.thebridgechurch.com/.

41. http://www.ginkworld.net/.

42. http://www.freewaybr.com/.

43. Celek and Zander, *Inside the Soul of the New Generation,* 126.

44. Eugene Peterson, http://www.theooze.com/articles/read.cfm?ID=42&CATID=2.

45. Sweet, *Soul Tsunami,* 425.

46. Ibid., 207.

47. Ford, 14.

48. Eric Sisk contributed to the research and writing of this section as part of a study group, "Church Planting in a Postmodern Age."

49. Sweet, *Soul Tsunami,* 89.

50. Guder, *Missional Church,* 45.

51. Beaudoin, ix.

52. Gibbs, *ChurchNext,* 129.

53. Mark Sayers from http://www.phuture.org/article.asp?ArticleID=56.

54. Gibbs, *Church Next,* 161.

55. Webber, *Ancient Future Faith,* 91.

56. Sweet, *Postmodern Pilgrims,* 72.

57. Guder, *Missional Church,* 37.

58. Gibbs, *ChurchNext,* 124.

59. Celek and Zander, *Inside the Soul of the Next Generation,* 67.

60. Gibbs, *ChurchNext,* 123.

61. Sweet in an interview with David Trotter and Spencer Burke in "The Ooze." http://www.theooze.com/articles/read.cfm?ID=142&CATID=4.

62. Sweet, *Soul Tsunami,* 31.

63. Grenz, *Primer,* 17.

64. www.cornerstone-sf.org.

65. www.cornerstone-sf.org, "Experience Cornerstone."

66. Beaudoin, 57.

67. www.ginghamsburg.org.

68. Guder, *Missional Church*, 103.

69. Gibbs, *ChurchNext*, 56.

70. Eric Sisk contributed to the research and writing of this section as part of a study group, "Church Planting in a Postmodern Age."

71. Long, *Generation Hope*, 133–34.

72. Celek and Zander, *Inside the Soul of a New Generation*, 58.

73. Long, *Generation Hope*, 50.

74. Ibid., 145.

75. Ibid., 146.

76. Gibbs, *ChurchNext*, 202.

77. Ford, 172.

78. Gibbs, *ChurchNext*, 196.

79. Celek and Zander, *Inside the Soul of a New Generation*, 59.

80. Sweet, *Soul Tsunami*, 170.

81. http://www.theooze.com/articles/read.cfm?ID=98&CATID=4.

82. Gibbs, *ChurchNext*, 198.

83. Grenz, *Primer*, 169.

84. Sweet, *Soul Tsunami*, 53.

85. Debbie Dornfeld and Ralph Greenwell contributed to the research and writing of this section as part of a study group, "Church Planting in a Postmodern Age."

86. Long, *Generation Hope*, 153.

87. From an unpublished paper written by Ralph Greenwell, no date.

88. Long, *Generation Hope*, 154.

89. Celek and Zander, *Iniside the Soul of a New Generation*, 32.

90. Sweet, *Soul Tsunami*, 301.

91. Celek and Zander, *Inside the Soul of a New Generation*, 33.

92. Sweet, *Soul Tsunami*, 220.

93. Sweet, *Postmodern Pilgrims*, 60.

94. Ibid., 59–60.

95. Baugh and Hurst, *Getting Real*, 47.

96. Ibid., 59.

97. Gibbs, *ChurchNext*, 107.

98. Ibid., 107–108.

99. Wayne Cordeiro, *Doing Church as a Team* (Ventura, Calif.: Regal Books, 2001), 176.

100. George Cladis, *Leading the Team-Based Church* (San Francisco, Calif.: Jossey-Bass Publishers, 1999), 39.

Chapter 13

1. Joe S. Ratliff and Michael J. Cox, eds., *Church Planting in the African-American Community* (Nashville: Broadman Press, 1993), 72.

2. Hozell C. Francis, *Church Planting in the African-American Context* (Grand Rapids: Zondervan Publishing House, 2000), 45.

3. Ratliff and Cox, Ibid., 17.

4. Ibid., 19–21.

5. Ibid., 21.

6. Ibid., 51.

7. Ibid., 91.

8. Ibid., 63.

9. Ibid.

10. Oscar I. Romo, *American Mosaic: Church Planting in Ethnic America* (Nashville: Broadman Press, 1993), 41.

11. Ibid., 28.

12. http://www.ccsb.ca/teams/robertson.htm.

13. Romo, *American Mosaic*, 29.

14. Ibid., 75–76.

15. Ibid., 32.

16. The last four references are from Richard Harris, *The Planter Update*, May 15, 2002.

17. Ibid., 27.

18. Ibid., 90.

19. http://www.nazarene.org/cg/research/ansr/articles/jen10.html is the original article. I edited down the version found at http://www.ethnichar-vest.com/links/articles/appleby_models.htm and included it here. The Ethnic Harvest Web site is a must for those who are planting ethnic churches.

Chapter 14

1. http://www.nytimes.com/2001/04/29/national/29PRAY.html.

2. Donald R. Allen, *Barefoot in the Church, Sensing the Authentic Through the House Church* (Richmond: John Knox Press, 1972). Electronically reproduced at http://homechurch.org/miscellaneous/allen2.html.

3. Wolfgang Simson, "Fifteen Theses Towards a Re-Incarnation of the Church" at http://www.house2house.tv/issues/wolfgang15theses.shtml.

4. Dick Scoggins, *Planting House Churches in Networks, a Manual from the Perspective of a Church Planting Team* (Fellowship of Church Planters).

5. Frank A. Viola, "Some Streams of the House Church," Present Testimony Ministry; 1405 Valley Place; Brandon, FL 33510; E-mail: Fviola3891@aol.com.

6. The Homechurch Homepage, Frequently Asked Questions, http://www.webcom.com/hchp/faqs.htm.

7. Nate Krupp, "Caution—Steps Toward Denominationalism," at http://www.radchr.net/stepstod.htm.

8. Charles Brock, *Indigenous Church Planting: A Practical Journey* (Neosho, Mo.: Church Growth International, 1994), chapter 2.

9. Ibid., chapter 4.

10. Wayne Grudem, *Systematic Theology: An Introduction to Biblical Doctrine* (Grand Rapids: Zondervan Publishing House, 1994), 857.

11. Roland Allen, *Missionary Methods: St Paul's or Ours?* (Grand Rapids: Eerdmans, 1962), 126.

12. Floyd Tidsmorth Jr., *Life Cycle of a New Congregation* (Nashville: Broadman Press, 1992), 91.

13. "The Church," at http://www.sbc.net/bfm/bfm2000.asp.

14. Westminster Confession of Faith, at http://www.pcanet.org/general/cof_chapxxi-xxv.htm#chapxxv.

15. http://www.breakawayministries.org.

Chapter 15

1. Donald A. McGavran, *Understanding Church Growth,* 3rd edition (Grand Rapids: Eerdmans, 1990), 163–178.

2. Revelation 7:9.

3. Rick Warren, *The Purpose-Driven Church* (Grand Rapids: Zondervan Publishing House, 1995), 170.

4. *Indigenous* means "from the area." It includes things like indigenous dress, music, language, etc.

5. Median is the "middle number." The median of 80 and 20 is 50.

6. Tom A. Steffen and David J. Hesselgrave, *Reconnecting God's Story to Ministry: Cross Cultural Story Telling at Home and Abroad* (Center for Organization and Ministry), 1997.

7. McGavran, *Understanding Church Growth*, 163–178.

8. Larry L. Lewis, *Church Planter's Handbook* (Nashville: Broadman & Holman Publishers, 1992), 27.

9. Ibid., 20.

Chapter 16

1. http://www.rockspringschurch.com/.

2. Personal interview with Chris Brewer, 26 April 26 2002.

3. Lunch meeting with Andy Stanley, 25 August 2002.

4. There are different versions of the Engel Scale. Malphurs describes a slightly different version than I have reproduced (Malphurs, *Planting Growing Churches*, 275).

5. Engel erroneously places repentance before regeneration. Theologians have historically held that regeneration precedes (and enables) repentance.

6. http://www.thegraymatrix.info.

7. http://www.brigada.org/today/articles/gray-matrix.html.

8. Robert Logan, *Church Planter Tool Kit,* audiotape 5.

9. LifeWay Prospect Services, 1-800-464-2799. This service sells lists of new babies, new movers, new marriages, and lists of new families with children.

10. Herb Miller, *How to Build a Magnetic Church.* Creative Leadership Series, Lyle Schaller, ed. (Nashville, Tenn.: Abingdon Press, 1987), 72–73.

Chapter 17

1. Bob Logan, "Church Planter Toolkit," tape 7, "Getting Your Ministries Ready for Birth," available from ChurchSmart resources (www.churchsmart.com).

2. Larry L. Lewis, *The Church Planter's Handbook* (Nashville: Broadman Press, 1993), 36.

3. Aubrey Malphurs, *Planting Growing Churches for the 21st Century* (Grand Rapids: Baker Book House, 1992), 320.

4. http://www.highpointechurch.org/.

5. The U.S. Postal Service requires a Business Reply Mail Automation System (BRMAS) account in order to receive business reply cards. Most post offices can explain the process of opening such an account. The permit costs US$205 and Canadian $465 at the time this was written. There is also a charge for each piece.

Chapter 18

1. Dale Galloway, *The Small Group Book* (Grand Rapids: Revell, 1995), 17.

2. Carl F. George, *Prepare Your Church for the Future* (Tarrrytown, N.Y.: Revell, 1991.

3. "Meta" suggests the idea of change. Thus, "meta church" is a "change" church, a church that changes or transforms in order to transform lives.

4. http://www.christthekinganglican.org.

5. http://www.christthekinganglican.org/docs/smgrps.htm.

6. Jeff Clark. E-mail, 2 October 2002.

Chapter 19

Adapted from Robert Logan and Steven L. Ogne, *Churches Planting Churches* (1995), 4, 10–11.

Ralph Moore, *Starting a New Church* (Ventura, Calif.: Gospel Light, 2002), 56.

3. http://www.inchristchurch.org.

4. http://www.fba.org/FBA/inchristchurch/index.html.

5. Postage has since gone up!

6. http://www.frontierbaptist-wny.com/.

7. Steve Sjogren and Rob Lewin, *Community of Kindness* (Ventura, CA: Regal from Gospel Light, 2003), 172–74.

8. Dan Ramsey, *101 Best Weekend Businesses*, Career Press, 1996, as cited at http://www.plantingministries.org/chapt3.htm.

9. http://www.plantthefuture.org/pdf/Growing_Past_the_Temptation_to_Quit_by_Steve_Sjogren.pdf.

10. Lewis, *Church Planter's Handbook*, 22.

11. In my own denomination, the Southern Baptist Convention, that usually inolves 8 percent to the Cooperative Program and 2 percent to the local Association.

Chapter 20

1. C. Peter Wagner, *Church Planting for a Greater Harvest*, (Ventura, Calif.: Regal Books, 1990), 118. Italics in the original.

2. Elmer Towns, *Getting a Church Started: A Student Manual for Theological Foundation and Practical Techniques of Planting a Church* (Lynchburg, VA.: Church Growth Institute, 1985), available at www.elmertowns.com, no page number.

3. From "The Barometer of the Southern Baptist Faith in America," a PowerPoint presentation. This research was done for the North American Mission Board of the Southern Baptist Convention and presented at the NAMB summer meeting in 2001. Its research covers several groups.

4. http://www.churchmarketing.com.

5. http://www.churchmarketing.com/articles/robert.html.

Chapter 21

1. Facilities for a growing new church will be discussed later.

2. http://www.nyjourney.com.

3. Portable Church Industries (PCI) can be contacted at 1260 Kempar Avenue, Madison Heights, MI 48071. Their phone number is 1-800-939-7722, and the Web site is www.portablechurch.com.

4. There is much litigation about churches using schools today. Since this may change, you can find up-to-date articles about U.S. and

Canadian laws at www.newchurches.com/legal. You can also find a sample letter that explains the law to school administrators.

5. Ian Buntain, E-mail, 9 January 2003.

6. Keith W. Hinton, *Growing Churches Singapore Style* (Singapore: OMF, 1985), 196.

7. http://www.seminolechurch.com/ourstory.shtml.

8. http://www.lifeway.com/.

9. For ordering information, go to http://www.purposedriven.com/.

10. Oldham Little Church Foundation, 5177 Richmond, Suite 1068, Houston, Texas 77056.

Chapter 23

1. Aubrey Malphurs, *Planting Growing Churches for the 21st Century* (Grand Rapids: Baker Book House, 1992), 335.

2. North American Mission Board church planters thinktank, 24–26 August 2002, an invitation-only gathering to discuss how to improve training for church planting.

3. Examples of different types of church planting mailers can be found at www.newchurches.com/mailers. Church planters who want to share their own mailers may do so there.

4. Norm Whan, E-mail, 9 January 2003.

5. www.tellstart.com.

6. http://www.easum.com/FAQS/new_church_plants.htm.

7. Norm Whan, E-mail, January 9, 2003. "The Phone's for You!" is available at www.cgdi.org.

8. This percentage of positive respondents occurs primarily in the South and the Southeastern United States. Millcreek Community Church determined that getting 200 persons to attend the initial service required 55,000 phone calls (or dial-ups), a rate of 3.6 percent. I know of one church in Boston that used this approach and had a 4 percent response rate. This means it would take almost 80,000 calls to get 200 people at the first service. I am aware also of a church in Rhode Island that had higher than a 10 percent response rate. Response rates do vary.

9. http://www.bigskychurch.com.

Chapter 24

1. Darrell W. Robinson delineates this threefold purpose: exalting the Savior, equipping the saints, and evangelizing the sinner; see his *Total Church Life*, rev. ed. (Nashville: Broadman Press, 1993).

2. Sally Morgenthaler, *Worship Evangelism: Inviting Unbelievers into the Presence of God* (Grand Rapids: Zondervan Publishing House, 1995).

3. "The Lord Reigns," Bob Fitts, Integrity Music, 1989.

4. Aubrey Malphurs, *Planting Growing Churches for the 21st Century* (Grand Rapids: Baker Book House, 1992), 187.

5. Though exaggerated, these problems were highlighted by James Michener's *Hawaii* (New York: Random House, 1959).

6. A theory of the source for this tune comes from Bill Moyers's PBS series on Genesis. There is little evidence that the tune comes from African slave ships. The American frontier was more likely the source of this hymn.

Chapter 25

1. York is a professor of preaching at The Southern Baptist Theological Seminary, Louisville, Kentucky.

2. Mohler's excellent article can be found at http://www.sbts.edu/news/ssmag/prejour.html.

3. http://marshill.fm.

4. http://marshill.fm/word/index.htm.

5. S. Greidanua, "Preaching from Paul Today" in *The Dictionary of Paul and His Letters.*, Gerald P. Hawthorne and Ralph P. Martin, eds. (Downers Grove, Ill., InterVarsity Press, 1993), 743.

6. Bailey, 99.

7. Michael P. Green, "Sermon Illustrations," in *Leadership Handbooks of Practical Theology, Volume 1: Word and Worship,* gen. ed. James D. Berkley (Grand Rapids: Baker Book House, 1992), 11.

8. Bailey, 81.

9. http://www.ecclesiahouston.org.

10. Interview with Chris Seay, electronically published on disk by Sermon Resources Incorporated.

11. John R. Claypool, *The Preaching Event* (San Francisco: Harper Collins, 1989), 87.

12. Bailey, 28.

13. Larry Moyer, "Evangelistic Preaching," in *Leadership Handbooks of Practical Theology, Volume 1: Word and Worship,* James D. Berkley, gen. ed. (Grand Rapids: Baker Book House, 1992) 11.

14. Lloyd M. Perry, *Biblical Preaching for Today's World,* revised (Chicago: Moody Press, 1973, 1990), 143.

15. Stott, 201.

16. Miller, 57.

17. Calvin Miller, *Marketplace Preaching: How to Return the Sermon to Where It Belongs* (Grand Rapids: Baker Books, 1995), 142.

18. John Calvin, cited in Stott, 128.

19. Ralph Moore, *Starting a New Church* (Ventura, Calif.: Gospel Light, 2002), 189.

Chapter 26

1. Aubrey Malphurs, *Planting Growing Churches for the 21st Century* (Grand Rapids: Baker Book House, 1992), 354–55.

2. Popularized by Saddleback Church; see www.purposedriven.com.

3. Available through LifeWay Christian Stores.

4. http://www.northpoint.org/.

5. Lunch meeting, 25 August 2002.

6. http://www.nhf.cc.

7. Ray Wickham, E-mail, 19 October 2002.

8. Dan Morgan, "Assimilating New Believers," unpublished paper.

9. Cited in Win Arn and Charles Arn, *The Master's Plan for Making Disciples: Every Christian an Effective Witness Through an Enabling Church* (Grand Rapids: Baker Books, 1998), 156.

10. An excellent resource for an addiction-recovery ministry is *Celebrate Recovery,* http://www.celebraterecovery.com/.

Chapter 27

1. Mailings should be taken personally by the outreach leader to ensure their timely arrival. This correspondence is so crucial that leaving it in the hands of subordinate team members may mean that mailings go out too late in the week—or not at all (I have witnessed this experience). They should go to the main post office to ensure that letters are not misplaced or delayed by a satellite branch of the postal system.

2. Lyle E. Schaller, *Survival Tactics in the Parish* (Nashville: Abingdon, 1977), 52.

3. Andy Stanley, *Visioneering* (Sisters, Oreg.: Multnomah, 1999), 85.

Chapter 28

1. Mandy Montgomery, my former student, helped research and write parts of this chapter.

2. Kim Sikes and Lori Haynes Niles, *The Warm and Wonderful Church Nursery* (Loveland, Colo.: Group, 1999), 5.

3. Personal conversation, 21 July 2002.

4. Thomas Sanders and Mary Ann Bradberry, *Teaching Preschoolers: First Steps Toward Faith* (Nashville: LifeWay Press, 2000), 17–18.

5. Cos Davis, *Breakthrough: Preschool Sunday School Work* (Nashville: Convention Press, 1990), 78.

6. http://www.vcfcolumbus.org.

7. Jeff Clark, E-mail, 24 October 2002.

Chapter 29

1. Lunch meeting, 25 August 2002.

2. Larry Lewis, *The Church Planter's Handbook* (Nashville: Broadman Press, 1992), 133.

Chapter 30

1. These ideas emerge from Paul Becker and Mark Williams, *The Dynamic Daughter Church Planting Handbook* (Dynamic Church Planting International, 1999), pages 11–15. It is available from Dynamic Church Planting International, http://www.dcpi.org.

2. Dino Senesi, E-mail correspondence, 24 September 2002.

3. Jack Redford, *Planting New Churches* (Nashville: Broadman Press, 1978).

4. Dino Senesi, E-mail correspondence, 4 September 2002.

5. A number of tools are available for this purpose. Among the better known are the Myers-Briggs Type Inventory, DISC, and LIF-O. The church planter assessment mentioned earlier is standard.

Chapter 31

1. http://www.imb.org/CPM/Chapter3.htm.

2. The church multiplication system is described here as explained by Kevin Mannoia in his book, *Church Planting: The Next Generation* (Indianapolis, Ind.: Light and Life Communication, 1994). However, the system has also evolved since Mannoia's book. Subscribers to Bob Logan's CoachNet can see a more updated version of the described system at www.coachnet.org. Cultivating Church Multiplication Movements (C2M2) is a ten-part system that helps church planting leaders develop a contextual strategy. Many denominations or agencies have adapted such systems to their own needs. The agency where I work, the North American Mission Board, uses a version developed for our context called the Church Planting Process. The CPP has greatly enhanced Southern Baptists' church planting potential. My Ph.D. dissertation focused on the development, implementation, and results of this system.

Index